D1279553

39-77

The following books are titles in the
Controversies in Education Series, Editorial Board
THE UNIVERSITY OF MASSACHUSETTS SCHOOL OF EDUCATION

Cooper—DIFFERENTIATED STAFFING

Hicks and Hunka—THE TEACHER AND THE COMPUTER

Lacey—SEEING WITH FEELING Film in the Classroom

Gentry, Jones, Peelle, Phillips,
Woodbury and Woodbury—URBAN EDUCATION: The Hope Factor

Mallan and Hersh—NO G.O.D.s IN THE CLASSROOM: Inquiry into
Inquiry

Mallan and Hersh—NO G.O.D.s IN THE CLASSROOM: Inquiry and
Elementary Social Studies

Mallan and Hersh—NO G.O.D.s IN THE CLASSROOM: Inquiry and
Secondary Social Studies

NO G.O.D.s IN THE CLASSROOM: INQUIRY INTO INQUIRY

JOHN T. MALLAN
RICHARD HERSH
University of Toledo

1972
W. B. SAUNDERS COMPANY
PHILADELPHIA • LONDON • TORONTO

W. B. Saunders Company: West Washington Square
Philadelphia, Pa. 19105

12 Dyott Street
London, WC1A 1DB

1835 Yonge Street
Toronto, 7, Ontario

NO G.O.D.s IN THE CLASSROOM: Inquiry into Inquiry   ISBN 0–7216–6000–2

Print No.:   9   8   7   6   5   4   3   2   1

3/27/74 Berkert Tgler cf. 7r

Who is to know something. . . .
must in nature and early training
far surpass the rest.
As a young man, he must have
a kind of erotic mania for truth.
as though inspired . . .
and when he has learned all
that has been held by
his most distinguished predecessors
he must judge and examine and test . . .
and turn himself away from what is
not in accord with evident phenomena.
For such a person I have much hope
that my work will prove useful.
In all, these will be few.
For the others, this book will be
superfluous, as a myth is to a mule.

Galen (A.D. 129–199)

I am not an advocate for frequent
changes in laws and constitutions.
But laws and institutions must go
hand in hand with the progress
of the human mind. As that becomes
more developed, more enlightened,
as new discoveries are made, new
truths discovered and manners and
opinions change, with the change
of circumstances, institutions
must advance also to keep pace
with the times. We might as well
require a man to wear still the
coat which fitted him when a boy
as civilized society to remain
ever under the regimen of their
barbarous ancestors.

Thomas Jefferson
(Thomas Jefferson Memorial)

"I don't ask for an immediate response, Lord. All I want is a commitment."

OPEN LETTER TO READER

It is difficult to write a letter, let alone a book, to someone we don't know. It presupposes a great deal on our part. We are aware of this, although the recognition does not lessen the discomfort. One thing we do know: you want to teach social studies, and within a short while you will be joining us. In this sense we are professional colleagues.

The book is part of a "triad." An "umbrella" book, *No G.O.D.s in the Classroom: Inquiry into Inquiry* attempts to deal with relating theory with practice and to provide the theoretical base within a decision-making context for social studies teachers. A second book addresses resources for teaching elementary social studies. The third will work with resources for secondary social studies teaching.

You will note that we have used a number of actual experiences encountered by teachers and that the selected resources, for better or worse, are those that have actually been used with students. We think that this is important to note. Teaching doesn't involve just lesson planning. Teaching is done within a larger context—one in which the professional lives day-to-day and one which influences what and how he teaches. In other words, we have tried to be honest about the backdrop, the stage, the audience, and the management. These things are "real" in the sense that they happened—and *not* in just one locale or one school system. And not all of it is pleasant, happy, and scented with roses.

The books were born out of experience in the classroom—elementary, secondary, and college. The hurts and the hopes, the frustrations and the satisfactions seep through... and we can't honestly apologize for this. One can become very critical of what he values, especially when there are glimpses of the potential. If one is looking for nice, neat answers simplistically wrapped out, they will not be found here. The nature of the content of social studies makes this impossible. And the natures of the learners would make such an attempt ludicrous. Add to all this the situational factors which every teacher encounters, and all one can hope to get from the book are some ideas (that will have to be modified, tested, changed, and even denied) and perhaps a better look at himself—his frame of reference, his strengths, his background, and the possibilities inherent in social studies teaching.

It is impossible to try to be all things to all people. We have *selected* certain aspects of teaching to emphasize, have *selected* experiences to pass on, and have *selected* various kinds of resources. As every teacher knows, there is a tendency to generalize to the "whole" from parts that are liked or disliked. Our own philosophy is that no one person has one life, but rather a countless number of lives—a part, and even a part of a part, of "life" stands on its own. We feel that this is also true of a book. Every book has countless subbooks within it, and thus a reader, in a sense, "makes" his own book. This is what teaching is all about.

Because content is such a permeating part of teaching, we have attempted to give it emphasis. It should be noted, however, that while we ask for *more* content we are NOT asking for more in the conventional sense. And we are naive enough to say that we may not know what good teaching is in all its dimensions, but we *do* know what constitutes poor teaching. One of our basic premises is at least as ancient as Dewey—it helps if a teacher has a good academic background. Courses taken in college can be of substantial use to the prospective teacher if there is a recognition of how to translate them for teacher planning. We don't separate content from process.

PREFACE

The authors have been in classrooms which supposedly addressed social studies learning. In over 20 years of teaching and observing at all levels, kindergarten through college, the conclusion has been reached that, in most cases, the teacher's role appeared to be primarily a Giver Of Directions. The mastering of this role finds its appeal through the security it offers the teacher.

This book is *not* designed to be a panacea for the social studies teacher in the classroom. The facts of life are too real. We well know the nature of the larger picture of the situation in which the conscientious teacher finds himself. He inherits a program, is told who to teach, what to teach, when to teach. He is concerned with student load and with different "subject" preparations. There are also the questions of discipline, evaluation, peer pressure, community pressures, and countless required administrative tasks. This often becomes more complex because his "subject" (social studies) has value orientations. If he is sensitive to the ethical dimensions involved in his attempts to change human thinking and acting—as he should be—he lives with an internal struggle to find a consistency among the intellectual, social, and psychological aspects of the teaching effort. There is no panacea, no guaranteed answer.

Realistically, one can only ask for some assistance.

After assessing what a teacher encounters in his daily routine, it is not surprising that a number of teachers resort to the role of "Giver Of Directions." It may, in fact, be tied to survival. But, survival for what?

There are a number of books and articles available that address the evils of education and plead for the educator to change. This serves a purpose. Unfortunately for the teacher who, day in and day out, lives with the problems and who is faced with the demands inherent in immediacy, these books and articles are not the sought after assistance.

The type of assistance that makes a difference is that which takes into account the de facto situation as it is and not as it *ought* to be or *might* be. It is practical. It can be used today and tomorrow. It is transferable to a number of teaching situations. It can be modified and adapted. It is food on the plate rather than pie in the sky. *No G.O.D.s In the Classroom* attempts to provide such assistance. Examples used in the book have been used with teachers and/or students in actual teaching situations. These examples relate *content with methods* which is "like it is" in the classroom. And they relate the concerns of an elementary social studies teacher with those of teachers at the secondary level.

The view that the social studies teacher is a decision-maker is the basic premise. Teaching is not a random activity. It involves ends and means. It involves knowing the variables at work in planning and implementation. It involves assessment, evaluation, alternatives. Teaching is not an isolated act. Rather, it is a system of behaving—a number of specific acts that are in constant interaction. A teacher, aware of this, can have more control over the system and, thus, make it more effective and satisfying. It can be creative, intellectually alive, and exciting for the teacher, and this may, in turn, be the most significant lesson he teaches.

This book attempts to practice what it teaches. It starts with a low level and easy involvement of the reader in assessing the teaching system and the interaction of the subactivities. It builds an experience base for conceptualizing, and developmentally establishes opportunities for the reader to be increasingly involved in working with materials and situations. For those who have not had teaching experience, this may serve as initial exposure; for those who have taught, it is hoped that new insights may be developed for the assessment of what has been done in the past and what might be done in the future. A stress on having each chapter reinforce and expand previously encountered concepts denies the usual segmenting and compartmentalization of teaching activities. Although concepts, skills, vehicles, and materials used are the main focus of separate chapters, the focus does not deter the reader from understanding how they interrelate. The prime purpose of each chapter is to bring the functional relationship to a conscious (awareness) level.

The content of materials used is directed at providing a base of familiarity with social science material. The examples of teaching strategies applied to selected content vehicles calls for the reader to use the skills and techniques incorporated in teaching methods.

The assistance offered the teacher is not intended to answer all the questions. It should open practical approaches and alternatives. And, hopefully, it will make the answer to the question "Survival for what?" something more than a problem of endurance.

It is one thing to talk about conceptual teaching, content, inquiry, social science, history, skills, discovery, and so forth, and another thing to share with others how such things have been translated and applied in teaching situations. Such sharing opens a vulnerability, for teaching is interdisciplinary and ethical. One cannot help but walk on a field of toes. Fine! Consistent with our effort to put some things together, we reply (and mean it!) that if one doesn't subscribe to the shared efforts and/or finds them in gross error, then come up with alternatives and share them! Be vulnerable—that's what teaching and learning is all about.

We haven't overconcerned ourselves with writing style. Maybe we should have. If at times we come on as overly pedantic, or flip, or in some overkill efforts our slip is showing, it is a slip that indicates that we are *not* neutral and that we have definite feelings about social studies teaching. If our slips work to closure then we are wrong. If they push you to feeling and to opening up of your *own* thinking, then there is no reason to apologize.

The main thing—have fun with the material—fun in seeking alternatives, fun in the process of building your own world. Which, after all, is what you are doing.

We are tempted to say that if you find errors we accept the responsibility. No... *when* you find errors, *we* are responsible. If you leave them as such, then *you* have assumed responsibility.

Have fun.

JOHN MALLAN

RICHARD HERSH

CONTENTS

NO
G.O.D.s

IN THE CLASSROOM

INQUIRY INTO INQUIRY

"*What's nice about being king is I dish it out but I don't have to take it!*"

INTRODUCTION

"With the jawbone of an ass ..."

Some two thousand years ago, the "Good Book" made it clear that with a jawbone of an ass one could slay thousands.

Within the last decade, there have been considerable data indicating that the most popular gadget used by teachers is relatively inexpensive but extremely powerful: the vocal cords. For some reason, if a teacher isn't verbalizing, isn't telling, isn't exhorting or explaining or needling or approving, he isn't *really* teaching. "Seek and ye shall find"—seek out teachers and see if you don't find that they somehow feel guilty if they are not perceived as being the focus of attention and a fountainhead of accumulated wisdom upon whom students may build dependency. Unless one "acts" like a teacher instead of *being* a teacher, he may be accused of such things as: not knowing his subject matter, not planning well, being too permissive, or not commanding respect.

THE TEACHER-SCHOLAR

We seem to be facing an interesting paradox.

Implied in the perception of what it is to "act" like a teacher is the expectation that the teacher is "academic"—a second class scholar—but still a scholar.

A scholar's behavior anchors respect and status in the processes he uses. The teacher finds acclaim in the product.

A scholar finds his "strength" in data, objectivity, qualification of finding, and skills allowing him to retrieve, manipulate, and relate data.

The expectations of the teacher role are cushioned in soft data, subjectivity, and knowledge claims. The "means" become incidental.

3

The scholar searches for truth; the teacher dispenses it.

The *expectations* of respective teacher roles may be a paradox, but the teacher and the scholar have different ends, different reasons for their activities. The teacher is not primarily concerned with research as an end. He is not primarily concerned with discovering and/or creating new relationships within a special discipline. His task, rather, finds focus in working with the findings of the scholar in a way that utilizes the general skills of the scholar.

The teacher, as a *public* professional, does not exist in the type of climate so vital for scholarly pursuit. The community and school environments, for the most part, are product-oriented. The products are often prescribed categorical "oughts." A fundamental fact of life for the teacher is that he lives in the real world, where opinions and romantic wishes supersede any commitment to inquiry. Voltaire's concept of infinity is said to have come from his observation of man's credulity. It is difficult to use objectivity, reason, logic, and data in a confrontation with emotion, magic, and myth.

The teacher senses the two hats he is expected to wear simultaneously. His instinct for professional survival warns him that any admission of doubt in regard to his subject matter, theoretical base, or instructional techniques is perceived as weakness. He is aware that he ultimately is evaluated and judged at the bar of nonprofessionals. This may partially explain the teacher's disposition to be the Giver Of Directions, of relying on gadgets, and of resorting to gimmicks. It is safe. As long as man is a rationalizing animal as well as a rational animal there is little apparent problem in his reconciling the irreconcilable.

There is one comment we can make with some degree of confidence: What the social studies teacher thinks he is teaching is often NOT what is learned by his students. There are numerous classic examples.

"INTERNALIZED" LEARNING —
To Know Good Is Not to Be Good

A secondary school was concerned about the number of students who were smoking. A program was launched to attempt to change the students' attitudes toward the habit. It was decided that a pretest should be given in order to determine what the students already knew about the evils of smoking. This device showed that a certain number of students already smoked. A teaching "unit" was prepared. Empirical findings were listed. Films were used. Testimonials about the dangers of smoking were solicited. The students studied the evils of smoking. Post-tests showed a substantial increase in the amount of information students had learned in the process *and that more students smoked after than before the study of the unit.* This raises an interesting question: What is the relationship among thinking, feeling, and actual behavior?

In another situation a school felt it wise to try to lessen prejudice patterns in early adolescents. Different groups of youngsters from different sections of the city were given the same educational program. Information, case studies, films, and planned discussions were part of the approach. Post-tests indicated that students from certain sections of the city *did* show a lowering of prejudice. Students from other geographic sections gave evidence of a significant *increase* in and reinforcement of prejudice patterns. The same program, the same ends—but different results.

A recent issue of *Social Forces*[1] presented evidence suggesting that however "neutral" a social science course might be, the student's acquisition and retention of social science data and findings were influenced by the political beliefs and attitudes he brought *to* the classroom. A student could resist what was presented in the course and would be likely to forget the information after the immediate utility (the examination) had ceased to exert pressure. Personal predispositions influence what is learned regardless of what the teacher intends to be learned.

Two unfortunate thoughts seem to nag at this point. The first is that there may be no necessary logical connection between *thinking behavior* and *functioning behavior;* the second is that most social studies programs and approaches *assume the connection.* It is as if the connection were a basic axiom. Do we assume that because a student memorizes part of the Declaration of Independence, can cite the names of the signers and describe in great detail the historical context for the writing of such a document, he will be a better and more democratic citizen?

We are told by Bertrand Russell that the one who deliberately plans and executes a learning experience for others may be committing the most heinous crime of all. What of a person who means well, plans well, executes well, but who has no idea of the consequences of that which is taught... or learned? At a committee

---

[1] Wasburn, Philco C.: Some political implications of students' acquisition of social science information. *Social Forces*, March, 1970.

meeting of a community action group, one irate parent directed her frustration at a school board member. "The law provides for dealing with the fast, incisive murderer. What about people like you ... committing a slow, torturous type of murder? The only difference is the immediacy of the result."

If it is any consolation, the social studies teacher does not stand alone. Starting with the "medicine man," the history of medicine reveals what human beings have done to themselves and to others in order to cure disease—a gruesome tale of horror. A student of medical history was asked to give an approximate date when doctors began to cure more patients than they killed. He replied that it might take another generation or so.[2] The history of war and the history of religious persecution would provide even more horrendous tales. "... [we] know not what [we] do!"

THE SIN OF COMMISSION

A well known Sanskrit tale had four brothers deciding to cover the earth in search of a new science. Each went on his separate journey. They had agreed to search for a designated period of time and then to meet together to share with one another what each had learned.

The first brother reported that he had learned to take the bones of a creature and from the bones create the flesh.

The second brother had learned the secret of growing skin and hair if the flesh were on the bones.

The third brother excitedly told the others that, given bones, flesh and hair, he had learned to mold these into a form complete with limbs.

"I," said the fourth brother, "know how to give life to a creature if its form is complete."

The brothers were quite pleased with their findings. They decided to find a bone with which to start. Fatefully they selected the bone of a lion, unaware of its origin.

The first gave the flesh; the second the skin and hair; the third molded a form and gave it limbs; and the fourth brother gave it life.

That which they had created turned and killed the creators.

The sad story was told to a King. The King asked those assembled: "Who was responsible for the evil that was created?" Having

---

[2]Knight, Frank H.: Science, society, and the modes of law. *In* White, Leonard D. (ed.): *The State of the Social Sciences.* Chicago, The University of Chicago Press, 1956, p. 14.

wisdom he answered his own question: "Only the one who saw the finished form and still gave it life. He is the guilty one."

Of course, the tale has its moral: Only if its roots are firm and watered with intelligence and worldly wisdom will the tree of human effort bear fruit.

The moral may stand by itself. But for those of us in social studies education there are subtle implications for what we do. In an age of specialization, the school is one of the few social institutions in which the data and findings of the specialists are inevitably used in some interaction. Knowing that bones and flesh and forms surround us, we also know that the accumulating data and findings are meaningless until we give them meaning — until we give them "life." We must note the choices implicit in the tale and, in so doing, acknowledge that, like it or not, the teacher's encompassing role is that of the fourth brother.

If we don't see the parts as some interaction in terms of the whole, if we don't have the fortitude to assist others — our "brothers" — to see more than the mechanics, are we not also guilty of allowing our fellow beings to create and possibly to destroy out of ignorance?

Francis S. Chase, former Dean of the Graduate School of Education at the University of Chicago, predicted several years ago an emerging problem for education in the massive, industrialized, modern society. He saw the danger of "higher illiteracy," which he defined as the inability to entertain ideas which seem to threaten one's own narrow view of the world. "While simple illiteracy is an easily recognizable barrier to the good things of life, . . . higher illiteracy is a serious, compounding factor." The higher illiterate refuses *to understand although he can see, hear, read, and learn.*

The teaching of social studies, at whatever level, is not a task for the tender minded or thin skinned.

SOCIAL CONTEXT OF EDUCATION

If a school is more than a building, it is truly without walls. He who enters brings the world. And he who leaves taking nothing has been robbed.

The process called education courts problems unless it heeds the signs of the times. The mind and the senses, working in conjunction, are like sieves — always sifting *parts* of new experience through a device honed by life. Hard as it may be for some educators to believe, there is a life of meanings outside the classroom.

This is as much part of learning—if not more—than any study the school provides in isolation. If one teaches, the signs of the times are an integral part of his preparation.

Education is not achieved in a void. The school itself does not exist in a void. The school's effectiveness may be determined by the extent it relates to the larger community and to the nature of the larger community. Educators recognize that subject matter just doesn't flow into a mental receptacle or container, that a student "screens" and "selects" the content. Parts of the sieve which allow the sifting are the social influences at work in society itself—influences NOT selected or controlled by the school. This should have particular significance for the social studies teacher.

There are a number of social "realities" at work influencing what is taught and what is learned. Some of these realities are listed below.

Conflict in Value Systems. Students (and teachers) live in a world of relativism and seemingly inconsistent values. The inherited prescientific value system of Western civilization is being challenged, and the challenge divides men into oversimplified antagonistic camps. The traditional "anchor" upon which to base behavior with a consistent world view apparently no longer is accepted as a guide.

Economic Changes. Students can no longer be assured that to be trained with a set of skills which will guarantee a life-long livelihood will suffice. The student senses a growing lack of economic security—even for the "educated"—and knows that what he learns in school guarantees little except the need for more, and more, and more training. Education as the means to the end of economic security is being questioned.

Labor Supply. With unemployment and underemployment so prevalent, it becomes no secret that one major role the school plays is that of a "delaying game" designed to keep potential labor from the labor market. Students are becoming increasingly more aware of this "baby-sitting" role.

Generation Gap. This appears NOT to be a gap based on age, but rather is related to the changing value systems and to varying world views. Credibility (individuals and institutions), integrity and a form of idealism seem to be the root issues—the difference between action values and verbal values. It has become obvious that many adults live by a dual standard and, along with it, support a third value system based on "playing games," with no other end than the "game" itself.

Social Class and Mobility Patterns. Traditionally the school has been used as a means of moving "up" and "out" — the available tool allowing an equality of opportunity. But, opportunity to do what? "Success" and ways of "getting ahead" appear to be questioned. The middle-class route is fuzzy, and the role of education as a means of social mobility is less honored than in former times. In many secondary schools different patterns of social class have emerged within the student population ("collegiates," etc.), and these patterns are not only distinct but influence the use of the school by the students.

Authority. The concept of "authority" is also undergoing challenge. The fact that someone occupies a position does not certify competence or ability. (What is the criterion for being an ambassador?) What a person *does* . . . and evidence of his doing . . . are in vogue. This fosters a challenge of paper credentials and raises issues for evaluation.

Time. Time used to be considered "on one's side"; it was thought that if one worked hard, in time, things would work out. Upon this base was built "having time," and this influenced even intellectual behavior premised on having time to define a problem, collect data, look at alternatives, make choices, act, and so forth. If denied this concept, then behavior often becomes more inclined to *reacting* and to a rejection of reasonable, rational methods. This puts an immediacy into demands.

Knowing About and Knowing. Schools are primarily concerned with "knowing about" something called the world, "knowing about" ways of making one's way through the world. Academic tradition is rooted in "knowing about." Through experiences outside the school, through mass media, through increased communication, through a "six foot" world, students are growing more concerned with *knowing* first hand. When there appears to be a discrepancy between "knowing about" and "knowing," the formal school may find itself losing out.

Family. The Women's Liberation movement, combined with a number of other societal factors, helps to underscore a changing view about the nature of the "family" unit and the functions it serves. As a microsocial system, the family finds leadership, role definitions, participation, shared relations, and so forth, undergoing radical changes. Sometimes the family offers *forced models,* which are rejected. Some families appear willing to let "society" share in what have always been family responsibilities.

Use of Chemicals to Effect Behavioral and Attitudinal Changes. The deliberate use of chemicals to modify behavior and outlook is going through growth "pangs." The potential benefits and destructive factors are in the process of being assessed, and with the assessment may come modification in legislation and efforts to put parameters on the "drug culture." The adult portion of society uses its own forms of stimulants and depressants. Youth (as far down as the middle grades, perhaps lower) are in the midst of an onslaught never before experienced.

Sex. This area of relationships is being influenced by the changes in value systems. Sex is seen as serving a number of functions, not the least of which are the "puberty rights" implicitly endorsed by an "X" society. Standards for some adults have changed, and sex, as a physical activity, combines with economic independence to equal adulthood. Sex as a socio-psychological activity infers "belonging," loving, and caring... aspects of self-concept, status and prestige so important to the young in the process of testing and forging themselves and their value systems.

Mass Media. Instant information is available, processed and packaged for consumption. Social problems are revealed, often with a communication process which relates cognitive-affective aspects. Problems of poverty, war, protest, racial tensions, violence, and human irrationality in many walks of life are no longer reserved to those segments of society immediately involved but are available as part of everyone's environment. The impact of the mass media poses problems for educators in methodology and in content.

Dichotomy of Situations. Most of us, including our students, operate with a primitive sense of justice. We move from the specific to the "whole." Problems are seldom solved without data, but injustice moves powerfully from a "feeling" level. Political rhetoric feeds the emotions and not the intellect and often suggests simplistic solutions to complex problems, thereby involving emotion with intellect. If the school accepts the emotive rhetoric stance, it has been converted; if it does not, effective motivation becomes a substantial problem.

Conformity. It is misleading to think that students are non-conformists. Many, if not most, of the students are willing to accept a perceived status quo. If there is nonconformity, it appears to stem from a form of conformity to subnorms which attempt to interpret and practice the verbalized norms held by the larger society. There is sometimes almost a puritanical aspect to the rejection.

Mechanization. Depersonalization and nonperson environments combine with the almost ubiquitous computers to develop a feeling that computers can do much of what the school expects of its graduates—faster, in greater quantity, and more efficiently. The largeness of organizations, business, government, and cities forces the single individual to use different cognitions in order to hack out "his" place. The old hacking tools, to some, are nothing but worn-out clichés.

Anxiety. As opposed to a specific fear, anxiety encompasses a broader apprehension. It is an apprehension shared by adults as well as youth. Single big Causes are increasingly elusive and thus "explanations" more difficult to formulate. A world of Probability is a far different world from one of Certainty—for the individual and for his species. There is a sense of loss of perceived control.

The above descriptions are arbitrary and make no pretense at being sophisticated. If there is any validity, then they at least provide an entré to the broad context within which social studies education is attempted. The student does not go to school leaving his informal education behind; he does not go to school without some screening criteria. In a sense the young person today is not unlike Voltaire's man of letters whom he compared to a fish skimming the surface. If he climbs into the air, he is eaten by the birds; if he dives, he is devoured by the sharks. Unfortunately it is in the soaring and the diving that man finds his life's education.

If an educator is content to skim the surface, then we are forced to ask again, education . . . for what?

IMPLICATIONS OF SOARING AND DIVING

The teacher's direct audience is comprised of the preadolescent and the adolescent. Not many years ago some professionals viewed this period of life as a particularly difficult one—a twilight zone in which one is neither child nor adult, a period when things got blurred as young people fluctuated between the protected world of childhood and the independence and responsibility of adulthood. But other periods of life seem to be difficult also, demanding adjustment, change, and modification in one's self-concept. The difference, perhaps, between generalized characteristics of one period and another may rest with the priorities ascribed to motives and needs, and available methods of accommodating the specific stresses and strains encountered.

Most teachers can tell battle stories about students whom they couldn't "reach" or didn't "understand" or "misread" or "packed it in on." (And all of us, having been students ourselves, could reverse the story telling!) Each classroom, each class, is a temptation to classify and to treat as a single entity; for example, the "fifth period" or "the American history class." Planning often is based on the single entity premise. The move toward individualizing instruction is, among other things, a move to break away from viewing students as a group, with each single part having identical characteristics and needs.

As we know, each *one* of us is in "a world of our own." A teacher who meets 125 or more students a day is really encountering a number of "worlds"—separate but dependent upon the others, being influenced and influencing others, interacting and transacting, and in the process of creating and satisfying individual needs. The classroom and the daily lesson may simply be a *means* to countless ends. We talk about motivation, relevance, small-group activity, individualized instruction, and student-teacher planning; such activities are more complex than many assume.

We earlier talked about the need for a teacher to be an intellectual leader. But the intellectual leadership is always exercised within a social context and this raises the key issue of how the teacher can effectively relate intellectual leadership *with* social leadership. If teaching is an "art," it refers to the teacher's ability to creatively *relate* the subject matter with students, to develop means by which the intellectual components and the social components become mutually supportive. And lest we forget, the teacher has his *own* needs, his *own* means for assuring his *own* relationship between the intellectual and the social; the classroom acts as a *means* for the teacher as well as the student.

The social framework or backdrop for teaching and learning involves a number of general needs which influence student motives and behavior. For example, one's self-concept depends to a substantial degree upon the concept others have of him, how he is treated, what status he is given or earns. The approval and acceptance by "significant" others becomes vital. "Belonging" and being wanted and needed often place the peer group in a position of greater importance than the adult figures in the school. Most of us carry this need during all the periods of life, but it seems particularly strong when one is in the process of *creating* his sociopsychological self. There is a difference between creating it and defending it. It is at the preadolescent and adolescent period that biological changes and role changes mesh, putting new demands on value choices and expected behavior. (Just for fun, recall your own dominant concerns when in junior high school.

Were they centered on world geography and the crops of Spain or on whether you were accepted not only by members of your own sex with all the implied roles, but also whether you were accepted by members of the opposite sex?)

The need for being socially "there" is strong. Along with this is a parallel need for greater autonomy—a wider range of freedom in choices and behavior, a chance to test the perceived adult attributes of mature self-determination and responsibility. As adults we know that a great deal of ego-tripping and face-saving is involved, and we know how we recognize and tolerate such mechanisms in our own *adult* relationships.

Part of this autonomy involves also the testing of attitudes and values, a testing of one's own through the testing of those held by others. To test is not necessarily to reject! Students are faced with a host of contradictory value systems dealing with moral beliefs, integrity, sex codes, loyalty, attitudes toward "differences" whether in individuals or groups, rules, ways of social control, even such things as manners, dress, and language. As a student's experiences bring him into greater contact with different groups and different norms, he sees inconsistencies in the value system of his own framework and within the framework of others. What may parade as cynicism may be an overt expression of a recognition of inconsistency, of the difficulty in forging a functional and satisfying value system.

The experiences that underpin the need for social acceptance, the desire for autonomy, the testing of value systems, all come piecemeal and all influence one another. The term "understanding" simply implies that one is aware of how things *relate*—the past with the now, this experience with that experience, the now with a maybe tomorrow. Sometimes the intellectual maturity of the preadolescent and the adolescent, the level of questions asked, a consuming interest in one thing—even for a short while, or an interest in the abstract world as part of the real world surprises and even threatens adults working with them. And when the students revert to the "ideas of youth" or to a naive idealism or to "silly unsophisticated interests," students are perceived to be behaving the way students "ought" to behave.

The audiences a teacher faces are diverse and complex. But it would seem that a teacher of the use of social studies has a "content" which would assist him in relating his subject matter *with* the social backdrop and *with* the primary concerns of his students. Many other academic areas do not, by the nature of the content to be taught, have a similar opportunity.

What are the implications for selecting concepts that are transferable? for determining student activities? for selecting and using different types of vehicles? for developing curriculum?

How *does* one effectively study about himself?

Realistically, what *can* a teacher do as an integral part of any teaching/learning situation?

What does a social study have to offer the preadolescent and the adolescent?

Let's look at a situation—real to others but, at this time, hypothetical to you.

So, you really want to teach?

Ask yourself:

What is the emerging role of formal schooling . . .?

What kind of an organizational climate encourages teachers and students to be "turned on" . . .?

What is the role of the professional in the process of having education redefined . . .?

If "knowledge is in transition," what implications are found in terms of the teacher being a student . . .?

To be a teacher in today's world takes intellect, imagination, creativity, stamina, sensitivity, and a commitment to become involved. It is not easy.

Our school community has done well when it comes to Merit Scholarships. Our graduates appear to be doing "well" after they leave the system. But, we are not kidding ourselves—education is more than this. . . .

We are not seeking starry-eyed visionaries.

We *are* seeking teachers who internalize the commitment they make and who have the courage to encounter problems instead of hiding behind a pile of jargon.

We *are* seeking teachers who will enter the dialogue basic to emerging concepts of "professional" and who will share with us a maturity, an intellectual excitement, and a political sophistication about the processes of change.

Our community is alive, interested, and interesting. It is active in its support of education. The students want to *share* in inquiry and are not anxious to be mere passive recipients of neat idea capsules. The teachers want to share their efforts with professionally alert colleagues.

If you would like to:

Teach in such an environment . . .

Share in the "hurting good" of the educational arena . . .

Commit your energy and intellectual competence . . .

Share in professional opportunity.

The advertisement shown on this page appeared in an issue of the *Saturday Review* (January 20, 1968).

Suppose that you are interested in seeking a position as a social studies teacher and that you wish to respond to the advertisement. Analyze your reaction to the questions raised and then raise some specific questions of your *own* which relate to the statements made below the questions listed in the ad. Put your thoughts together in the form of a letter designed to inquire about specific vacancies.

Suppose that your letter elicits a response. The response has two enclosures. One includes what the system believes to be the characteristics of "effective educators" and you are asked to react to what each item listed under each major category means to *you;* the request asks that you be fairly "specific." Assuming it is worth the effort, how would you respond?

CHARACTERISTICS OF EFFECTIVE EDUCATORS

Social Maturity
1. Emotionally stable.
2. Cognizant of individual behavior in larger social context.
3. Acceptance of ambiguity.
4. Recognition that "conflict" involves a number of levels and need not always be negative or threatening.
5. Less emphasis on personal "win-lose" attitude when dealing with students and with overall professional concerns.
6. Positive sense of humor (as a reflection of use/attitude).

Human Relations
1. "Open" in the sense of expressing own ideas, beliefs, etc., and *listening* to the ideas and beliefs of others.
2. Sensitive to the needs of others: students, colleagues, parents.
3. Supportive of others in their own struggles for self-actualization.
4. Cognition that education is a social process involving transactions among people and the acceptance of the fact that most professional problems involve human relations.
5. Recognition that the role of the teacher is to facilitate learning (self and others) in all areas involving human interaction.
6. Acceptance that difference from oneself is not the measure of absurdity.
7. Honesty in one's dealings with others—behavior constantly aimed at developing a trust level base for human interaction.
8. Recognition of one's own needs (social), and the refusal to judge others according to one's own needs.

Inquiry Oriented
1. Accepts fact that no decision is ever made on the basis of having complete information.
2. Ideas are hypotheses to be constantly "tested" even

when being implemented. This assumes a form of self-reliant humility.

3. Willingness to identify the sources of the information one has upon which action is proposed.
4. Applies inquiry processes in teaching and in professional relationships.
5. Ability to apply the rules of logic in formulating and testing conceptualizations.
6. Is aware of the functional relationship between affective and cognitive experiencing and can identify the two areas.
7. Sees the teaching/learning act as an experience involving both inquiry and the processing of the results of inquiry.
8. Is "open" to the "public" test; that is, personal "win" or "lose" is subservient to acting upon the best information available. This implies a willingness to welcome sharing ideas with others and welcoming "challenge" as well.
9. Can identify assumptions, logical inconsistencies, and inferences from data.
10. Does not accept "private" concepts without identifying them as such.

Teaching

1. Aware that teaching and learning are forms of human transaction and are facilitated through communication skills.
2. Views teaching as a planned experience to facilitate learning on the part of the student; that is, "teaching" is not basically an expository process.
3. Accepts the view that teaching is learning, that the teacher, in this sense, is another member of the class and is also a student.
4. Recognizes that teaching is a form of planning experiences designed to change human behavior. The ethical nature of the act is to make the experience a planned one: knowing the ends-in-view, the justification for the ends and the means to be used, and willing to make the planned experience "public."
5. Recognizes that the teaching act must be based on a theory of learning to which the teacher subscribes. This should be explicit.
6. Accepts the fact that program development is an ongoing process taking place through daily lessons and through larger formal attempts to guide the daily teaching.
7. Recognizes that "teaching" is not done solely within designated areas called "classrooms" but permeates the entire relationship with students: in classrooms, activities, etc.
8. Is cognizant that education (hence, teaching) has rami-

fications for the larger society and must be related to other social institutions.

9. Recognizes that a primary task of the teacher is to facilitate the student's ability and desire to experience; that is, to support the individual and his own efforts to come to terms with his world as it relates to himself.

10. Realizes that the teacher is viewed as a "product" of educational experiences and becomes a working model for what it means to be educated. (This has implications for actual behavior which infers attitudes, skills, learning, etc., to the student.)

11. Is sensitive to the role that group dynamics play in the teaching/learning act and that the groups within which one lives and works are, in themselves, teaching/learning experiences.

12. Has a willingness and an ability to internalize that a learning experience is never fully "completed" or "terminated." Teacher expectations for self-role and for students must be an open, creating, and becoming form of aspiration.

13. The term "discipline" is always related to perceived "ends." In any disciplinary act, the teacher should be cognizant of how he/she relates ends and means.

14. A zest and real excitement for his/her field and for the teaching of the respective field becomes crucial. This implies the need for teachers who "know," who realize they "don't know," and who are willing to be alive to the questions yet unanswered and the questions yet to be formulated. If it is worthwhile "teaching," it must be worthwhile living.

Involvement

1. Skills and ideas are to be used — that is, applied and tested in a real world of action. Willingness to commit and to become involved in social concerns and issues is part of the teaching act. If something is important, the test of its importance is whether or not one is willing to act.

2. Membership in organizations is not necessarily being involved. Emphasis on active work within organizations or on one's own outside the strictly "educational" scene implies the degree of commitment.

3. Accepts willingly and out of conviction the need to work to improve the profession, since the improvement of the profession has a direct bearing on how effective the teacher may be: curriculum, salaries, working conditions, benefits, etc.

Creativity

1. Desires freedom to try different approaches, ideas, and methodologies and is alive to deriving different kinds and varieties of relationships.

2. Alert to (and willingness to implement) teaching

strategies which encourage creative experiences to
be encountered by the students. Such strategies involve the students in active (and often self-directed)
activities involved in the "normal" teaching areas.
3. Views creativity as basic to human behavior and
recognizes the individual nature of creative processes.

The second enclosure relates to an opening in the social
studies department at the high school. It states that the department has done away with prescribed courses of study and that
each teacher will devise his own course within a framework of
departmentally sanctioned broad areas. Enclosed is a one-page
"framework" listing four umbrella guide areas.

At a recent meeting of the department, teachers wrestled with
identifying the broad major areas in which a teacher of world
history establishes his course. There seemed to be a general
agreement regarding the broad areas, and I am passing on
the "notes" to you for your consideration. We would appreciate any comments you wish to make in terms of clarification,
revision, changes, etc.

ASSUMPTION: Every individual and every group throughout
recorded history has been concerned with goals and the means
of attaining the goals. These goals have gone through a process of change and modification. The means of attainment have
also been subject to change and modification.

Assuming the above, and assuming that the major guide
lines should be related to the basic assumption, the department identified the following four major areas:

1. Man's relationship with the function and justification
of the state.
2. The meaning and content of the social sciences.
3. Man's perception of the nature of man and his place
in the universe.
4. Man and his social and economic institutions.

Note: These areas were identified as guide lines for the teacher.
They were not designed to prescribe any one method of approach. If there is anything which concerns you and which
you feel should be taken into consideration by the department, please indicate the specific concerns so that they may
be relayed to the rest of the department. Thank you.

The letter asks you to list "considerations and concerns"
which you would feel would be important under each of the four
major areas. You are NOT expected to write a course of study but
simply to react. What things would you consider important?

You are told in the letter that this is a "screening" aspect of
recruiting and that, if satisfactory, you will be contacted at a later

time for a personal interview. What are your specific reactions to the recruiting program of the system? Would you feel comfortable in applying?

Don't be scared off. Most experienced teachers would have a difficult time trying to respond to what was asked. And things are not always what they seem. For example, one social studies teacher already teaching in the system which placed the advertisement, responded to the ad. "Where are you located?" he asked. "I would like to teach in such a system." Another teacher in the system wrote a public criticism of the advertisement and objected to the type of person to whom the ad was pitched. He objected to language such as "turned on." A college professor (mathematics) wrote saying that the advertisement was not professional and was an insult to teachers and to teaching. Another professor wrote that the approach was "refreshing." A school board member in the system liked it so much that he wanted to be in on the interviewing, whereas another board member, sitting on the same board, raised doubts and wanted a financial comparison made between this kind of recruiting and visitations to campuses as was formerly done. So. . . .

At any rate, it might be interesting to see how you would respond *after* having wrestled with the material in this book!

SOME GOALS, PREMISES, AND DEFINITIONS

Following are some of the goals which the authors feel relate to social studies training, as well as some premises and definitions of terms used in *No G.O.D.s in the Classroom.*

SOME GOALS FOR SOCIAL STUDIES TRAINING

1. To "sharpen" and refine the reader's awareness of the role a teacher assumes as a decision maker.

2. To assist in bringing to the cognitive level the variables influencing teacher planning.

3. To provide an opportunity for the reader to relate planning with classroom decision making.

4. To assist the reader in developing a rationale and strategy for planning.

5. To provide an opportunity for the reader to relate ends and means.

6. To provide an opportunity for the reader to make educational terminology "operational"—instruments which help in planning and decision making.

7. To develop a greater awareness of the use of materials as instruments to desired ends.

8. To provide an opportunity for readers to become more aware of the significance of *skills* in social studies education.

9. To refine the participant's awareness of the overt and covert problems encountered in social studies education.

10. To develop a greater awareness of the *roles* that evaluation (in the form of feedback) plays in planning and decision making.

SOME BASIC PREMISES

1. The effectiveness of social studies teaching is related to the teacher's *own* cognitive organization, orderliness, and critical thinking ability.

2. Social studies teaching is more than semirandom activity within the framework of a textbook or within the context of selected multiple materials.

3. The teacher is an administrator in the sense that he is involved in giving "leadership" to classroom management and academic decisions.

4. In instructional management, the teacher is working with a "system" of which he is part. His decision making functions at various levels: broad planning and specific planning *prior* to implementing a lesson, immediate decision making while "on-the-spot" during implementation, and evaluating the implementation in order to modify subsequent broad and specific planning.

5. Efforts at planning and executing formal schooling are instrumental; that is, are *means* to perceived ends that transcend the immediate class lesson.

6. Social studies teaching appears "polarized" into either/or camps: concepts *or* facts, coverage *or* skill development,

content *or* process, cognitive *or* affective, behavioral *or* nonbehavioral objectives, indoctrination *or* education, inductive *or* deductive methodology. The "camps" are intellectually and pedagogically untenable.

7. An effective social studies teacher needs his own consistent *rationale* which gives direction to planning, selecting, use of materials, and evaluation.

8. Effective social studies teaching calls for organization. New information does not only call for addition to conventional programs but calls for, as well, the reorganization of conventional data—not just deletion.

9. The social studies teacher is an important part in the system. His impact upon the students depends on such things as: types of questions asked, data made available to the student, materials selected, and ideas/facts elaborated upon or passed over. The teacher's functioning implies what is of value.

10. The social studies teacher must mediate among the academic scholars and among learning scholars, and must translate the mediation to functional usage.

11. The teacher is a decision maker.

DEFINITIONS OF TERMS*

TEACHING: An isolated "act" of teaching incorporates a number of *interrelated* activities. Teaching is *doing*. It is doing such things as planning, selecting, evaluating, communicating, adapting. It is the processes of decision making and being able to see how each "part" of the teaching act influences, and is influenced by, the other parts of the teaching act. It is a "systems" approach deliberately designed to change human behavior. The teacher designs the "system" and administers all the interacting "subsystems" or parts. (It is perhaps the most complex undertaking known to man.)

SOCIAL SCIENCES: The term is applied to human activity which uses a scientific approach to understanding how and why human beings relate to one another and with their environment. To make the study more manageable, different "disciplines" bring a focus on specific aspects of human behavior. "Disciplines" are subsystems;

_____

*A warning: Not everyone in the field of education uses the labels in the same way. Hence, there are difficulties. We have used labels and in one case created a label (vehicle) because they appeared to be of value to us in working with teachers and students.

they are related with one another and have no absolute boundaries. The older subsystems are labeled: economics, history, political science, and geography. The newer subsystems are sociology, social psychology, and anthropology. The world of human behavior is an interacting world. Other animals treat it as the "whole" that it is; man artificially divides and labels it for more effective study. The social sciences are human tools. The processes of science are the basic components of the tools.

SOCIAL STUDIES: The label refers to the use of findings of the social sciences in areas of concern to the individual and society. It is studying the interrelationships among the findings and acting with intelligence in regard to others. This necessitates some degree of predicting the nature of the relationship as well as knowing the objects or events being related.

CURRICULUM*: This is the *totality* of actual experiences and data which influence what a student learns. The experiences and data influence one another *and* the student. Some of the experiences are *deliberately* planned in order to influence. Others are randomly encountered. For example, the study of violence in literature is planned; a street fight may just be encountered.

EDUCATIONAL PROGRAM*: This refers to the total *planned* experiences and how each "part" is deliberately related with the other parts and with the whole. A social studies program, K–12, has grade level courses and specific "topics," and deals with skill development.

COURSE OF STUDY*: The label refers to a specific aspect of the educational program and acts as a guide to assist teachers in planning and implementing experiences designed to modify behavior.

THIS WHOLE RELATIONSHIP IS NOT STATIC:
IT IS MOVING, CHANGING, ADAPTING,
MODIFYING, DISCARDING, ADDING.

CONCEPT: A concept refers to a mental organization of information and/or experiences *and* how the information and/or experiences relate. We usually give the organization a label. For example, "nation" or "conflict" or "due process" or "geography." Conceptualization is the ability to organize information and/or experiences into a pattern of relationship. (To merely learn the "label" is not necessarily to learn the concept.) A concept becomes a tool through which "new" information and experiences can be, in turn, conceptualized. A concept is a tool—an instrument for continued learning.

GOAL: A broad statement of the larger "end" or vision. It is not unlike Browning's "a man's grasp should exceed his reach." As found in educational programs, a goal would be: "To develop a sound,

---

*Many people think of curriculum as simply a course of study. *Curriculum* refers to a larger fabric of influences (planned and unplanned). The *Educational Program* refers to the deliberate part of the curriculum. The *Course of Study* is a part of the program, and a lesson plan refers to the instrumental plan for implementation. The lesson plan is the *action* plan while the course of study helps to guide the action in terms of the program. The program helps to guide in terms of the curriculum.

happy individual." *A goal exists to assist in establishing specific objectives.*

OBJECTIVE: The term refers to specific "ends" that are realistic in terms of accomplishment and evaluation. It is *assumed* that if a student can achieve the objectives, he is closer to achieving the broad goal. If evaluation is desired, specific objectives must be identified. *Example:* Goal: To be among the top ten archers in the world. Objective: To hit the bull's eye five out of ten times on this specific target at this specific distance and under these specific circumstances.

SKILLS: The term refers to what a person is able to do in getting and relating information in order to form concepts. To be a "tool," the functions and application of a skill must be conceptualized. The ability to phrase questions which allow for factual answers is a skill. When a student knows (conceptualizes) how, when, and why the ability is functional and can phrase such questions, he has learned this skill. As with concepts, a label is not a skill. Telling time is called a skill. But what skills are necessary in order to tell time?

VEHICLE: This label refers to "content" areas. It is the information and/or experiences which are *selected* for use in *carrying* or *transporting* a student to ways of deriving or testing concepts. It indicates the parts which are to be organized and related. It identifies the raw material to which skills are applied.

METHODS: These are the strategies a teacher determines to use in working with vehicles, concepts, and skills in order to achieve desired and specific objectives. An inductive-deductive strategy would assist in determining how to use, for example, a particular vehicle, concept, and skill.

ACTIVITY: An activity is a specifically planned experience which complements the other aspects of the teacher's strategy. For example, *reading* may be an activity. But this may be related to a vehicle; for example Jefferson's First Inaugural Address. The vehicle is related to selected concepts and objectives. The activity likewise is related to planned skill development. An activity is NOT an end in itself; it is a means.

MATERIALS: Anything used in an activity is referred to as "Materials." This may take the form of films, filmstrips, records, tapes, books, articles, case studies, pictures, maps, and so forth. The vehicles, methods and activities help to dictate what materials are most effective in terms of objectives.

EVALUATION: This refers to the activities used in determining how a teacher or student knows he is achieving an objective. Knowing this, a teacher or student can *diagnose* what the difficulties are and where they might be, so that achievement can take place. *Evaluation is not a judgment so much as a tool designed to help one to learn better.*

SYLLABUS: The term refers to a brief (four or five pages) adaptation of a course of study by a specific teacher working with a particular class or focus of study. A course of study usually applies to all teachers of a subject at a designated grade level. The syllabus is a refinement in terms of the individual teacher and situation.

"You can't talk to that crowd—they've all got extra Y chromosomes."

1

TEACHING CONCERNS

". . . a stranger in a strange land."

Tale of a Tub

Seamen have a custom, when they meet a whale, to fling him out an empty tub by way of amusement, to divert him from laying violent hands upon the ship.

JONATHAN SWIFT

PUBLIC/PRIVATE PROFESSIONALS

Not many professionals exhibit their abilities for public scrutiny. Few people have an opportunity to watch a surgeon operate. A dentist's expertise is a private affair. Occasionally a lawyer can be observed. The public usually observes the professional's product but not his processes.

Actors and teachers are different. Their processes and product are interwoven. Others can observe, in both cases, the professional doing the things that make him a professional. Many people have observed actors performing. Most people have observed teachers in the act of teaching. A trained drama critic may show sophistication in his observations and, in a sense, help to sharpen the observations of others. Critic teachers seldom make public their criteria for observing, nor do they make public the observations. These are interesting phenomena. Students observe teaching for a number of years, but the schools have not seen fit to make this activity a focus of study for students. It's like being a steady theatergoer and having absolutely no idea of what to look for, be it the writing, the directing, the sets, the timing, the tone, the affective pull, the audience input, and so on. One simply either likes it or dislikes it, is entertained or is bored.

Although many people have not technically observed teaching, it is fair to assume that, as former students, most have at least witnessed and/or played some supporting part in the teaching effort.

Assume that you are a teaching critic. You are going to observe five classroom situations. The situations are not the usual classrooms. Homework in the form of text reading has not been assigned, and the teacher does not ask 20 questions to see if the assignment was read. (The "What did General Washington do then?" syndrome is difficult to explain.) The description of the classroom situations are real in the sense that the activities did actually take place in social studies classrooms. If you were a teaching critic (like a drama critic) what observations would you make?

MINI-TEACHING SITUATIONS

SITUATION ONE

Senior High School. The teacher is working with a low ability group. He is using the same curriculum guide used with the average ability groups. The text has a lower reading level. The teacher observes that the students in his class appear to have no trouble learning the words of popular songs. They do as well as the "average" and "fast" students. He lists the English Reform Bills and the respective dates on the board. He puts the Reform Bills and the dates to the melody of a camp song. The students learn it quickly. The teacher and the students sing away: "1832 — the middle class came barreling through — working on the suffrage," and so on. This particular teacher is able to get his class "through" the departmental final examination. He teaches his data through music. The students seem to enjoy it.

SITUATION TWO

Intermediate Grade. The desks and chairs are all pushed back against the walls. In the middle of the room lies a huge tractor tire. The tire is filled with sand. Pocket mirrors appear as bodies of water. Strips of cardboard act as railroad tracks. Sponges, painted green, are dotted over the sand and represent wooded areas. Two students act as generals of opposing armies and describe to the rest of the class the strategy they would use in a particular battle, which actually took place in the war between the states. The other class members apparently have read the same material describing the battle and can ask questions. Three class sessions have been spent on the lesson. One day on getting the tire and accessories ready; one day on reading the material; and one day on the battle strategies.

SITUATION THREE

Intermediate Grade. The teacher is using a slide projector. She has taken pictures of paintings of the battle of Lexington from *American Heritage* and had slides made. The paintings of the same battle had been painted years apart. In the chronological order of the appearance of the paintings, the teacher shows the slides to the class. The students are asked to brain storm what they see in each picture. The teacher makes separate listings of the observations on the board. After the lists of observations are complete, the teacher asks the class to identify what each painting seems to have in common with the others. Some common factors are, according to the class: the same buildings are in each picture, all must have been painted at the same time of day as the shadows are the same, the troops in all pictures are in the same position, and so forth. The teacher then asks the class to tell what is different in each picture. The students note that in each slide the colonial troops seem to be getting stronger, to be fighting back in a more determined way. The teacher asks a question: How can you explain that paintings made a hundred years apart could be alike in some ways and different in others?

SITUATION FOUR

Junior High School. The class is in the auditorium rehearsing a play to be given before the rest of the school. The teacher tells you that putting on the play helps with language arts skills and teaches poise. The play itself helps the students to learn American history. Students have written the script. There have been a props committee, a lighting crew, a costume committee, and an advertising committee. The students start rehearsing. Francis Scott Key promenades across the stage—now a deck. At the back of the stage red lights flash and sounds like cannons firing are heard in the background. Key sees the flag still flying and over the sounds of the cannons you hear a voice repeating, "Oh, say can you see..."

SITUATION FIVE

Senior High School. The students are in groups of four. They are spending the class period playing cards. The teacher made up the game, which seems modeled after "go fish." Each card has a separate date and event on it. Students have partners, make contracts, keep score. The teacher assures you that the dates will be learned in no time and that the students will have enjoyed learning.

All five situations are descriptions of actual classrooms. In all five cases the teachers are considered to be "good teachers" by the administration, parents and youngsters. The teachers are said to be "creative," to plan well and to care whether the kids get the material. Their classes are enjoyable.

A Proffer: What often looks like good teaching *may* be a shallow type of random activity. If you will, Swift's tub. Everyone has a whale of a time. In all but one of the above situations, one sees specific techniques or activities (gimmicks?), but it is difficult to observe a larger, well thought-out, teaching strategy. Techniques and activities may be entertaining and/or a form of diversion and may assist a teacher in competing with television appeal, but unless they are part of determined strategy, it is questionable if they contribute to professional teaching.

What did the teachers in the five situations do that anyone just walking in off the street could not have done provided he liked kids?

Another Proffer: What is not worth doing is not worth doing well.

TO PLAN OR NOT TO PLAN

The fellow who lives a few houses down the street is a decent sort of fellow; dependable but a bit carefree. The neighbors have him tabbed as "hanging loose," with a sort of "nondirective" approach to his own affairs. Sometimes it can be bothersome to others. For example, he requested an estimate on painting his house and then gave the painter the incorrect address. You can imagine how his next-door neighbor felt when he discovered a stranger walking around his house to check for a needed paint job — on a house painted the summer before.

The vacation plans the fellow makes seem to support his non-

My Day·
By Mike

Mike wrote "My Day" for an English class in a large suburban high school. Obviously he can communicate. Knowing him, one could imagine him on a college campus—his manner is pleasant and courteous, his test scores and performance place him in the lower quartile of the regular track. But he will never get to college. His education has been largely irrelevant.

Comments in the margin, made by a "department chairman" during a typical teacher candidate interview, reflect the general attitude of the school.

MY DAY

To teach in our district is rewarding. Students are of high average ability. And the community wants excellence in education and is willing to pay for it.

When I get up in the morning I walk into the John and brush my teath (big thrill!) Then I get dressed, have breakfast and a cigaret. (this all happens in a span of about 15 minutes) Then I do the least important thing in my life I go to school.

The whole child and his total development are never forgotten.

The class of '66 had 36 semi-finalists—the class of '67 had 37 in the National Merit Scholarship Program.

The people that run the school say that school is moast important and everything else is seckondary but they are full of it. Thair is only one thing that will help you get through life sucksessfully and it is not school. It is called common sence and you can't learn it, you acquire it through experience. This gets so involved with politicks that I'll drop it right here and go on to more important things. After school I go to work.

Our students recognize that their teachers are the finest in the nation.

75% of our students are college bound, and college preparatory subjects are strongly emphasized.

We do have a work experience program, but it is not significant in that only 20 out of 2800 students are involved.

Work is first in my life because it is intresting and profitible. I enjoy working very much and try never to miss it. It is a big bisness and we never get enough help. If you subscribe to a newspaper you probably get it from us The News Agency. I am what you might call a foremin.

Seniors wrote 309 APP Examinations in 10 subject areas; 76% secured college credit.

I am in charge of the afternoon paperboys which may sound easy but one must considder a few things about this job before deciding its just a kids job. First of all, before I came to work thair the afternoon routs were a mess and were being handled by a man. Seckond my present rate of income is probably more per hour than a teachers. Third since I took over I've made a vast amount of improvement and cut the complaints nearly in half. I consider my small sucksess to only one thing, Common sence. Of cores an edjucation did help a little but only so I could count and read.

Each high school student's education is secured by more than $82,000 in taxable wealth, a tax base which ranks with the highest in the nation.

We hope to develop in our students the challenge of original, independent research and investigation and to train them in this method.

After work I go home eat dinner and go out (in my new car that I paid cash fore) and goof around till about 12 or so.

In order to provide a rich experience for the child, last year we had a total of 75 extracurricular activities for our students.

After 4 years in our school, we feel each student has a foundation that will enable him to participate successfully and constructively in a democratic society.

My goofing around (since that is what you seem to be moast intrested in) consists of a little drinking and just plain doing what Im inspired to do. for instance one time I was drivin along when a bus cut me off. I pulled ahed of him and stomped on the brakes. that dope almoast put all of his passangers through the front window. I have a pashon for car raceing (professional) and do it nearly every sunday. A frend of mine (lawer) has a car that cost him $10,000.00 and is a blast to drive.

Every door is open to educational progress, and professional growth, and to the expression of talent.

Closeing statement.

Teenagers are careless, indifferent, lazy (occasionly) unmannerly, disorganized, silly, restless, noisy, and just intristed in doing as they please.

WHO ISN'T!

One of the most rewarding experiences for the teacher is that after endless effort, the student finally develops insight about himself and his relationship to society.

Submitted by JON R. KINGHORN (508, Ball State University) assistant principal, West Division, Niles Township Community High Schools, Skokie, Ill.

(Reprinted by permission of the author and the KAPPAN.)

directive approach. He informed his friends that he was going to take a three-week vacation. He needed one. Where was he going? He didn't know — he would just load the kids into the car and take off. They would go according to impulse. Stop when they felt like it. Reservations? He'd take his chances. Costs? He'd play it by ear.

For some people this is getting away from it all.

It is interesting to compare him with his next-door neighbor. The neighbor is viewed as a rather sensible chap. He plans his vacation. He decides what he wants to do, where he has to go to do it, and plans for the trip. For example, last year he wanted to see some stage productions. After weighing alternatives, New York City seemed to afford the most variety and easiest accessibility. He weighed the advantages (and costs) of flying or driving. The car emerged as his choice of vehicle. It would take him longer but would allow his wife to do some antique shopping along the way. Besides, he had relatives in Syracuse and he could make that an interim stop. He got a road map, assessed alternative routes in terms of toll costs, speed potential. He had his car checked. And he figured out mileage, costs, number of stops, and so forth. He made reservations — some were definite and booked as late arrivals. Other arrangements were tentative.

In a sense, this is what this book is all about. A teacher can have a broad goal such as "teaching students how to think" and then use a "by heck and by hunch" random approach to getting there. Or, a teacher can have a broad goal and then make *plans* for reaching that goal. Plans do not necessarily have to mean that each "step" is tightly structured, but they help in making decisions along the way, in evaluating where one is, and in noting alternatives open at any particular time.

Any approach to "methods" must take into account a host of interrelated activities. To approach social studies methods as a collection of prescribed gimmicks is like having a first-aid kit in the glove compartment: it is a small (and perhaps necessary) part of the planned trip, but in no way to be viewed as the total entity.

Poor as such analogies so often are, let's look at what major component parts the planned vacation considered:

> **Goal:** To take a vacation. (This presupposes need, desire, time, funding, etc. But it is not a *specific* target. It remains a broad goal until refined.)
>
> **Objective:** To view legitimate theater. (Now the broad goal is refined into more specific terms. One can measure whether this one part has been accomplished. This objective allows for further planning.)

Alternative Subobjectives: From among a number of alternative places, New York was selected. (Note: the selection of the subobjective is consistent with the Prime Objective and supports it. And the Prime Objective is consistent and supportive of the goal.)

Vehicle: What kind of transportation is most amenable? (If the trip is not an end in itself but rather a *means*, what vehicle is most appropriate? Further subobjectives such as stopovers with relatives and antique shopping help to determine the vehicle selected. A host of variables go into determining this selection: Do the kids get car sick? Costs?)

Map: A guide for effective use of the vehicle which is used to get to the objective which, in turn, is used to achieve the goal. (This acts as a guide in decision making and further planning.)

Anticipated Activities: Considering how all the above relate, the activities selected may also prove supportive. (Planning to see summer stock along the way, reading reviews, selecting certain plays, listing the ones desired into order of priority, etc.)

One can assess how he is "progressing" (and make adjustments) along the way, as well as after the vacation has been concluded. The findings may assist in subsequent planning. It should be noted that keeping the youngsters amused during the trip in the car may call for a number of gimmicks—harmless in themselves if they do not detract from the goal, objectives, vehicle, map and activities.

Planning is a human activity. It takes making decisions, and knowing the basis upon which the decisions are made. It takes foresight, data, skill, and effort. *It moves beyond chance to probability.* It puts man's intelligence as an intervening variable between himself and his environment. It gives him *power* to become and not just be. Perhaps this is what education is all about.

COMPLEXITY

Consider the following incident: A young boy asked his father to take him to see the university in a nearby town. As they neared the main administration building the boy asked, "Is that the university?" The father replied, "No, that is the administration building." As they were approaching several high-rise dormitories the youngster asked, "Is that the university?" The father replied, "No, those are buildings where students live." When they entered a new multimillion dollar library, the son again asked, "Is this the university?" And again the father replied, "No, this is the library." "Well, where is the university?" the boy demanded. "University is the word we use to refer to all these buildings, plus the students, and the teachers all together."

While one cannot say with certainty that the young boy understood his father's explanation of "university," the story does suggest an important concept with regard to this book. The word "teaching" functions like the word "university." Teaching is not just taking attendance, lecturing, correcting papers, having discussions, writing lesson plans, disciplining students, motivating students. Teaching is a collective word, a "one" concept, if you will, which implies a collective set of relationships between singular parts. By looking at one part we do not "have the concept" because the whole is, indeed, greater than the sum of any of its parts.

"Social studies" also functions like the words "university" and "teaching." Is political science, social studies? Is economics, social studies? Is sociology, social studies? Is geography, social studies? Is psychology, social studies? Is anthropology, social studies? "No" is the appropriate answer to those questions. Social studies is the one *concept* used to designate the study of *me,* of *I,* and the extended study of me's and I's, that is, the study of man. Each of the above social sciences is a disciplined way of studying man, each insufficient by itself in the quest for total understanding, yet when related in an interdisciplinary whole — called *social studies* — they begin to put the puzzle of man together.

Many teachers do not understand the underlying complexity of such a study of man. Nor is there extensive understanding about the need to relate one discipline to another in attempting to gain explanatory power concerning the whole. Even though a doctor examines each part of us separately, he remembers that the parts interrelate and influence the functioning of other parts and the whole. If he commits the reductionist fallacy of believing that one part equals the whole, he may be sued for malpractice. The reductionist fallacy is also tempting for teachers who, out of necessity, must simplify complex understandings. The problem seems to be one of simplifying while at the same time not losing sight of the de facto complexity.

Many of the major changes in education have been initiated "outside" the educational community; for example, the prayer in the schools issue in New York, the court rulings on desegregation, and informal parent pressure groups demanding more say in education throughout the country. There are performance contracts which find business contracting to "educate," and there are alternative schools attempting to provide different educational opportunities for students. The "outside" influences demand that the educator take a long look at his own effort. Sometimes the look is not at all comforting.

The following finds the social studies teacher the issue at stake: Mr. Collins calls Mrs. Riceman for an appointment in order to discuss his son's work in her American History class. The appointment is made and Mr. Collins shows up with another gentleman who is a citizen of the community. In a simplified way, the conference ran as follows:

Collins: Now, just so I understand what we're talking about — your course deals with what subject?

Riceman: It's American History.

Collins: Yes, but certainly you don't teach *all* of American History.

Riceman: That's true. We take certain important things and teach them to the students.

Collins: Fine. How did you determine what the important things are?

Riceman: Well, it's here in the curriculum guide for 8th grade, and the curriculum guide ties right in with the text we're using.

Collins: Then, do I understand you to be saying that you and your social studies colleagues didn't select what would be taught?

Riceman: In a sense we selected from what others — good historians — selected.

Collins: According to what criteria?

Riceman: I don't understand. We teach much more than just what's in the book. It is only a base.

Collins: Fine. Give me some examples . . . of the other things . . .

Riceman: Democracy, sound thinking, good citizenship . . .

Collins: I'm afraid we are not communicating. I'm simply asking why are you teaching what you're teaching. Why this and not that?

Riceman: The course of study . . .

Collins: Let me see your final exam. Perhaps it will help.

Half an hour later, Collins and his friend are in the principal's office. Collins tells of their conference with Mrs. Riceman. The principal asks why Collins is concerned. Collins says that he and his "witness" are going to bring charges against Mrs. Riceman. "A professional who does not know why she is doing what she is doing is incompetent — be it a doctor or teacher. I plan to press charges." The principal defends Mrs. Riceman as being a good teacher, well prepared, conscientious, and dedicated to the children. She had been observed by himself.

Collins: "Being prepared, conscientious, and dedicated is not enough if these things aren't put to work. As for your observations, what criteria did *you* use?

This kind of hassle is not a remote possibility. The day is here.

Emerson said that a single drop is like a small ocean. Let's take a look at a single situation (one that actually took place) and see if we can't detect the factors at work with one another.

THE FACTS OF LIFE – THROUGH
THE EYES OF THE BEHOLDER

A first year secondary social studies teacher had his problems. Art, one of his students, had yet to turn in any written work and they were well into the first semester. He was no problem in class.

1. *"Do you believe in complete freedom of thought?"*
2. *"Sure."*

1. *"And you believe in freedom of speech?"*
2. *"Yep."*

1. *"Would you allow a Comunist to teach a 3rd grade class in America Comunism?"*
2. *"Not a 3rd grade class, maybe a high school class."*

1. *"Why not a 3rd grade class?"*
2. *"Because they wouldn't know enough not to except it."*

1. *"Would a high school class know not to except it?"*
2. *"Sure."*
1. *"Why?"*
2. *"Because they have had more time to learn democracy."*

1. *"But the 3rd graders might become Comunist?"*
2. *"Right."*
1. *"And you don't want them to become Comunist?"*
2. *"No."*
1. *"Why not?"*
2. *"They're my kids, aren't they?"*

1. *"Then you want them to believe what you believe?"*
2. *"Yes."*

1. *"Then it's all right for a Comunist to preach Comunism as long as nobody listens to him?"*
2. *"Sure."*

1. *"Then in America you want freedom to become democratic but nothing else?"*
2. *"Sure. That's the American way."*

He sat there, apparently paid attention, but never seemed to "turn on" or to have any desire to make a contribution. The first marking period he had received an "F," and this seemed justifiable in that no assignments had been completed and there was absolutely no participation in class.

After one period had concluded, the teacher observed Art dropping a piece of paper into the wastepaper basket on the way out of the room. Curiosity got the better of him and he retrieved the paper. The following was taken from the wastepaper basket. (It is reproduced *exactly* in the form in which the student had prepared it.)

The teacher couldn't wait to share it with his colleagues. Two periods later he had his moment of respite in the faculty room. He shared the work and asked his fellow teachers to "try to guess" who did it and under what circumstances it was done. They entered into the spirit of the inquiry. "It was copied from Jules Feiffer." "It was done by the art teacher as a dig at the social studies department." "It was done by a student." (The teacher confirmed this, thus narrowing down the guesses.) "Ah, it was done by a student with 'communistic' tendencies." "It was a slur on democracy." "The kid can't spell." "I wonder why they (students) waste their time this way." "I'd give him an 'F' and tell him to shape up." "I hope you didn't show this to a board of education member. . . . They'd have a fit."

The facts in the case:

1. The student (Art) was in a "slow" class.

2. He had received "F's" in all subjects on his report card.

3. He had not handed in any written work because "teachers always return the papers telling me how lousy my spelling is."

4. The particular paper found in the wastepaper basket related to the class discussion that had been carried on in the class.

5. Art had a collection of such papers. He never showed them to anyone.

6. The teacher wanted to give him an "A," but the other teachers denied that he had earned an "A." He had not handed in the assignment calling for each student to write a composition on democracy.

7. Art dropped out of school.

Using the student's art work as a vehicle, what questions emerge?

What ideas did the student attempt to express?

Did he suggest some elements of learning theory?

Did he imply some purposes to public education, and specifically for social studies education?

Did he build his case in a logical way?

Are there other ways to express an idea other than just in written form?

Is there an issue raised about who determines what is taught, to whom, and when?

What basis does one use for evaluation? What function does it serve?

We have attempted to share with you some concerns and some realities. Teaching is not for the thin-skinned and tenderhearted. Sheer negativism can lead to a generation of snipers when, in fact, we need positive and constructive architects in all areas and especially in the social studies.

SYNTHESIS AND PROLOGUE

Education is a strange land. We have tried to provide an outline map of some of the tourist traps and spots of interest. It's becoming known less and less as a vacation land. We have provided the opportunity to observe some of the native customs and ceremonies. The two neighbors bent on having a vacation exposed some of the ingredients that go into a teacher's life. And, as is true with most people, we must judge them eventually by what they do and not what they say. We have seen that some of the natives are not too sure about themselves and about what they are so busily doing to others. And we have observed that some of the young natives, held captive in this strange land, resort to secret messages asking for help. Decoding is a lost "Art."

The next chapter moves us from tourist class to immigrant status. We move in to study these "fishers of men" and attempt to see the different ways they go about planning their work and educating their young to live with knowledge, wisdom, resourcefulness. Be neither too harsh nor too critical until you know their ways . . . and yours!

"If you throw me back in, I'll give you three wishes. On the other hand, if you eat me, you'll probably get mercury poisoning."

2

MAKING DECISIONS

"... fishers of men."

Show us not the aim without the way,
For ends and means on earth are so entangled
That changing one, you change the other too:
Each different path brings other ends in view.

FERDINAND LaSALLE

The fisherman usually seems to be an odd combination of the romanticist and the empiricist. In one sense, he is the epitome of modern man. Look at what he does. He has a dream of catching the "big one." He studies the environment into which he will intervene. He knows the influence of the temperature of the water and of the depth and speed of the current, and he can identify the natural feeding spots. He knows how to motivate and how to get attention. He knows his quarry's habits—what he likes and dislikes, when he feeds and when he dozes, whom he hangs out with, and even his mating habits. The fisherman allows for individual differences and accordingly takes great pains to use the right lure or bait. He shares some of his thoughts and findings with others, but never *all* his information. The thrill is in the strike, the play, and the landing. He may catch *a* big one ... and even spend moments admiring the catch. But *the* "Big One" will always be the next one. So he readies himself for the next strike and anticipates the thrill of the landing.

Some fishermen are pretty keen philosophers. This is not to say that they know philosophic schools nor to deny that some would think Plato was a Walt Disney character. A short while ago we had this confirmed in a direct way. Not far from a university being visited was a small fishing village. We had a chance to meet an "old timer" who just ached for a chance to reminisce and to discuss the whole world. We asked him about the local university and how he felt about education.

"You know," he said, "those educators are a lot like fishermen. Only they're not as bright. It's a big ocean and most of us only have

39

a small boat. A fisherman knows this. The educator forgets. An educator is lucky if he even gets to the rail to drop a line. He's not used to the roll and the pitch. And, you know—he won't use the net. Guess he wants his own thrill more than the catch. And he doesn't pay much attention to what can help him—the weather, the wind, the gulls . . . he's a gambling man more than a thinking man." The old man paused for a while apparently waiting to be disputed. When this didn't happen, he continued. "I feel kinda sorry for the man. He must be unhappy. He expects too much and spends a lot of time on things that don't really help him." He decided that he wouldn't take a professor's job for all the salt in the sea.

If you ask a fisherman why he does what he does, the chances are that he'll feign not understanding the question or dismiss the whole thing because "it's just common sense." If you ask a teacher, the answer becomes more complex. Students are not large mouth bass. And *they* have been known to do some baiting themselves. The *interaction* involves human exchanges. The fishing analogy breaks down. Acting is not *just* reacting, but forces modifications and changes in midstream. A well planned lesson must include a *base* for making decisions in the midst of the action. In a rapid-fire, decision-making situation, a teacher must be sensitive to the opportunities for choice as well as able to predict the consequences of choosing this alternative over that. Each on-the-spot decision influences a range of subsequent choices. This may partially account for the two extremes of teaching methods so often encountered in the classroom. The *Giver of Directions* decides in advance to narrow the range of on-the-spot choices by limited interaction to predictable student reaction. The "love me, I'm trying" teacher goes to the other extreme and gambles that increased interaction may lead to something worthwhile for the students. *The teacher's own needs play a major part in deciding what classroom procedures are used.*

There is no question that one of the basic inclusive acts in the total teaching "act" is that of making decisions. This is at the heart of planning and of putting the plans to work in the actual classroom situation. Let's try to pin this down a bit.

A colleague who teaches a social studies methods course shared with us a tape he had made of one of his classes. He was anxious to get some feedback on how well the class was able to relate content and process. The instructor's decision-making role and his importance as an intervener (or intruder) in the class functioning was vivid. We played the tape a second time and recorded the explicit or implicit decisions he made during the hour class. He made over 70 decisions—at least as implied from hearing the tape. For example, his initial posing of a problem got limited feedback so he apparently decided to rephrase the proposition. He had to decide *when* to intervene, *how* to intervene and with *what* to intervene. He had to decide what questions to honor, what points to use immediately and what points to "bank" or challenge. He had to select the timing of synthesizing, methods of analyzing data with the class, who and what needed clarification. He also considered when to interject his own reserve of data, when to let which student "go," and when to redirect. He even had to decide what moments of silence were worth keeping.

We then went through each apparent decision and asked him to explain it. What was he trying to do? How did this relate? What alternatives did he have in terms of a specific act or reaction? Most of his responses were in terms of the "Big One"—the major objective he had had for that particular class session. But each specific decision was tied somehow to intermediate objectives which he tried to build into a consistent and cumulative relationship with the major objective. Many of his responses were a form of rationalizing his own interest in a particular student or idea as disassociated ends in themselves. In some cases he acted—he deliberately selected a particular thing to do in terms of a desired end. In other cases he simply reacted without deliberation. We were not concerned with whether acting or reacting was right or wrong, but rather with determining the almost unbelievable decision-making role a teacher plays. A sensitive teacher, over the course of any day's teaching, makes more decisions than most executives. And for the teacher, time is not easily manipulated into an ally. A class session allows little leisure time for protracted contemplation. Decisions have to be made and *are* made. The question is . . . how?

Can a teacher develop a framework to assist him in making classroom decisions? Taking time to be aware of his goal and specific objectives gives a crucial reference base. This becomes a compass and helps to guide each move in the general direction. It puts up initial boundaries to protect from random activity. (Recall from Chapter 1 the two men planning their vacation?)

Some of us recall dismissing the whole concept of lesson planning. It was kind of "old fashioned" and "too restrictive." But to say that lesson planning is not appropriate is to say that thinking in advance of acting is inappropriate. Some may reject the nature and form of the "old" lesson plan. Fair enough. But to reject the lesson plan concept because it is "too restrictive" is to make some basic assumptions about the *uses* of a lesson plan. It *is* possible for one to plan for flexibility and change.

We are providing a case study which was used as a *vehicle* at different grade levels. Consider the study for possible use in a social studies classroom. Can you determine a number of possible uses? Would you label it history? Or would you call it anthropology? sociology? economics?

CASE STUDY: SENIOR HIGH*

On the subtropical north coast of Australia lives a tribe of native hunters and fishermen called the Yir Yoront. Like most primitive Australians, long cut off from other cultures, the tribe enjoyed great stability. Customs and beliefs were standardized and before any change was accepted, a myth had to be invented which proved that one's ancestors did things that way, and thus the change was really no change at all.

Up to the turn of the century, the tribe was still living in the Stone Age. An important tool, a short-handled stone ax, was used to build huts, cut firewood, and make other tools for hunting, fishing, and gathering wild honey. The stone heads came from a quarry 400 miles to the south, and were obtained from other tribes in an annual intertribal fiesta. The handle was fitted with great skill and care and attached with bark and gum. The completed article—or artifact—was far more than a tool. It had become a symbol, a totem, a sign of the owner's masculinity, to be cherished and handed down, and loaned only with the greatest circumspection. The stone ax was not only useful, it was a kind of keystone in the belief system of the Yir Yoront.

About 1900, steel axes began to filter in along the tribal trade routes. They were welcomed at first as more efficient; one could cut down a tree much faster. By 1915, missionaries were distributing the steel axes as gifts and rewards. If a man worked especially hard he might get an ax, and so might his wife or young son. The missionaries hoped by this means to induce people to plant and fence gardens and improve their diet.

The idea was excellent, but it overlooked the culture concept. The steel ax destroyed a most important symbol in the belief system of the tribe. A man lost his importance and dignity; his very masculinity was threatened without his stone ax. Women and children, now possessing axes themselves, became independent and disrespectful. The entire system of age, sex, and kinship roles was thrown into confusion. The old trade relations were disrupted and the intertribal fiesta was robbed of significance and charm. Stealing and wife lending increased. The ancient totem system was shattered, for it could not be decided whether the steel ax should be a totem of the Sunlit Cloud Iguana Clan, as the stone ax had been since time out of mind, or the totem of the Head-to-the-East Corpse Clan. . .

---

*From Chase, Stuart: *The Proper Study of Mankind.* New York, Harper & Row, 1963, pp. 112–113.

Anthropologists, studying the situation in the 1930's, found that the culture had not broken down so completely as in the case of certain other tribes more exposed to western influences, but it was shaky and insecure. The major reason was the change in the composition of one artifact, from stone to steel, and a change technically for the better.

A junior high school social studies teacher read the case study and categorically denied any positive use for it. She was teaching geography and could see no sense in interjecting such material. It had no bearing whatsoever on what she was trying to teach and would divert the students from learning geography.

A senior high school teacher reviewed the case study and saw it as being useful as an example of how other people live. When asked what he thought his students might specifically get out of the study, he responded that it would help to bring "better understanding and tolerance." He decided to use it and to share his plans for making it an effective vehicle.

He passed out the case study at the end of a period and assigned it as homework. (When something is assigned, most students automatically assume that that means simply to read it and to be familiar with the information.) The teacher then elaborated, in writing, his plans for the next day's session. The first part of his plan appeared as a list of questions:

1. What kind of climate would you find on the north coast of Australia?

2. The name "Yir Yoront" refers to what group of people living in Australia?

3. What did the Yir Yoront have to assure themselves before any significant change could come about?

4. If we observed the Yir Yoront around the turn of the century, we would place them in what "age" of man?

5. Give three uses of the stone ax.

6. How often did the Yir Yoront hold an intertribal fiesta?

7. Give two ways in which the stone ax was important to the tribe.

8. The year 1900 was important to the Yir Yoront for what reason?

9. What did the missionaries do in 1915? What did they hope to accomplish?

10. Give two reasons why the tribe might have resisted the missionaries.

11. What was the importance of the Sunlit Cloud Iguana and the Head-to-the-East Corpse Clans?

12. What did the anthropologists find in 1930?

The individual student written assignment to be completed in class:

Write an essay showing that although the change was helpful in technical matters, other problems were created. Give an example of a similar thing happening in the United States today.

This general approach probably looks familiar. It is by no means the exception. Teaching social studies often is a matter of getting students to recall information and of making an attempt to show that the information is somehow important to the students. It must be noted that the teacher *did* plan. And he, in fact, *did* implement the plan.

Let's review the type, extent, and implications of the planning effort.

The case study was recognized by the teacher as being something that he could use with his students. It could be a *vehicle*. It was appropriate to a social studies class because it did discuss "other" people and some of their history, geography, customs, economics, social structure, and problems. Although not singularly labeled as such, the social sciences were incorporated into a social studies lesson in an indirect way.

The teacher *did* have a broad goal or purpose for using the case study: it was an example of how other people live. This example could contribute to the students' having more "understanding and tolerance." In other words, the case study was not used just because it was available. It served a purpose.

At this level of planning it is difficult to argue. The teacher could demonstrate what he was doing and why. But too often we stop at this level. The teacher has planned and implemented. Therefore, he is doing his job. . ?

Let's move to the next level.

The teacher has made several giant leaps of logic which may be questionable. It can be inferred from the questions that the teacher believes that the "knowing" of specific details in the case study is somehow logically connected or related, in a causal way, to this goal of understanding and tolerance. His planning was at the "fact" level and focused upon recall. The planning did *not* identify *specific objectives* and did not address planning directed at concepts and skills.

His plan *did* address an extremely broad area, allowing for the relating of some of the data into conceptual form. This was to be done in the written assignment. The teacher could argue that he gave his students an opportunity "to think" and to make the data relevant. Refer back to the assignment. It is fairly broad. The students do not have specific targets.

The planned activity of question-response (act-react) and the individual written assignment imply a closed process system, a system that is teacher directed toward preset and closed ends. There is a "right" answer. The teacher acts as a *Giver of Directions* in a number of ways. He has established the framework for appropriate data, a structure for response, and a prescribed channel for communication. He uses questions to focus attention upon specific data and gives pointed directions by accepting or rejecting a student response. The G.O.D. role also seems to be underscored in the individual writing assignment. The assumption seems to be made that thinking and learning are not necessarily a cooperative "building" experience by individuals in conjunction with others. No opportunity was given for pooling shared data from sources other than the case study.

The controlled situation did not allow an open flow of feedback and thus denied an opportunity for the teacher and other students to check their data, thinking patterns, logic, inferences, generalizations, need for more data, and so on.

Does his plan provide for student, teacher, or vehicle evaluation? Has the teacher any way of knowing if he has approached his stated goal?

Without a doubt, the class would be firmly "managed." This was built into the plan and raises the question of the possibility that a real and subtle goal in the plan is to secure a quiet, well disciplined classroom in an appropriate study climate.

What did the students learn?

And, perhaps of equal importance, what has the teacher allowed himself to learn?

". . for all the salt in the sea."

CASE STUDY: INTERMEDIATE

A student teacher, three weeks into her school experience, was also given the case study. She read it and *enjoyed it herself.* In her own words, "My mind couldn't stop running all over the place." This was her problem. She saw a number of uses for her particular class. She faced too many alternatives from which to choose. Her own reading implied a variety of interests and she could see a myriad of possibilities.

She identified several concepts appearing in the case study and listed them (in different forms) for *herself* prior to making an effort to plan for classroom use. She had to "... straighten out my own thinking before I could pick and choose." She shared the list (in note form):

> The whole concept of myth. It's more than nice stories. Definite influence on the way people see the world and what they do in the world.

> Some cultures have legitimatized ways of introducing change and this keeps the tension off — we don't embrace a violent overthrow of the government, but we do allow freedom of speech?

> The whole idea of invention and technology and how a change in one thing brings about a whole host of changes not directly related. What does it mean to the status quo?

> Roles. The masculine role and the feminine role as a learned phenomenon. The feminist movement.

> The question of complexity. You fool around with one part — it looks innocent enough — and then the whole thing starts to shake. "Parts" and "whole" concept. Question of planning change.

Newspapers and magazines provided other examples which seemed to feed the issues she had raised. And these were examples a student could find in his own world — if he knew what to look for. For example, the local paper carried an article on Ralph Nader in which the influence of the automobile on our way of living was assessed. Initially the automobile increased the efficiency of transportation. But, for several related reasons, the *number* of cars increased to the point where it took almost as long to cross New York City by car as it did by the horse and carriage around 1900. Progress? Insurance rates reflect some of the "side" effects of the car. This one article alone could provide living examples of multiple causation and multiple effect in the students' own culture. And, the student teacher found other examples: Has the introduction of sophisticated weapons brought about change in international relations, in coexistence strategies, in the domestic economy, in people's value systems? In medical technology, how are such things as death rates, population growth, birth control, abortion legislation, and moral values influenced?

What the student teacher was experiencing is interesting.

Technically she was not yet a blue-ribboned, certified teacher. She was still a student and approached teaching as a *student* rather than as a self-perceived teacher. She was becoming overwhelmed by the possibilities of the case study. And she recognized that she had no disciplined and systematic approach to help in the formulation of plans for classroom use. She wasn't afraid to ask for help; she discussed her dilemma with her supervisor. She was fortunate. He propounded a sound lesson. A potentially good teacher has many more problems than does an average or poor teacher in the classroom. It is the intellectually alive, alert, concerned and sensitive teacher who is aware of the overwhelming number of positive alternatives open to him. *It is complex.* And the complexity demands of the conscientious teacher a more organized system of planning than is usually assumed.

In this instance the supervisor suggested that the student teacher visit a lower grade classroom in order to observe what the teacher would do with the *same* case study. And he suggested that the student teacher work with the teacher in planning a lesson. The suggestions came as a surprise. Why would a teacher preparing to teach at the secondary level spend part of her training within an elementary situation? Why would the reverse move be effective? A secondary level teacher can find assistance in approaching planning by "reducing" his thinking to teaching appropriate for younger students. A primary or intermediate teacher can find help in viewing secondary materials as potential resources for her own planning. The organizational structures of a school system often box out valuable planning experiences.

The elementary level teacher knew that the case study, in its secondary form, was too difficult in reading level and its data too complex. However, the material could be used at a different grade level *without losing integrity, meaning, and a recognition of complexity. In a basic sense, every lesson attempts to do just this.* A teacher who can effect such a "reduction" has an untapped wealth of potential materials at his disposal. There is a difference between wildly searching for and pouncing on data, and intelligently selecting and modifying data to be used.

The intermediate level teacher adapted the case study to her grade level needs. Printed in primary type, the case study appeared as follows:

ON A COAST IN AUSTRALIA LIVES A TRIBE OF HUNT-ERS AND FISHERMEN. THESE PEOPLE HAVE NOT HAD CONTACT WITH OTHER PEOPLE. HOW THESE PEOPLE LIVE HAS NOT CHANGED MUCH OVER THE

YEARS. THEY STILL BELIEVE THE SAME THINGS THAT THEIR GRANDPARENTS BELIEVED. THEY STILL HUNT FOOD AND FISH THE SAME WAY THEIR GRANDPARENTS HUNTED AND FISHED. BEFORE ANYTHING CAN CHANGE, THE PEOPLE MUST TELL THEMSELVES THAT THE "NEW" THING IS NOT REALLY NEW. THEY HAVE TO CONVINCE THEMSELVES THAT A CHANGE IS NOT A CHANGE.

THESE PEOPLE HAVE AN IMPORTANT TOOL. IT IS A SHORT-HANDLED STONE AX USED TO BUILD HUTS, CUT FIREWOOD, AND HELP SHAPE OTHER TOOLS FOR USE IN HUNTING AND FISHING. THE STONE HEAD OF THE AX COMES FROM A STONE QUARRY OVER FOUR HUNDRED MILES AWAY AND IS RECEIVED FROM OTHER TRIBES DURING A FIESTA. THE HANDLE OF THE AX IS WORKED ON WITH GREAT CARE AND IS SECURED TO THE STONE HEAD BY BARK AND GUM.

THE MAN WHO OWNS SUCH A STONE AX IS CONSIDERED TO BE AN IMPORTANT LEADER. CELEBRATIONS ARE HELD WHEN THE OWNER PASSES THE AX DOWN TO HIS CHILDREN.

MISSIONARIES CAME UPON THE PEOPLE AND GAVE OUT STEEL AXES. A MAN MIGHT GET A STEEL AX. HIS SON MIGHT GET A STEEL AX. HIS WIFE MIGHT GET ONE. THE MAN NO LONGER LED HIS FAMILY. BUSINESS WASN'T GOOD. THE FIESTA WAS NO LONGER NEEDED. CRIME INCREASED.

As the student teacher and the teacher reviewed the reworked study it was recognized that it might cause a reading problem for some students. However, as long as the students were not to be tested on it, *any* questions about the story—words or understandings or whatever—would be fair. This would not be a problem.

The mutual planning started. The teacher and her class had already worked with two concepts: (1) man *learns* to behave and act in different ways; and (2) a change in one thing causes changes in many things. The teacher wanted to see if the students could "transfer" these concepts to something new. The case study could do two things: it could reinforce the concepts, and it could be used as an evaluation instrument for the teacher to see how well she was doing.

The class had also been working on some skills. The students had worked on trying to identify facts, how to put facts together into an idea, and trying to answer the question, "So what?" after an idea had been made.

The first thing the teacher wanted to do was to review the concepts and the skills. She suggested using a couple of "warm up" vehicles *before* passing out the case study. But the warm-ups *had* to be selected in terms of the concepts and skills. After some weighing of alternative vehicles, they decided to use two. The first would be taken from Oscar Hammerstein's *South Pacific*.

> You've got to be taught
> To hate and fear,
> You've got to be taught
> From year to year,
> You've got to be taught before it's too late
> Before you are six or seven or eight
> To hate all the people your relatives hate,
> You've got to be carefully taught.

The students would be asked if there were any facts in the song. They would be asked if there were any ideas? (And if an idea is made up of a lot of little facts, is the idea a fact?)

The second warm-up vehicle, the student teacher and teacher made up. It appears as a situation:

Child A comes into a drugstore. He is crying. He buys a chocolate ice cream cone and stops crying.
Child B comes into the drugstore. She is crying. She buys a chocolate ice cream cone and stops crying.
Child C comes into the drugstore, is crying, buys a chocolate ice cream cone.

This would be used as follows:

The students would be asked to predict if Child C would stop crying. (Differences of opinion among the students were anticipated.)

The students would be asked to give the facts in the story.

The students would be asked to put the facts into an idea.

The students would be asked how they could "test" the ideas to see if they *work*.

Then the case study would be passed out. The teacher would put what she and the students called the "diving board" on the board. In this case it would be three things:

Facts?
Ideas?
What Ideas Can We Trust?

After reading the case study with the students and clarifying any problems, the teacher would pose the following questions:

IF YOU WERE GOING TO BRING ABOUT CHANGE IN THIS TRIBE, WHAT WOULD YOU HAVE TO THINK ABOUT? WHAT CHOICES WOULD YOU HAVE TO MAKE? CAN YOU BE SURE THAT YOU ARE DOING THE RIGHT THING?

The student teacher had a unique experience. We know too well that it doesn't happen often enough. She had a chance to go through the processes of planning with the teacher. She had the opportunity to view planning as a building process and not just as separate activities hung together through the grace of sequence in time. She also had a chance to work with the teacher's system of keeping records. The teacher used 5″ × 8″ cards. Each vehicle was put on a separate card and the intended use was noted. These were filed away in a shoe box. On a separate 5″ × 8″ card, the teacher roughed in a general guide to the lesson—the concepts, skills, intended use of the vehicle, the warm-up vehicles, and the related activities. This was on the front side of the card. The reverse side was used to record what *really* happened when the plan was tried. A different way of lesson planning?

The student teacher still had a nagging thought. The teacher appeared to be trying to do too much in a single lesson—in a sense, she had *transferred* her own concerns to the new situation. At this point a crucial factor emerged, and the teacher helped to clarify it. A lesson plan is artificial if one assumes it will automatically fit neatly into a set time block. If this is assumed, teachers often end up "forcing" the plan and in so doing make it ineffective. The plan can become a trap.

In this particular situation it was anticipated that two class sessions would be needed. The teachers would have to see how far they got in the first session and then make necessary adjustments in the broad plan.

The stone ax case study seems a natural for teaching social studies. There are a number of social science concepts in the study and it seems like a logical, reasonable vehicle to use.

MATERIALS AVAILABLE

Ah, the rub. Teachers have told us that they cannot find such studies. If one reads and observes and, if one knows what he is looking for, such materials are more plentiful than imagined. It may call for some adaptation and modification. In Chapter 7, Vehicle Selection, we will suggest specific ways of identifying such materials and of preparing your findings for use.

At this point, however, it is important to realize that some material which might not initially *appear* to be social science oriented may, in fact, prove to be of substantial help in the classroom. Again, it calls for knowing how to plan.

The teacher in the next situation was able to use such material. He taught a secondary course in *Problems of Democracy*. It was an elective for juniors and seniors. One of the primary goals of the course was to have the students gain a better understanding of the relationships among science, technology, and values.

His students had complained that school and society were becoming increasingly depersonalized. They blamed the "metallic spurs" of technology—the IBM cards; scheduling, ways of reporting, and so forth, were now specific holes in cards. You were a number, not a person. The teacher decided to utilize the issue.

He started a class by asking if the students believed that computers should replace our jury system. The initial reaction was to treat the issue superficially—to assume it was a joke. But as the class started to play with the idea, it became a real issue. The teacher argued that the jury system is predicated upon: the ability to differentiate fact from hearsay; the assumption that peers will reason, and will use logic and objectivity in reaching a verdict that would go "beyond reasonable doubt." He pointed out that until now a verdict by peers seemed the better way, considering all the alternatives. "If a jury deals with the question of *probability* of guilt, the difficult aspect of serving on a jury is that of collectively determining reasonable doubt." People being human, he argued, are obviously influenced by much more than just the facts. Case in point: *Twelve Angry Men**, a film the class had seen earlier in the year. Past experiences, different value systems, fatigue, other obligations, and a number of other variables influence the perception of reasonable doubt.

On the other hand, we could use computers. The lawyers and judge could determine the admissable evidence. A reasonable doubt probability level could be statistically established. The case could be programmed, and the computer could establish the odds. "And that's what it's all about," the teacher maintained.

---

*The Critic and Film Series, British Film Institute, London, England.

Some of the students were upset. This would be another step in dehumanizing man. Some of the students played with the idea. One maintained that if he were guilty he would want a jury of humans "because I could get a lawyer who could appeal to their feelings." Interestingly, most of the class agreed. One argued that the motivation of a defendant in breaking a law was an important factor, and she couldn't understand how a computer could react to that kind of data. Another student wondered how anyone could judge "intent."

The next day a student brought a newspaper clipping to class and shared it with the comment that "computers might not replace juries but were on the way to replacing teachers." The article again raised some of the issues the students had previously encountered.

HOW TO RUN A BANK?
COMPUTER A TEACHER

The best way to learn how to run a bank is to run one for a while and see what makes money and what loses.

But bankers are dubious, to say the least, about any trial and error process where real money is concerned.

The Cleveland chapter of the American Institute of Banking has a banking school course that sets young men managing mythical banks — then tests their decisions against a computer.

Teams of four or five students are being taught by John B. McCarter of Central National Bank. The students are given a set of facts about a "paper bank."

They decide what to do about the bank in the coming financial quarter. Will interest rates go up or down? How about loan volume? Is it time to revise some investments?

Their decisions are put into an IBM computer. The computer calculates the results of the decisions. The team finds out if it made money or lost it — or if its bank is out of business.

The same process, using the computer's new picture of the bank's condition, is repeated for the next financial quarter.

(Cleveland Plain Dealer)

The teacher wasn't too sure where to go with the whole issue — if any place. In a sense he was like the student teacher. He was aware that the questions raised were loaded with possibilities.

They related to his broad goal, but just "playing" with the article in class was not enough.

The newspaper clipping brought in by a student and the resulting discussion in class reminded him of an article on bridge playing he had clipped out. He liked bridge so it had caught his eye, but it had done more than just trigger interest. The way it was written was a lesson in applied skills, and he had saved it because it appeared to be a description of a scientific way of thinking applied to man's thinking about a social situation. What would a computer have done if fed a program of similar data and procedures? He decided to use the article as a vehicle and had it dittoed for the students.

HOW BRIDGE CHEATERS WERE CAUGHT*

New York. At least 10 bridge experts played a part in investigating accusations of cheating in Buenos Aires that have rocked the world of international bridge.

Among those who played key roles in the investigation at the recent world contract bridge championships were two American players, two nonplaying captains, officials of the American Contract Bridge League, the British Bridge League and the World Bridge Federation and this writer.

Terence Reese and Boris Schapiro of Britain, acknowledged as one of the world's greatest partnerships during the last 15 years, had been accused of signaling to each other by illegal methods during the tournament.

Ralph Swimer, the British nonplaying captain, voluntarily benched the two players and conceded two matches. As a result of the concessions, the United States ended in second place, behind Italy, and Argentina was third.

Reese and Schapiro denied the accusations. Schapiro, on his return to London said: "I will never play again."

Interviews and discussions with many of those involved in the investigation have contributed to the following account:

On Monday night, May 17, B. Jay Becker, a member of the American team noticed that Reese, the opponent at his left, was holding his cards in what appeared to be an uncomfortable and awkward fashion. He then looked to his right, and saw a similar mannerism by Schapiro.

During the rest of the session he noticed that his opponents held their cards in a variety of ways, and that one, two, three or four fingers showed at the back of the cards. He said he felt

---

*Truscott, Alan. Copyright 1965 by The New York Times Company. Reprinted by permission.

sure that Reese and Schapiro were passing information to each other, but had no idea what the signals meant.

He mentioned his observations to his partner, Mrs. Dorothy Hayden. Three days later, on May 20, they again played against Reese and Schapiro. They testified that they observed the same mannerisms on that occasion.

Becker shared his suspicions with this writer and with his non-playing captain, John Gerber of Houston, Texas. He asked both to regard the information as confidential. He hoped to avoid a general scandal, and planned to deal with the matter on a player-to-player level.

On Friday afternoon, May 21, the four people who were in on the secret, saw Reese and Schapiro in play against the leading Italian pair, Pietro Forquet and Benito Garozzo. The same finger mannerisms were observed. Notes were made by Mrs. Hayden and Gerber of the number of fingers shown by each player on each deal.

In the early hours of Saturday morning a conference between Becker, Mrs. Hayden and this writer reached an explanation of the meaning of the signals. The official records of the bidding and play were compared with the notes already made of the observed finger movements. It was found that the connecting link between the records and the notes appeared to be the number of hearts held in every case.

Four hours later this writer presented the evidence to Gerber. Feeling that his duty to his team and to the other teams required him to do so, Gerber communicated the details to Robin MacNab, president of the American Contract Bridge League, and Walldemar von Zedtwitz, the league president emeritus.

It was agreed that Swimer should be informed, and this writer was requested to lay the evidence before him. In cases of this sort, the records of the bidding and play can be examined, and they were.

It appeared that Reese and Schapiro had an almost perfect record in bidding situations relating to the heart suit. Not once had they missed a good heart contract, and only once had they reached an unsound one.

The same night Reese and Schapiro played against Argentina, and records of finger movements were kept by Swimer and Geoffrey Butler, the chairman of the British Bridge League. Again the number of fingers shown proved to correspond, almost exactly, with the number of hearts held.

Early Sunday morning, May 23, a meeting of the World Bridge Federation's appeals committee was held and all the evidence collected was considered. Reese and Schapiro were called to the meeting and denied the allegations absolutely.

Meetings of the full executive committee of the World Bridge Federation, including Gen. Alfred M. Gruenthers, the federation's honorary president, continued for the rest of the day. The committee had to consider the appropriate course of action in circumstances without precedent in bridge history.

The decisive action was taken by Swimer.

Working together in class, the students and the teacher sequenced the specific events as related by the article. In so doing, they evolved an outline of the problem-solving processes involved. Obviously the teacher did not care if the class learned all the names of people involved or the organizations or dates. He *was* concerned that the vehicle (in this case the article) provide for two things: (1) an opportunity for students to be cognizant of the role of the computer as a decision maker in human affairs; and (2) an opportunity for students to be cognizant of the skills involved and the methods used in getting and relating data. He believed the specific article would allow for both ends *and* would allow for both ends to be *related*.

What did the sequential outline indicate:

1. A single observation of an unusual incident. In this case an awkward way of holding cards. (What does this suggest about the "screening process" man uses in making countless observations in his daily activities?)

2. Noting of *another* observation of a similarly unusual incident at the same table and by the same people. (How does one form an initial test on something observed?)

3. The relating of the two observations (pieces of data) into a possible relationship. (Is this what we mean by conceptualizing?)

4. Checking the observations to see if the "relationship" continued? (Checking to see if it might be "chance." What role does repetition play?)

5. The initial observer informed his partner and asked her to make her own, independent observation. (How do others help?)

6. The two separate observations supported one another.

7. The two initial observers requested additional observation by two other people.

8. The specific ways of holding the cards were *recorded* by one observer. (What is the importance of recording data rather than relying on memory?)

9. The recorded notes on observed finger movements were compared with official records. (What is the importance of relating two different kinds of recorded data?)

10. The comparing of recorded observations and official records indicated some relationship between finger placement and the number of hearts held.

11. The relationship now took the form of a *hypothesis:* The number of fingers shown correspond to the number of hearts held. (What role does a hypothesis play? What does it allow people to do?)

12. The hypothesis was used in checking against a number of hands (17) and the relationship held. (What is the difference between a possibility and a probability?)

13. A "public" record was now available. The two who were suspected had "an almost perfect" record in heart bidding situations. (What about the exception?)

14. The two who were suspected played another team. Records of finger movements were made by two *different observers*—including the captain of the team represented by the two suspects. Again, the relationship was consistent

15. The two accused appeared and were confronted by the evidence. They denied the allegations.

16. The two players were benched by their captain.

The teacher could have done such an outline himself and then passed out the results. But the students in going through the process of making the sequential outline voiced some significant questions which, in turn, led into a pertinent class discussion.

Why didn't the first player simply accuse the two other players of cheating? What's the difference between "private" evidence and "public" evidence? Can't you "just feel" something is right? How can one's personal involvement possibly distort perceptions? Why weren't the two accused after "step" six? What might have influenced a player's perceptions?

The whole issue focused upon data and probability. Were the two guilty? The teacher reported having read another newspaper article which was a follow-up. This article suggested that the two had no reason to cheat and, furthermore, if they were going to cheat there were a lot more sophisticated ways to do it. It was supportive of the two accused.

The students tried to reach some agreement. The data had been validated—to a point—by a public test indicating a positive correlation between finger movement and success with the heart suit. Recalling the number of incidents and tests, what was the probability of the finger movement being sheer coincidence? Could the students say with absolute certitude that the two were guilty?

No, the class could not. There just was no certainty to be had. All the students might agree upon would be a method of determining the probability and a statistical cut-off point for establishing reasonable doubt.

It became obvious that no matter what the verdict, it was possible that it might be wrong. This upset some members of the class.

Then, they went back to the jury situation: What alternatives did they have other than the method described in the bridge article? What about the role of computer and man?

TEXTBOOKS AS MATERIALS

The bridge vehicle allowed the teacher to discuss the skills involved in handling quantitative data, and skills involved in interpretation and analysis. A social studies teacher is confronted with a multitude of situations in which the processes can be used—even to the point of having skill development become a prime focus of a particular lesson. There are countless opportunities at all grade levels. For example: A standard elementary social studies textbook states: "In our country we are free to choose the place where we will live. We are free to buy any house we can pay for." Note: This is presented to the students as a *statement of fact.* It implies that specific empirical data have been related, that the relationship is consistent, that the statement is beyond the hypothesis stage. What could a teacher do with this?

The phrase "in our country" refers, in context, to the United States. "We" apparently is a reference to *all* citizens of the United States and is not qualified with "most" or "some" or "many." Logically the statement holds that all citizens in the United States can buy any house they can pay for. Following the processes, what kinds of data would have to be collected? How could the data be related? Could we form a hypothesis? How could one test it? What exceptions might we find? How might the data on exceptions be related?

Obviously most textbooks do not provide a data bank for the kinds of information needed in this type of teaching approach. Just as obviously, to teach such a statement as an accurate description of fact is to teach something that is not valid. This suggests that, in some cases, we may be doing substantial harm.

It is important to note that the bridge article is different from the case study taken from *The Proper Study of Mankind*. The latter addresses the social sciences while the former was intended as a report of an event. In this particular case an enterprising teacher saw a possible connection between his objectives and the article — even though the "content" of the article was not social science per se.

But it should be clear that his use of the article was not a random activity to provide some diversion. On the contrary, he knew his objectives and *then* was able to work at creating meaning.

"He's a gambling man more than a thinking man. . . ." A thinking man is also a gambler when he translates thoughts into action. But he knows the odds. This is what planning is all about . . . and there is *no guarantee!*

SYNTHESIS AND PROLOGUE

Analogies are never complete in the sense of being an accurate parallel. A fisherman uses common sense in planning. A teacher has to use this also but must go far beyond. We have attempted to provide opportunities for you to become involved in the decision-making processes involved in teaching. You have had a chance to see it from a number of different angles — the college professor and his tape, another approach that deals primarily with recall, the student teacher who met the problem all good teachers must live with, the elementary teacher who knew what she wanted to do and used planning as a building process, and the teacher who approached planning as a form of skill development. If all this suggests anything, it appears that a social studies teacher has a number of alternatives open to him. The selection of alternatives, the decisions made in planning and in the classroom presuppose that the teacher knows what he wants to accomplish — not in terms of broad and nebulous goals — but in terms of specific objectives. The creating of a rationale is what we consider in the next chapter.

We have used the terms concepts, skills, and vehicles in context. Don't worry about pinning the terms down at this point. It should become evident that certain personal characteristics are almost prerequisites for teaching: intelligence, intellectual curiosity, ability and desire to do divergent and convergent thinking, energy, and a willingness to risk. In varying degrees most people have these characteristics. To some extent, they can be developed. In a sense, this is what teaching is all about—for the teacher as well as for the student—for these are two ingredients that are invariably mixed if either is to have an identity.

To the rationale . . . and a base of reference for decision making.

"Damn it, Conrad, I'm for peace,
too—but not as an end in itself."

3

DEVELOPING A RATIONALE

The Almighty has His own purpose

The first breakthrough many teachers need to achieve is a clear formulation of their own convictions. One source of social studies weakness is the scarcity of teachers with mature convictions about social studies goals. Teachers need not all agree on their goals, but they should be consistent with themselves.

DONALD W. ROBINSON

IN OUR WISDOM

Ogden Nash wrote, "God in His wisdom made the fly. And then forgot to tell us why." A disgruntled parent leaving a conference with a social studies teacher was overheard to say: "The people in their wisdom made the schools. And left them to the quirks of fools." Apparently the conference had not gone too well. The perplexed parent might have been more relevant had he bemoaned that "Colleges in their wisdom make the teacher. And then turn loose this random creature."

At a regional social studies meeting, one speaker commented to the assembled group that if happiness were, indeed, the art of self-deception, then he "must be addressing the happiest people in the world...people who don't know what they are doing or why they are doing it and yet persist in the effort, expecting plaudits from appreciative taxpayers."

When asked why he felt that he had received such a warm ovation upon conclusion of the unmasked attack, he claimed that "social studies teachers applaud style more than content." He did appreciate, however, the audience's willingness to confirm his observations.

In a heated exchange in another situation a school administrator in an urban situation took a similar type of swipe at social studies teachers.

> Look... most of the black parents are more "middle class" when it comes to schooling than are the second generation suburbanite. They want their kid to first of all know how to read. This is the basic tool — the tool for digging their way out. If a school can't show success here, forget the rest of it. And I want the kid to have a marketable skill... something that can put food in the gut and guts into getting out. *Then* you social studies teachers come along. If you insist on studying Rome and can't tell me why it is better for the kid to study this than to learn survival skills and ideas so he can make it today, you're in the way. Do us a favor — stay out of the way. As it is now, you're doing more harm than good.

The administrator didn't receive applause for his style — only a few side comments such as, "What can you expect from an anti-intellectual?" and "Don't worry.... He's probably a former coach."

It is becoming more and more apparent that the "gentleman's agreement" for professionals not to take on fellow professionals in terms of their functioning proficiency has been called off. The public arena is not a placid, pleasant, professional plateau. Administrators are finding it increasingly difficult to hide behind status and position and simply account for bodies, budgets, and buildings. And teachers can no longer have assurance that hats will be tipped instead of bricks thrown if they can't articulate more than a call for blind faith on the part of parents and lay public.

What do you *do*?

"I teach social studies." (Or, as is often the case, "I teach kids.")

This used to end the dialogue. Now it is just the beginning.

WORKING WISDOM IN THE CLASSROOM

A teacher who has thought out what he is trying to do and why he is doing it is a rare commodity. When he does exist, he is often more prone to extinction than distinction. Jonathan Swift's "Confederation of Dunces" is easily threatened by one who knows the questions to ask and who is willing to ask them of himself.

Following is an example of this wisdom in practice:

Testament to Teaching

There was empirical evidence that an influenza epedemic was sweeping the country. The Asian Flu, as it was named, was contagious and aroused concern among school people. Some administrators of public schools considered health to be relatively more important than one week of schooling; their schools were closed for a week.

For some reason teachers were viewed as not being susceptible to the foreign virus and were told to report for duty as usual. Busy minds and busy hands abort potential trouble, so it was decided that the one week of nonteaching would be spent having each department prepare a presentation for the rest of the staff. The presentation would serve to inform the others what each department was attempting to do, what procedures it followed in teaching, what courses it offered, what standards it maintained, and so forth. In this way each teacher could be provided with an opportunity to see the "whole."

Each department met separately to plan its presentation. The social studies department made little progress. Serious debate was encountered for each of the following issues: (1) Should each member give a brief description of the courses he taught? (2) Should the overhead projector be used to show that audio-visual materials were used? (3) Who would make the transparencies? (4) What kind of transparencies should be used? (5) Why shouldn't the department chairman make the public presentation? (6) Why was the administration doing this to them? At this point the planning session broke down. There was heated discussion about doing more important things like averaging grades or putting files in order. There was evidence of resentment that professionals should have to "show and tell" just to keep the community off the administration's back.

One member of the department, a second year teacher who was not overly respected by his immediate colleagues, suggested that the social studies department give the staff an examination: a "final" exam, one worth one third of the final grade. And why not use an *actual* examination? It would be fair because they could give the final given to last year's slow senior class. The examination would show what the department valued in content and what it felt a graduating student of the low level *must* have in order to function as an effective citizen in the world as it really was.

The reaction to this suggestion was extremely positive. The exam was in the departmental file. The stencils were already cut, so with some minor changes it could easily be prepared. The master correction form would simplify correcting.

The slow senior final examination was given to the staff.

It was taken with some grumbling. Two teachers flatly refused. One apparently intentionally answered all the questions "wrong." Some did not finish the 200 short answer items. By a show of hands, the staff made it clear that it did not want the results posted. A number insisted that no names appear anywhere at any time!

The administration of the examination became hectic. The results? A music teacher walked off with the honors. The highest grade was 76 per cent. Twenty scored in the 60's; the rest failed. The horror and the embarrassment! The teachers had failed an actual final examination given to slow seniors, an examination of what a person *had to know* in order "to function as a contributing citizen."

The "honors" music teacher was ecstatic. But lonely. There was a demand on the part of the staff to know how the social studies department interpreted the results. This caught the department completely unprepared. Questions came from the floor — and even from colleagues considered friends. Was the staff considered "stupid" because they couldn't remember all that "trivia"? Did the department really mean that a person couldn't function as a citizen if he failed the test? What was the department trying to do — embarrass people? What was the purpose in giving it in the first place?

The Almighty has his own purpose. . . ?

PLANNED INTERVENTION AND HIRED HELP

Many of us shy away from the facts of life. Or, if we are not the shy type, we substitute gentle and disarming terms to describe what we are intent upon doing: intervening in human lives. We are paid to intervene. We do this *on purpose.* Whatever teaching is, it embraces some form of manipulating the environment and people in order to accomplish desired ends. We often use some of man's most subtle forms of seduction to accomplish the ends: charisma, sex appeal, emotional blackmail, institutionalized patterns of recognition and ostracism, competitive comparisons, promises of mobility, status, prestige—all become carrots on the educational rod and are dangled in forms subsumed under the gentle term "motivation." We motivate or establish certain learning experiences in order to bring about desired changes which society believes essential and necessary for the student in society.

If not this, what?

People who argue vehemently that they do not want "social engineering" in the schools are really saying something else. Schools are designed and supported for social engineering. The issue is not whether the schools will engineer but, rather, toward what ends the engineering efforts will be directed. What are the purposes of planned intervention in human life... by paid professionals?

Every teacher has some implicit and/or explicit purpose for teaching. The purpose may range from having a personal ego trip, to zealously pursuing missionary work, to developing reasonable and rational human beings. The purposes may overlap.

The individual teacher's purposes interact with institutional goals, and the questions of what *should* be taught and how the "should" *can* be taught most effectively are at the heart of any teaching/learning effort. Social studies teachers appear more vulnerable than other teachers. Granted, teachers of mathematics, reading, language arts, and physical education encounter the same questions, but the social studies teacher lives in a world of values, attitudes, taboos, "Knowers," and pressure groups. If he takes the questions seriously, he finds himself stretched in many directions when trying to respond.

If the educator is not aware of his *own* intent, it raises some basic ethical issues. If he *is* aware but neglects to share this with his colleagues, students, and the public, he is seeking success in the art of seduction. The consequences of his purpose influence others. We intervene in human lives *on purpose*. Whose purpose? Why this purpose and not that?

THE PRO AND THE CON

Whenever one teaches, he makes judgments. The alternative selected implies not only what is deemed important but *most* important in the given situation. A teacher does not randomly select from an array of ends.

Teaching is making choices. Is it better for a youngster to know about the history of Rome or to know about contemporary political processes? It is not that the history of Rome is not important but, relatively speaking, some knowledge is more worthwhile than others. The choices imply what is of value.

Over 25 years ago we were told that if we asked teachers for the reasons why they teach as they do, "few would fail to have at hand some ready answer." But if they were asked the reasons for their reasons, the further answers would no doubt come more slowly and with more hesitation.[1] It was realized that the quest for such reasons was perplexing and annoying but that only when the reasons for the reasons were explored could a teacher place confidence in relating his methods with his objectives.

There is considerable difference between confidence and a confidence game.

The confidence game too often played by the teaching profession is based on the "Four H" approach: Hope, Hunch, Hush, and Hoorah. We "hope" that we are doing something worthwhile. We have "hunches" about what the worthwhile activity should be. We aren't confident about the hunches so it is prudent to "hush" efforts designed to make our ends and means public. And when something works, we "hoorah" it to the winds of public opinion— almost as a diversionary tactic.

The confidence in this game is gone. A century ago there were complaints that "historic trivialities" were committed to memory not because of any direct benefits but merely to escape social contempt.[2] The Four H's were fairly safe in a context that gave emphasis to using education to enhance the social graces and thus find status and honor in the discipline of memory. As we move away from the old anchors of status, position, and prestige we become less concerned with the "cut of the suit" and more concerned with how it wears during day-to-day use.

There is need for the individual teacher to identify and articulate a rationale. Although there is no scientific way to determine the broad goals and more immediate objectives, a rationale should be made explicit so that it is subject to evaluation[3] and stated to reflect that "we *ought* to act in such a way that what *is* true can be verified to be so."[4]

The problem with social studies teaching is that we now face more viable alternatives than ever before. These demand that we look at purposes and ways of implementation as never before. What we *should* do is no longer an abstract, esoteric, academic question. The question is asked within a framework that suggests we *can* do practically anything. What we *should* do is "the principal moral implication of our new world."[5]

"The challenge to education is . . . staggering," wrote Emmanuel Mesthene in the *Saturday Review*. Asking teachers who were brought up to cherish that which is stable to work with children of parents raised the same way and to "teach them that the stable, the unchanging, is unreal, constraining, a false goal . . ." is asking a great deal. But, survival depends on how well one can understand and master and control change.[5]

Science, its processes and products, has moved man beyond the Enlightenment to a period in which he stands face to face with himself. "Pure science has moulded [man's] philosophy of life, and applied science has determined . . . his chances of life or death, poverty or affluence, freedom or slavery. . . . Natural science is by far the greatest movement in modern history. . . ."[6]

In an academic area well rooted in the study of history, one must ponder if a student is functionally illiterate if this "greatest movement" is not considered. Over 30 laboratories in various parts of the world are working with chemicals believed to be involved in the transfer of learning. Life is being produced in laboratories. Life and death are in the process of redefinition. What could be more fundamental to the human choices faced by man? What should we do?

If we look at social studies programs and social studies teaching, we find ourselves in a pastoral setting "pinned on the assumption that each generation will generally live amid the conditions governing the lives of past generations."[7] This assumption feeds the passing on of knowledge about the past, knowledge to meet the "permanent" conditions. It appears that we are intent upon heaping piles of dead ashes when we should be determining ways of carrying *fires*, not ashes, from the altar of the past.[8]

Intent upon introducing human rationality into the use of the technological products of man's thinking, we shy at chances to introduce the products and processes of human intelligence into the realm of social affairs and conditions. In a fascinating and, to some, disturbing paradox, man orders his physical world while leaving his home in chaos. In making choices there is no guarantee, no certainty. Choice making is future oriented and lacks the security of the past. There seems to be an unwillingness to "play at odds" with individual lives while, at the same time, there is a fascination to "playing at odds" with that individual's environments.

The challenge to the social studies teacher *is* staggering and does involve making choices. The functional value of freedom is implicit in the ability to choose and the willingness to act to implement the choices made.

Science, the permeating force in modern history, assists in providing data and tools for making choices but it does not portend to be a diviner of what choices should be made.[9] Freedom is a mixed blessing! For example, the teacher Socrates sat crouched in jail not because he knew about muscles and tendons but because he *chose* to. Hemlock comes in many containers and satisfies many tastes.

The need to articulate a basis for making choices and to indicate desired ends and means is not new to us. Herbert Spencer, writing over 60 years ago, found no "deliberately derived rationales" for education.[2] Education guides consisted simply of "mere custom, or liking, or prejudice." There was little consideration about "the enormous importance of determining in some rational way what things are really most worth learning." Spencer pointed out that all knowledge *may* prove to be worthwhile—even that which comes from gossip over the back fence—but one has to choose, "to play at odds," that some knowledge has a greater probability of utility than other knowledge. The criteria for selection depend upon assessing the information available, the situation in which one is to function, and then finding "most worth" in that information which seems most probable to assist in the functioning. If you will, determining that which one must be able to *do* and then determining what one must know about in order to assist in the *doing*.

Aristotle argued that education is too important to be pursued in a random way. Legislators should make education a chief concern for, if neglected, the "constitution of the state would suffer," . . . and people must be educated to suit the constitution. "All do not take the same view about what should be learned by the young... nor is opinion clear whether education should be directed mainly to the understanding or mainly to moral character. If we look at actual practice, the result is sadly confusing."[10]*

We face choices about human life and human functioning. What we *should* do is a philosophical question. Only when this question is responded to can we effectively address the issue of how we *can* do what we *should* do. Expanding sources of knowledge feed cumulatively expanding information. Our information base changes; our situation changes. Our criteria for what is most worth knowing must change responsively.

WHAT DOES A RATIONALE DO FOR US?

What Is a Rationale? It is a consistent and integrated awareness of one's *world view*, which guides a consistency and integration of one's *teaching view*. It is a cognition of what one accepts as "given" — a cognition of the basic premises upon which one con-

---

*As social studies teachers, you should be wondering why we used a historical citation at this point. The use of a citation implies some concept about the use of history. The citation could be used for several reasons:
1. It might be that Aristotle (as translated) posed the problem far better than we could. He phrased it in such a way that we felt it communicated exactly the point being made. FUNCTION: To effectively communicate. (Would we have used it if Al Capone had said it just as well?)
2. It might be that Aristotle is "the man," *the* Authority. If he said it, it must be worthwhile. FUNCTION: To provide acceptable *evidence*. (What if Ho Chi Minh had said it?)
3. It might be that we assume history repeats itself and want to suggest that there is nothing new. FUNCTION: To prove an accepted idea. (What if Nasser had said this?)
4. It might be that we assume each period of history finds different situations in which value decisions must be made or that it is difficult to infer purpose from observing practice. FUNCTION: To test an idea. (Would we have used the quotation had Adolph Hitler made a similar observation?)
5. It might be that we assume Aristotle's quotation is familiar and thus likely to add credence. Or that Aristotle is legitimately viewed as a profound thinker. Or that Aristotle's credentials are such that an educated person would find such a source as a confirmation or denial of an idea. FUNCTION: To cushion a risk within the womb of a recognized authority. (What if Sammy Jones, the guy on the street corner, had said the same thing as Aristotle?)
6. It might be pragmatic. It might just add to an aura of being academic. FUNCTION: To help overcome hurdles in order to get the book to the reader.
One can *use* history: to help to communicate, to prove, to test, to raise issues, to legitimatize, to imply value systems, and/or for strictly pragmatic reasons.
Question: Might an idea be worthwhile exploring *regardless* of the source?

structs meanings. It is a cognition of the types of evidence one is willing to accept, of purposes one harbors for himself and others, and the extent and limitations of what one knows. The implications for teaching are of vital importance. The teacher contributes to the selection of what to teach, how to teach, who to teach, when to teach, and how to evaluate.

Why Is a Rationale Important? An individual teacher's *own* private world view may prove psychologically satisfying *to him*. But what ethical issues are raised if he unwittingly foists *his* "givens," his belief system and his concepts upon others? What if he were wrong? We are *not* suggesting that a social studies teacher be stripped of his biases, prejudices, personality predispositions, and beliefs. It is naive to assume that a teacher stands aloof and impartial in the midst of the stream of life. A social studies teacher who is told to teach both sides of any issue may also be assured that he will be supported as long as the "right" side is clearly shown to be right. This situation may account for the apparent lack of need to have teachers publicly articulate their rationale for teaching and for teaching a particular subject. Teaching without a rationale, however, is not justifiable.

If a teacher has *deliberately* evolved a rationale, he should value it to the extent of making it public, acting consistently within its conceptual base, being willing to repeat his actions *or* modify the rationale, and be willing to subject his teaching framework to public scrutiny.[11] Obviously, who wants to be wrong? Who wants to live with inconsistencies? Who would rather be secretly wrong than publicly modify his views and actions? Perhaps a politician or a school board member or a parent or a lawyer, but certainly not the social studies teacher who is committed to rigorous scholarship, the pursuit of truth, integrity, and wisdom.

Several basic premises underpin the need for a teacher to have his *own* articulated cognitive organization *PRIOR* to finding himself on the firing line in a classroom.

> The effectiveness of social studies teaching, as measured by what students learn, is related to the teacher's own sense of purpose, awareness of alternative ends and means, systematic planning, and ability to "model" reflective thinking.

> Efforts directed at planning and executing social studies lessons are instrumental: that is, are *means* to perceived ends, means that transcend intermediate objectives in a particular lesson.

> Effective social studies teaching calls for organization in

classroom *and* academic activities. New information calls not only for adding on to or deleting from existing programs but demands *reorganization* of conventional data.

The social studies teacher's *own* functioning implies to the student what the teacher values in content, thinking, and functioning, as differentiated from what the teacher *says* he values, thinks, and does.

The teacher is a decision maker. He operates at a number of different decision-making levels: broad, long term planning *and* reactive decisions in the classroom.

If a rationale helps a teacher to "put it all together" into a framework for teaching, what does the teacher *do* with what he has deliberately articulated. If we may borrow a legal phrase, he makes a "proffer." That is, the individual teacher makes public his rationale: to his colleagues, to parents, *and* to his students. No games. If we recognize that no teacher is completely able to divest himself of his bias and accepted "givens," then the next logical step is to *accept this as a fact of teaching* and to make public the teacher's rationale or framework so that others — colleagues, parents, *and* students — are at least aware of what the teacher is trying to accomplish, how he will attempt to proceed, and how he will evaluate. The others have some options: acceptance, challenge, indicating inconsistencies, and/or even rebutting with their own thought-out rationale.

When this is done in a school system, each teacher has his rationale in concise syllabus form for each course. All this is asked for, in a move away from the Four H approach, to identify what the teacher is trying to do, to help him to be consistent, and to give some indication of a thought-through approach. This is a move toward professionalism. If the rationale in syllabus form is accepted by his professional colleagues as being professionally sound, the teacher can be evaluated only in terms of whether he is doing what he says he wants to do and *not* in terms agreeing or disagreeing with his general approach. Theoretically we allow for individual student differences. In this way we can dignify the adult by allowing for individual teacher differences. This incorporates freedom with responsibility; it builds in professional accountability. It asks only that the teacher do the thinking and practice the use of analytic skills that he trusts his students will be able to do and practice.

Following is a Syllabus Form which has been used by one school system. You will note that it is designed to put a rationale in a specific course area into articulated form. A completed syllabus is seldom more than five pages in length and its possible uses are indicated. Some of the terminology used in the form will not be clear at this point. These will be considered in later chapters that deal with concepts, skills, vehicles, etc.

SYLLABUS FORM

A syllabus is a plan. It should encompass a long period of time and thus act as an "umbrella" for specific subplans within the whole. A single lesson plan thus will be related to the syllabus. As a plan, the syllabus points out a general base for purposes, ways of approaching end results, and for decision making as one moves along. The syllabus need be no longer than four pages and parts of it may change without changing everything. This makes curriculum development an ongoing process.

Possible Uses:

1. Assist teacher in planning.

2. If distributed to students, suggests that teacher has thought through what he/she is trying to do and allows the student to see the broad "whole" of his encounter.

3. If shared with other teachers, it can keep different ideas and approaches transfusing throughout the staff—a mild but exciting form of ongoing inservice by one's peers.

4. May be used to discuss areas with parents who have concerns.

5. May assist the guidance counsellor in assigning students to classes that may be directed at the student's particular needs.

6. If given to the librarian, may assist her and/or media people in selecting materials related to curricula ends.

7. May assist new teachers in thinking through their own purposes and means... "a model" to be followed—at least in form.

8. Allows the viewing of a course of study as being a compilation of the syllabuses being used.

Form:

A. Descriptive title of the course.   Teacher's name.

B. Statement of teacher's major assumption regarding course content, methods, evaluation.

C. Statement of major goals: Goals are general statements of purpose or intent; they are not related to a specific period of time, and they are not measurable in any way other than a broad subjective assessment.

D. Specific objectives: Objectives, which are desired measurable accomplishments within a time framework, are developed.
These objectives:
Relate to a goal
Are measurable
State the method of measurement
Indicate the evaluation criteria
State the time period for achievement

E. 1. Concepts: Identify major concepts to be derived and/or tested.
   2. Skills: Identify skills to be emphasized and evaluated in the course.

F. Major vehicles and subvehicles (a vehicle is a *means*, a boundary around a data bank): The data are used (skills) to construct concepts or to test concepts. When the goals, objectives, and criteria have been defined, the next step is to develop a program outline that will attain the objectives. A program is a group of interrelated activities directed toward accomplishing goals. The course is arranged in an outline structure, an arrangement that demonstrates the relationship of activities to goals and objectives.

G. Example of methodology.

H. Approximate time divisions.

I. Proposed methods of evaluation.

J. Resources (required and complementary).

Once a rationale has been thought out and the reasons for the reasons indicated, a syllabus constructed, what does this do for the teacher?

1. It provides a systematic general framework for long range *and* short range planning.

2. It provides a thought-out base for determining goals and for relating objectives to the goals.
3. It provides a framework for synthesizing content, materials, methods, and situational factors.
4. It provides a base from which to solicit and use feedback, a base for self-evaluation and monitoring.
5. It provides a guide for making "reactive" decisions while "on-the-line" in the classroom.
6. It provides psychological security in that the teacher has worked out the "whole" and has noted part-whole relationships. What is done in the classroom, is done *purposefully* and can be *educationally* justified.

THE PRO AND THE CON: MOSTLY "CON"

It would be less than honest if it were implied that social studies teachers welcome the opportunity to make and use a syllabus. The resistance to making public proposed ends and means has been vehement in some cases. One teacher, for example, said that what he did "was *his* business" and he "didn't have to give reasons to anyone." Another commented that it would "limit academic freedom." Others felt that the syllabus approach opened the door to invidious comparisons among teachers, to unfair evaluation methods, to parent harassment, to "showing the hand when it should be placed close to the vest." This tells us a great deal about the teaching climate, the social studies field, and the profession as a whole. To the committed Four H'er, public scrutiny *is* a threat. To those who feel they have to "bootleg" their teaching in certain situations and communities, this *is* a threat. And to those who are aware that in some situations the profession exists in name only, that the *individual* cannot count on professional standards and support, this *is* a threat. On the other hand, those who are willing to take the risk find this to be an individual and professional tool of strength, direction, change, and professional growth. The sharing of syllabuses proves to be a continual form of in-service in one's own field. It takes a psychological "set" to be open, willing to share ideas, willing to be wrong, willing to modify, willing to seek out new data and new methods, and willing, if necessary, to reconceptualize the teaching effort— the characteristics, if you will, of a good student.

Social studies teachers are not alone in this struggle to make sense of what they are doing. Legislators face some of the same dilemmas: How does one's basic conceptual framework or rationale influence and guide the making of legislation? Blum and Funk-houser did a study of legislators involved in creating drug legis-lation.[12] It was found that the philosophical position, or what the authors called "personality predilections," of individual legislators played a vital part in determining the nature of any social legis-lation — legislation directed at influencing human behavior. "Moral absolutists" tended to reject the findings of the social sciences and stayed with the "common sense" premises. The "pragmatists" appeared to lean more toward accepting data from the social and behavioral sciences as a basis for legislation.

The acceptance or refusal to accept empirically based data in regard to such things as capital punishment or drug use may have serious consequences in education as well as in legislation.

A syllabus reveals the personality predilections. This is prob-ably the biggest threat of all. Teaching can be rational and at the same time extremely unreasonable. If premises remain hidden, there are few rules in the confidence game.

OLD ANSWERS AND NEW QUESTIONS

It is an old question: What does it mean to be an educated person? If the American view of man and his world is anchored in 18th century premises,[13] then the social studies curriculum will stress reason (in a classical sense), rationality, and an approach to knowledge that will focus on Western classics and on a careful study of the past. An educated person will not "presume to create his own norms... [nor]... search for new principles of action." Right behavior prescriptions will be found in the Golden Age of the past. The educated person will be a "traditionalist," measured against a criterion that existed at least to the 19th century.[14]

A conventional social studies curriculum is likely to find its rationale rooted in such a premise. A teacher working in such a curriculum will be expected to have an individual rationale which will relate to the basic views. A conventional teacher is prone to assume that to "know about" is a necessary condition to functioning effectively as an educated person. The challenge comes from those who determine first the probable life demands upon an individual and *then* select knowledge. The emphasis is reversed. Instead of asking, What do I have to know about? and then relating this to functioning, the question becomes, What will I have to *do* to function effectively and what knowledge will be of most help in my functioning?

Both sides will rest their cases on "acting in the best interest of the individual." The reasons will be identical. But the reasons for the reasons may imply entire ranges of teaching and learning activity diametrically opposed to one another. It is the reasons for the reasons that provide the operational guides to teacher behavior.

Today's social studies teachers face the standard issues: change, function, and a rationale directed at what it means to be an educated person... in the *20th* century. But there are some added dimensions in rationale consideration, dimensions teachers a decade ago did not have to encounter. *Today's student is aware of his own changing rationale.* Until recently we could assume that the student's rationale was in the process of being formed, not articulated, and not a contributing factor in the teacher's rationale. The student was perceived as accepting education as a "given" — taking it on faith. Education was assumed to be worthwhile — a "key to the kingdom."

This act of faith is not so readily made by today's students. The kingdom, as *we* see it, may not be a paradise to be entered. The key may be coupled with a lock rather than an open gate. Crudely, vaguely, and often with difficulty, today's youth at *all* levels are at work forging their *own* rationales. They do this often, despite our efforts. If the schools', the teachers', *and* the students' groping for a sense of the whole are *all* crude, vague, nonsystematic, and not logically articulated, discourse erodes and battle lines are formed under the banners of power, coercion, and fear.

Until recently the *one* stock in trade that a teacher had going for him was that he had some expertise in an academic area. A social studies teacher was assumed to know more in the areas of history, geography, and government than the average lay person. The basic foundation of the professional teacher's qualifications was content — some body of information. The teacher's task was to take portions of that important information and somehow make them available to the students.

What happens when that basic building block of content is categorized as being unimportant? What happens to the role of the teacher when *knowledge itself* is under attack? What happens when students relegate intellectual effort to a minor role?

Writing in *Daedalus*, Herbert Blau argues that, admitting all outrage, "what the students have done beyond reproach is to make us question the wholeness and accuracy of our teaching and to measure our precious values not dispassionately against one another but in real-life situations, urgently, against ourselves."[15] What gets lost are our habits of thought. The "agreements with life" are made below the intellectual structures which seem to bind us.

At the ground level we are starting to see what Vytautas Kavolis calls the "Post-Modern Man."[16] This P.M. Man, with an "underground personality" has predilections that *repudiate some of the major basic premises upon which education and teaching have been built for the past two thousand or more years.*

What do we find repudiated? Organized impersonal systems, formalism in language, fragmentation, specialization, logic, controlled prediction, selected content, traditional concepts of time and meaning. Modern, technological, rationalized, and hierarchical institutions are repudiated. In short, most of what we call the organization and process of formal education is repudiated.

In its place? Spontaneity; improvisation; the irrational, informal, mystic, romantic, expressionistic, sensuous experience; wholeness. Each moment is whole and complete. To know is not to absorb intellectual data compiled and systematized from human experience but rather to have a unique, singular, feeling experience. The P. M. Man doesn't want complex wisdom and delayed abstraction. He wants simplicity and with it a firm reference point.

What we find being rejected is *even the traditional framework for evolving a rationale* . . . for living and for teaching! Thinking without feeling is no longer tenable. But feeling without thinking?

History and the social sciences hold little import to the postmodern. History is remote and abstract and disjointed from the new and complete here and now. Social science deals with groups, prediction, statistics, probability, controlled and systematic inquiry, rules, and patterns. Who needs it?

The Scranton Report on campus unrest was issued in 1970. The Post-Modern Man is again encountered. The report talks of the "penchant for pure idealism," for the return to the old: the classical notion of the autonomous, self-determining, uncluttered, authentic individual whose instincts are in harmony with the inner self. "Confidence is placed in revelation rather than cognition, . . . in sensation rather than analysis, . . . in personal rather than the institutional." Natural man is thus found pitted against value systems that embrace competition, dress codes, correct speech, hair length, credits, rules, "success," poverty, war, pollution and systems with the potential to control human ends and means — political charades, the playground of payoffs.

And, if the teacher teaches this value system? Either the teacher is said to lie in a nonauthentic and calloused hyprocrisy or he is less than human. No matter which, who needs it? Who needs *you*?

In one sense the social studies teacher might feel complimented. Often he has underpinned his teaching effort upon a romantic concept of the autonomous, self-determining, authentic individual struggling with effecting a pastoral dream. The teacher stresses the work ethic while collectively bargaining with local boards of education to help to save him from his calling. He demands for himself few restrictions under the mantle of academic freedom. He resists being evaluated. He has renounced success and materialism just by entering the profession. He refuses a merit system or suggestion of competition and material differentiation.

One might say that the teacher has modeled in action, if not in words, the Post-Modern Man. The perceptive teacher recognizes the dimension of the problem. He finds himself in the middle of the subject matter of human behavior and he must ask himself, What have we learned from the human experience to date? Has the effort assumed that one can think *without* feeling? If this has been implied, does it justify a continued split, with the pendulum now swung to the feeling aspect of experience? In forging a rationale, he addresses the old questions but must respond in terms of what we have learned about human behavior—learnings that may not have been available in the 19th century.

A rationale for contemporary social studies teaching must take into account the dimensions of a changing world. The teacher though, must recognize that he does not stand apart from interacting with the changes. Considerations basic to a contemporary rationale must also include an assessment of what one thinks he knows about the learner. What about the learner?[17]

He can learn. That is, he can modify his thoughts and behavior.

The stimulation of his senses is crucial to his learning.

He *creates* meanings by processing human experience.

He is plastic and open to a wide variety of physical and social environments.

His *feelings* play a substantial role in screening what his senses feed him. He sees what he wants to see and hears what he wants to hear. His attitudes and values work with experience in creating and monitoring meaning.

He is able to "take" abstracted parts of experience and mentally organize them into mental constructs or "ideas." He simplifies complexity.

He and his kind have created social needs. What he has created is sometimes more important to him than are his physical needs.

He is capable of interpreting and of creating myths and fantasies — which he treats as real.

He is introspective and can learn about his own functioning: how he learns, how he thinks, how he perceives, how he communicates, and how he depends upon others.

He is a maker of symbols and language and has a tendency to substitute these creations for reality.

He can project, plan, and implement relationships between ends and means.

As a human, he is a social being. Others influence his values values and goals, his actions and reactions. The small groups about him are instrumental in his defining of himself. He seeks approval, respect, prestige, status, and acceptance — often more than virtue or truth.

He tends to take the familiar to be "natural" or "correct."

His human nature is rooted in potential rather than in set patterns. His nature is described in terms of change, plasticity, variety, and ability to adapt.

He does not separate thinking from feeling. HE THINKS WITH FEELING. (But he can also feel *without* thinking.)

This learning creature, defined in terms of potential, has evolved patterns of group behavior: government, family, economic institutions, ideologies, legal systems. Twentieth century man has learned that these patterns are NOT explained simply in terms of biological or instinctual drives.[18] Motives, values, and ideologies are learned. And what of language patterns? "How far is our discussion... distorted by habitual attitudes towards words, and lingering assumptions due to theories no longer held but still allowed to guide our practice?"[19]

Should a social studies teacher take the findings about man and include them in a deliberate, planned approach? Should the social studies teacher offer each finding in terms of probability and not "law"? Should a social studies teacher hit head-on the tendency of man to confuse *feeling* with certitude, simplicity with truth?[20]

The 1971–72 college freshmen have strong feelings about social issues, but an increasing minority of the students agree that "realistically, an individual person can do little to bring about changes in our society." Three quarters of the freshmen have a personal goal of developing a meaningful philosophy of life.[21] To what extent should social studies teachers assess with their students such things as political and social action, changing strategies, effective involvement? What should the role of the social studies teacher be in providing issues worth philosophizing about as well as opportunities to philosophize? To what extent does a teacher explore the relationship between thinking and feeling within the context of history and the social sciences?

New data about the human being and his social functioning work to modify the old questions which guide our response to, What *should* one teach?

"To teach what is not very useful, not very well, to the not-very-interested" leads to a dislike of the subject and issues by both teachers and students.[22] Inheriting and using old frames of reference offers little effective guidance in determining objectives, methods, and content. What a teacher needs to develop is his *own* suitable frame of reference, his *own* rationale, in order to have a thought-through base for course planning.

The difficulties faced in developing a rationale are complex— as complex as teaching. A rationale simply points up that "the basic issues of education are simply the basic issues of life in an educational context."[23]

Much of life is random and predicated upon chance. Educational efforts are not exempt from this real arena, but neither is such an effort exempt from addressing the arena of life *as it is.* Formal education is deliberate, planned, selective, and valued. A teacher's rationale, made public through a course syllabus, is an "open invitation" to others to speculate on the ends and means of education. The R.S.V.P. on the "invitation" asks that the rationale not be judged with "ambiguous language, unexamined assumptions, ignored entailments, logical contradictions and non sequiturs."[24] Pollution takes many forms!

In other words, let's start by "telling it like it is"—at least like it is to us—so that teaching and learning can find *some* base for disciplined discourse and disciplined "discovery."

The Almighty may have his own purpose. But it is no longer secret and it is no longer strictly His own. His purpose works in concert with the purposes of others.

APPLIED EXAMPLE:
OBSENITY, PORNOGRAPHY,
AND TEACHING

The Commission on Obsenity and Pornography is an example of how acceptance or rejection of empirical data plays a role in determining what should be done in a specific social situation . . . *and* in social studies classrooms. The example attempts to indicate how one's teaching rationale may influence decisions made.

The report was issued in 1970. The Commission found *no* empirical evidence that pornographic materials played a significant role in causing crime, deviancy, or severe emotional disturbances among youths or adults. The Commission majority declared that "Extensive empirical investigation, both by the commission and by others, provides no evidence that exposure to or use of explicit sexual materials plays a significant role in the causation of social or individual harms." If you recall, the commission majority found no reason for continued governmental interference with the full freedom of *adults* to read, obtain, or view such material. Other points to recall:

1. The administration disavowed the findings in advance of the report.

2. A three-member minority of the 17-member commission issued their own report, which held the recommendations to be "shocking and anarchistic" and refusing to deal with the issue of to what extent society may maintain certain moral standards.

3. The recommendations included the prohibition of commercially distributing sexually oriented pictorial material to young people because "a large majority of Americans believe that children should not be exposed to certain sexual materials."

The social issues involved in the commission's report are apparent. If one does not use empirical data, what alternative sources of evidence are open? Is it necessarily anarachistic to modify a conventional and deeply rooted idea? If enough people hold an opinion, even if contrary to verifiable evidence, does it justify continuation of rules and regulations? What are the sources of moral standards? Do standards change? If so, to what extent should society establish and maintain morality? Is there a double standard for determining legislation for adults and youth?

The same material was used in two completely different ways in social studies classrooms. One teacher used the report as an example of the "moral breakdown" being compounded in American society. The other teacher used the report with secondary students to raise questions about the different kinds of evidence people seem willing to accept and to explore the logical implications of such acceptance.

Each teacher screened the material through his own frame of reference. Each had some implied rationale for using the article, for using the article in a particular way, and for relating the use to some larger goal beyond just the material itself. If both had been asked why they had used the Commission's report, it is likely that both would have responded that "it helped make better citizens." But if asked why they speculated in such a fashion—the reasons for the reason—it might have been difficult to evade encountering the Four H explanation.

Parenthetically it is interesting to note that the first teacher received no "flak" from the administration or community. The second teacher's use triggered some concern over intent!

Perhaps we should be exploring what rationale guided others *not* to use the report in their social studies classes. What framework of ends and means and what situations worked to rank Ancient Egypt and the Age of Exploration in preferential position?

REASONS FOR THE REASONS

Although still categorized as "perplexing" and "annoying," there have been efforts made to have teachers identify the *one* social studies idea or concept they would teach students if that idea would be all a student would get from a public school education. As is to be expected, the responses have varied a great deal. After the idea had been selected, teachers were asked to review the process gone through in deriving the response. Most ideas were seen as "umbrella" ideas allowing a number of subideas to be related in the process of teaching.

Below are two representative responses. Each is accompanied by the subideas encompassed by *the* major "real," worthwhile idea to be taught.

People are basically good

1. If everyone in the world lived by the Golden Rule there would be peace on earth.
2. If you are honest and work hard, people will recognize you for what you are.
3. There is too much distrust, anger, and violence in the world. People don't care for one another.
4. History shows that when the chips are down people come through.
5. If man is made in God's image, he is good. We've got to emphasize the positive.
6. Young people should be surrounded with optimism. There is too much negativism.

Science can help man to solve his social problems

1. Science is a process, a method, and not a dogma.
2. Science can be applied to the study of social behavior.
3. Facts don't speak for themselves. People have to have an attitude which will use science as a way to help make decisions.
4. The methods of science involve a number of activities that can be learned: asking questions which return data, observing, make hypotheses, checking information, etc.
5. Everything man does is with not enough information to guarantee that things are certain. Man has to be willing to live with probable "laws" and not certain "laws."

Do the responses imply some philosophical position which might influence one's approach to teaching? Review the subideas under each response: Does anything imply a view of human nature? purpose(s) of life? source of knowing? values? change? Does anything suggest a view about the role of social studies in school? the role of the social studies teacher? Could both response give as a reason: To help people to become more human? Would the reasons for the reason differ?

SYNTHESIS AND PROLOGUE

We have visited an area in which angels fear to tread and which the demigods and demagogues ignore.

Teaching is at base an ethical activity. It involves intervening in the lives of others, manipulating people and experiences, and motivating people to desire certain ends. The educator is intent upon attempting to change people—*on purpose* and *with purpose.* The formal educator gets paid to do this.

A thought-out rationale attempts to make explicit the nature and purpose of the intervention. It helps teachers become more honorable and more efficient at the same time. It exposes what teachers are trying to do and why they are trying to do it. It guides planning and helps to implement designs. In *syllabus form* it makes public ends and means and puts internal, integrity in a form allowing for long range and short range planning. It breaks down "discreet dilences" while exposing the nature of commitment.

We have noted that the basic premises of formal education which have guided schooling efforts over centuries are being challenged. The teacher of social studies can use the findings of his own "content" area to help to reassess with students what we think we know of the nature of the human experience. This reconstitutes education as something to be used.

The framework or rationale for the intended uses suggests the nature of the content to be used. Teachers *select* content, hopefully, on purpose.

We now move to the area of content selection and to various types of raw material to be used in teaching. We will look at history and the social sciences and ask what they each can do for us. It should be noted that our implicit rationale will determine the questions we ask.

REFERENCES

1. Brubacher, John S.: Comparative Philosophy of Education. NSSE Yearbook, 1942.
2. Spencer, Herbert: Education. New York, D. Appleton and Co., 1896.
3. Ackoff, Russell L.: Design of Social Research. Chicago, University of Chicago Press, 1953.
4. Bronowski, J.: Science and Human Values. Julian Messner, Inc., New York, 1956.
5. Mesthene, Emmanuel G.: Learning to live with science. Saturday Review, July 17, 1965.
6. Taylor, F. Sherwood: Science and Scientific Thought. New York, W. W. Norton and Company, 1963.
7. Whitehead, Alfred North: Adventures of Ideas. New York, The Macmillan Co., 1933.
8. As quoted in Gerard, R. W.: Intelligence, information and education. Science, May 7, 1965.
9. Compton, Arthur H.: Science and man's freedom. Atlantic Monthly, October, 1957.
10. The Politics of Aristotle. (Translation and notes by Ernest Barker.) Oxford, Oxford University Press, 1958.
11. Raths, Louis E.: Clarifying values. In Curriculum for Today's Boys and Girls. Columbus, Ohio, Charles Merrill Books, Inc., 1965.
12. Blum, Richard H., and Funkhouser, Mary Lou: Legislators on social scientists and a social issue. J. Aapplied Behavioral Science, Vol. I, No. 1, 1965.
13. Brinton, Crane: The Shaping of the Modern Mind. New York, New American Library, Mentor, 1953.
14. Ward, John William: Cleric or Critic. The American Scholar, Winter, 1965.

15. Blau, Herbert: Relevance: The shadow of a magnitude. Daedalus, Summer, 1969.
16. Kavolis, Vytautas: Post-modern man: Psychocultural responses to social trends. Social Problems, Spring, 1970.
17. Berelson, Bernard, and Steiner, Gary A.: Human Behavior: An Inventory of Scientific Findings. New York, Harcourt, Brace and World, 1964.
18. Tumin, Melvin M.: If war is a transitory aspect of human behavior. Saturday Review, December 19, 1970.
19. Ogden, C. K., and Richards, I. A.: The Meaning of Meaning. New York, Harcourt Brace, 1923.
20. Dewey, John: The Quest for Certainty. (Gifford Lectures, 1929.) New York, G. P. Putnam's Sons, Inc., 1960.
21. National Norms for Entering College Freshmen. Washington, D.C. American Council on Education, Fall, 1970.
22. Powell, Thomas F.: Reason and necessity in the social studies. Social Education, December, 1963.
23. Virtue, Charles F. Sawhill: General philosophy and philosophy of education. Educational Theory, October, 1958.
24. Gayer, Nancy: How to get the fly out of the bottle. Phi Delta Kappan, April, 1962.

"It's not that you're not funny—it's just that your stuff is too intellectual for our court."

(By Herbert Goldberg. Copyright 1969 Saturday Review, Inc.)

4

CONTENT SELECTION

I have heard with my ears...now I see...

I like to say there is no scientific method as such, but rather only the free and utmost use of intelligence.

PERCY BRIDGMAN

UNSPOKEN WORDS

She was a first year teacher—young, fresh, and attractive. They said the kids would crucify her, and she got all sorts of advice from all the caring others who would not take the "slow" class in 8th grade social studies. After all, seniority must mean something,... and one learns best by getting "in there" and "seeing what it's like to teach kids like that." This way a new teacher "learned how to keep order first and worry about teaching last"—"learning how to survive is the teacher's dum-dum weapon."

At any rate she ended up with the "slow" pupils who were located in this particular building because it was the only one that had room. The basement wasn't too bad; at least the confusion and bustle were kept to a minimum.

She came into the principal's office one day. He was discussing renewals of contracts and the likes with the school system's personnel man.

"Well, my kids got the finger today," she said.

The two administrators glanced at one another. Did this young thing, fresh out of college know what it was to "get the finger"?

She allayed their doubts by giving the sign.

And then she explained how her students had come in from the playground and told her that the other kids in the school were giving them the finger.

"We'll have to stop this," said the principal.

"Gee, I hope no one else saw them," said the personnel man.

"What did you do?" asked the secretary in a tone implying anticipation of a vicarious and thrilling experience.

The young thing just kept right on going. She explained that the "finger" was a form of nonverbal communication, so she had used it as a jumping off place to discuss ways people communicate without using words.

"You actually used it for a lesson?" the personnel man asked.

"Why not?" It was rhetorical. She kept on going. "We got into the way people use hand signals and posture to "speak," and she explained how the class "got into" the Ainu of northern Japan, how American Indians sometimes pointed with their lips, and how laughter may mean different things to different people living in different cultures, even into a discussion of tribes that viewed spitting as a way of curing people.

"We ended up talking about it taking two to dance, and two to make messages. This gave them some options." She was glad that she was "finally able to use some cultural anthropology with them. It turned into a darn good class."

The principal, believe it or not, was nodding his head in approval. The secretary felt cheated because the description had taken an academic twist. The personnel man kept silent.

After the teacher had left to meet another class, the personnel man asked if the principal condoned such things. Obviously, not the finger, but teaching about the finger.

He did. Apparently he thought "it was a damn good lesson."

Personnel man: "But, we pay her to teach social studies — history — and not that kind of stuff. Since when have we moved the street corner into the classroom?"

This story appears to spotlight some basic issues involving content and methodology. Is the teacher of social studies really primarily a history teacher who occasionally flirts with political science and physical geography? Or is the teacher of social studies involved in the social sciences in an attempt to bring the findings of the social sciences to bear on human behavior? Is this simply a game of semantics in ritualistic form, of little import to the teacher in the classroom?

THE TEACHER AND THE HISTORIAN

Social studies teachers have placed an immense burden upon history and upon the historian. A number of assumptions have hardened into unexamined habits which demand fulfillment of untenable demands. The resulting frustration may lead to cynicism about history and human experience. Unrealistic and non-negotiable demands may lead students to a rejection: a rejection unfair to themselves, to society, to historians, and to the larger human experience.

The following dialogue attempts to show the dilemma faced by the historian when the teacher of social studies demands that which cannot be ordered, packaged, and delivered.

The social studies teacher and the historian were seated in the living room of the historian's home. It was a cold, February evening but the living room was warmed by the embers of a fire that flickered shadows among the books lining the room. The historian was carefully tending the fire, its sporadic "snaps" and pops punctuating his efforts.

Historian: Ah. A fire is good. It warms a man. And not all fires are made of logs. There are fires of experience which feed man's contemplation and belonging. My life has been spent tending such fires and warming to the glow of human experience. (HE REMEMBERS HIS GUEST AND TURNS) . . . but, you know what I mean. As a teacher you bring people to the fires. What can I do for you?

Teacher: I don't know what you can do for me. I am not sure that my task is to bring students to the fires. I am not sure about very much any more. And I am not sure about understanding you.

Historian: It is a perplexing time for all. Let's talk about your situation and let's think as we talk. As one of my colleagues has said, "The thing that is important is that one think about the situation in which he stands." None of us is "free" in regard to the situation. It is a person's master, his oracle, his god. One can ignore it, but it will not neglect the ignorance. An insult is never left undone.[1]

Teacher: You're saying that the situation in which man finds himself influences his vision, that it must be taken into account?

Historian: By *all* means. A fact of human life is that man is no longer freed from making choices. His freedom is to choose from among possible choices, and this moves man back into a responsible position.

Teacher: At least that is what I teach my students — freedom involves responsibility . . . at least to *some* degree. (HE LEANS FORWARD AS HE TAKES HOLD OF AN ISSUE.) Let's look at the dimensions of *any* situation. You have faced these dimensions in your work and your studies.

Historian: To be sure, it is not a new question. But that does not make it the less aggravating. Contemporary man — and some of you educators — talk about the "open mind." An open mind is not an empty mind. Sometimes the two are confused. Being open to a situation is not enough. Any historian recognizes that *he* is part of any situation . . . even in studies of ancient times . . . that he brings something to the situation, that he *interacts* with it, and that from this transaction "meaning" is created. (HE STOPS. LOOKS EMBARRASSED.) I'm sorry. I ramble a great

Historian: deal. Did I lose you? All I am saying is that each one of us is part of the "situation" in which we stand—a part of it and not apart from it.

Teacher: No, I follow you. In teaching we say that we take a student where he "is" and I suppose that means we are aware of what he brings to his situation—to his studies.

Historian: That makes sense. It seems silly to make an obvious point, but often the obvious is overlooked. A student at any grade level is an actor (it is in acting that one finds consequences—your Dewey knew this), and the options open in any act are enhanced if one is aware of *what* he brings to a situation, *why* he brings it, *how* what he brings can be used. If he can assess the situation in a valid way and if he knows how he and the situation will interact, he has greater control over the situation.

Teacher: You know what you have done?

Historian: I'm never sure.

Teacher: You've put together the components of the area of "social studies." You've suggested what it's all about: being aware of what one brings, being aware of the situation, being aware of how he and it interact and make meanings, and being aware of the choices open to him.

Historian: Fine—as far as you go. But one must learn how to *do* such things. This has implications for what one teaches and for how one teaches. But then, this is your field of competence, not mine.

Teacher: Oh?

Teacher: (A FEW EXTENDED MOMENTS OF SILENCE PASS. WITH A NOTE OF HOSTILITY.) You historians bother me. History bothers me.

Historian: Some sage commented that he did a man a favor and was hated for it ever since. What bothers you about me and my work?

Teacher: Well, you're supposed to be a "service study and not a self-sustaining discipline",[2] at least when it comes to social studies teaching. And now you say that this is not in your line of competence! Where does that leave me and the social studies?

Historian: I am well aware that when you talk of social studies you usually mean some form of history with perhaps a sprinkling of geography and government. You've used history as the major vehicle to accomplish your ends. It is a heavy burden. And, perhaps, if you will pardon me, a little naive and unrealistic.

Teacher: Of course history has dominated the area.[3] We really don't play much with the newer social sciences.

Historian: Don't be kind and skip over my concepts of naiveté and unrealism in terms of your *use* of history. A teacher friend of mine made some material for use in the elementary grades. It wasn't bad. It dealt with population. Some history was used and put into chart form, and even Malthus was included. Her *purpose* was to raise some issues about prediction and change. Her social studies coordinator returned the materials with this note (HE RUMMAGES THROUGH HIS DESK, FINDS IT, AND READS ALOUD). "How come we are now talking about predicting the future when we haven't even begun to finish up the discussion of the past?" What was this coordinator saying about history?

Teacher: Obviously, that....

Historian: That it is possible to *finish* a study of the past? That the purpose of teaching social studies is to study the past? Studying *all* the past is necessary before one can predict—act in a new situation? One cannot move in and out of history but MUST use it in a linear progression. This is what I mean about being naive. How can you *use* history until you grapple with what it is and with *ways* in which it can be used? You teachers have a tendency to assume an awful lot, and then to damn me and my colleagues when your assumptions fall short.

Teacher: But admit it, friend, it is the uselessness of the content against which students have rebelled.[3] The kids are turned off. They don't care about history and see it as being useless.

Historian: You prove my point. If *you* don't use history well, it means that history has no value? I suggest checking your logic.

Teacher: You're copping out. You're absolving yourself of responsibility.

Historian: No! My responsibility is in certain clearly defined areas. If you view history or sociology or *any* content area as a partial *means* to get to your ends, then *history is not taught but the use of history* is taught. This distinction between teaching history and teaching the use of history is a vital distinction—a distinction you have not made. You see, there are two different kinds of professional functioning. This historian may not be concerned with the *instructional* use of his efforts. He may view utility of his work as that which allows *him* further inquiry.

Teacher: I suppose these differences suggest that there are two different frames of references, conceptual bases, skills, and methodologies.

Historian: Precisely! Not to recognize this is to put a burden on me that my credentials and functioning ill equip me to handle. (HE LOOKS INTENTLY AT THE TEACHER.) I don't assume that you are qualified to determine for me and my colleagues a focus of work and methods of inquiry. Similarly, don't expect me to make professional judgments for you.

Teacher: In a way, you are right. We say we want to *use* history, but end making it master.

Historian: Please don't misunderstand me. I am not faulting anyone. There is a long tradition. And such things as N.D.E.A. workshops and the likes have put *me* in a very uncomfortable position.

Teacher: It has just always been assumed that history—and particular aspects of history—have been the best vehicles for achieving the ends of social studies education. We build on this from elementary school right through graduate school. And, if I understand you, you are suggesting that we should become more familiar with history before we expect it to be all things to all people.

Historian: Ill founded expectations can kill a person. You teachers live in this arena—with your students. Words have a habit of detour-ing human curiosity from further exploration. You think of a rose, and we often forget the complex aspects of its organic operations and its ecological balance systems.[4] The term "history" often operates the same way. It blocks under-standing.

Teacher: Would you mind taking the detour sign down from the term history. This might help me to move away from the question of "What have you been?" to the one that really concerns me... "What can you do for us?" And by us I mean social studies teachers.[5]

Historian: History has a history, and in this way it is no different from any other human development. It is significant for teachers to realize this.

Teacher: It's important for historians to realize it too. One of your colleagues argued that you historians, some of you, look back upon the Greek's as spiritual godfathers. If I recall, Greek history was written for the intellectuals and even reflected a hostility to its own history.

Historian: Ah...perhaps true. We have been a bit snide about con-temporary history, but it is well to recall that most Greek history was contemporary history with little sympathy with past generations and past accomplishments.[6] One should honor one's lineage, but not at the cost of oneself.

Teacher: This is all very interesting, but what can you do for us?

Historian: First of all, we cannot offer you any guarantee of certainty. We always try to state past reality in terms of assurance, but all that historians can do is to give their own impressions. The person-ality and predilections of colleagues are at work in the situation. The simple truth is not so simple.[7]

Teacher: You're saying that you cannot be expected to know the whole truth—you *don't* know the whole truth about Waterloo, or Munich, or Fort Sumpter.

Historian: That is correct. You can see how upset we might get when people move away from our concerns and then assume we have something to say in matters of morality.[9] As individuals we may have some say. But as historians, no. We are human beings. Why expect more?

Teacher: But, we infer to our students that the present is a product of the past.

Historian: It can equally be said that our created view of the past is all a product of a present situation. We create our conceptions of history out of present needs and purposes.[10] Look at Augustine, Toynbee, Spengler.

Teacher: But what does history offer?

Historian: You are still looking for neat, nonhuman certitude? This is a psychological problem, not a logical one. History (along with teaching) eventually comes before the bar of philosophy.[5] Through popular usage there has been a transfer of meaning of the term history—a transfer *from the historian to the material* with which he works, to the events themselves. This just promotes the view that history is something existing outside of the mind of the historian; something apart and independent of human activity.[7]

Teacher: But, there must be some patterns. There must be some framework for what historians select to study, how they discriminate among countless human events.

Historian: Perhaps you better than I can answer your probe. Do your history texts deal with subjects or monarchs? vicars or Popes? workingmen or captains of industry? with the spectacular and dramatic and sensational—crises, battles, castastrophes, heroic deeds, crimes, war? Do your texts include the annals of the poor, the tedious struggle of daily living? The poets, artists and folksingers take the poor and the misery. Literature takes the little specimen and makes it whole.[9]

Teacher: Come on, now, the spectacular and the hero and the monarchs moved history.

Historian: History or the historian?

Teacher: What about causal relationships?

Historian: Do you assume that because one thing follows another in temporal sequence that the one thing is caused by the other? Does mere sequence explain a relationship?

Teacher: But, human values?

Historian: You forget about the historian not being a man of cloth. Nothing possesses value because it has grown, was made a long time ago, or emerged from a long process.[5]

Teacher: You are destroying every premise I've had for my social studies program—*you*, the historian. Unbelievable!

Historian: But when in your preparation for your professional function did we take time to meet? If the relationship is so vital, why now—only when students say that history is useless—do you and I take time to meet?

Teacher: Let us not talk of past neglect. I teach *now*. My situation is TODAY! Again I ask, What do you offer?

Historian: And, again, you ask the wrong question. I am not a professional psychiatrist!

Teacher: Are there no generalizations from your work that a teacher of social studies can use?

Historian: Now we are back to terms. In literature, generalization means covering of too much territory too thinly to be persuasive and convincing. Are you asking if history is literature? In science the term generalization refers to a principle that has been found to *hold true* in *every special case experience*. Are there relationships that remain constant that we can state as generalizations?[14] If we view history as literature, there are some. If we view history as science? *Maybe*, but it is more likely that you will find no certainty, no assurance, no stated principles, no ways of testing such principles—*no* scientific generalizations.

Teacher: Your devastation lends credence to the student's complaints. History is *useless*!

Historian: Only when you make it so.

Teacher: Well, then, what?

Historian: Historians have access to countless case experiences. It is possibly the largest proving grounds known to man. It can be used *to test* a theory, even those theories historians have contributed to making. Generalizable concepts can be found in the social sciences, and we work with the social scientists in collaborating, testing, feeding the generation of new theories.[7]

Teacher: Aren't you discouraged by being put in such a position?

Historian: You don't understand. Our function is significant and necessary, *but* we never claimed to be God—only humans working with other humans to try to understand—the human experience. And the profession is more than alive. At our latest professional meeting (AHA) we found the life juices flowing. We discussed, at times heatedly, what we've been discussing tonight:[12] social engineering, propagandizing, academic and scholarly standards, the movement toward our social science colleagues, the hopes...and the doubts. As the outgoing president said, "The profession of historians are not sure what the profession is." So, you see, we too stand in a situation. But we are alive.

Teacher: We have our problems, too. Your history joined the loose confederation of disciplines called social studies in 1911. Our structure hasn't changed much since the reorganization report in 1916 and has been dominated by history. We are told it won't change much because we can't move too far ahead of teacher competency and public attitudes.[12]

(A PERIOD OF SILENCE. HOSTILITY IS GONE AND IN ITS PLACE IS A COMMON RECOGNITION OF SHARED CONCERNS.)

Teacher: You know, I feel a little foolish. I've asked you what we in social studies education should do. I've asked you to simplify an obviously complex realm of concerns. I wanted your apples so I could make a banana split.

Historian: I must admit to some frustration. It reminded me of Peter Marin telling how he traveled across the country with his young son and a friend. They stopped at a restaurant in Kansas and as they walked in—bearded, wearing dark glasses, sporting strange hats and with a long-haired boy—one matron whispered to another that she'd bet the two men had kidnapped the little girl. Marin related: "I took a deep breath and started to speak, but I didn't know where to begin or how to explain."[13]

Teacher: I feel that way every time a student asks a question. Education seems committed to simplifying. Maybe the only hope we have is to make sure the students are aware of the simplifications—while knowing the complexity.

Historian: This may be your major role—to point out what we *don't* know for sure. But let me get back to you. The area you call social studies is designed, you say, to help a youngster come to terms with the contemporary world. This means working with certain cognitions and skills. If this is so, and if the teacher is a teacher of the use of the social studies, then the questions you ask of any contributing academic discipline must be in terms of *your* determined ends.

Teacher: True, but we still haven't been weaned from the other questions. We are told that history instruction works with tested principles and generalizations, with inquiry, with creative thinking, with dealing with intellectual and ethical ways of addressing pressing social concerns.[14] We haven't reached the point yet when we can drop the term "history" and simply talk about principles and generalizations, verification, use of human intelligence, and so forth, and *then* tap any source of help we can. We're still suckling at history's bag.

Historian: Well, we talk about every youngster being his own historian.

Teacher: But, he's more interested in moving beyond just the verifying and recording of the past. He wants to *use* it to make his own history. Why not? Our problem is to make it a viable tool.

Historian: What is history for?[1] To know what it is to be a man, a certain kind of man, and a unique man. Part of what man has done implies what he is capable of becoming. This is the warming fire in my soul.

Teacher: Psychology, sociology, political science, anthropology, economics, social psychology — they can help to answer the question too.

Historian: By *all* means. Just don't anoint any *one* discipline. And, don't claim too much for your area of study. To do so breeds cynicism and contempt for study. Maintain integrity!

Teacher: There is much to do.

Historian: There always has been.

TWO SIDES OF THE COIN

We are including two articles which appeared in the *New York Times*. The articles reflect two fundamentally different positions and raise issues addressed in this chapter; issues that confront a teacher in the social studies area.

The articles are included for two reasons: (1) to indicate that the issues are relatively current and part of the situation in which you stand or will be standing; and (2) to be used as vehicles for exploring the dimensions of the situation and the implications for teaching.

We have used such material with teachers and, on occasion, with students. Some of the questions raised in the use are included with each article. It might be worthwhile to try to identify the "focus ideas" implied by each article and to determine activities which would allow you to test, modify, refine, or delete the focus ideas. It might also be worthwhile to try to determine what kind of a rationale one might evolve given the positions reflected by each article. Can you determine what each article implies in terms of the *use* of the social sciences and history in teaching? Once determined, do the implications have any bearing on *how* one might teach? What does a teacher do when encountering honest men, both scholars, who disagree about the nature of their field? What implications does this problem have for teaching in terms of content and method?

A CRITIC FINDS SOCIOLOGY HAS A FAR WAY TO GO BEFORE FULFILLING ITS CLAIMS*

Sociology has become a power in the land. Since Gunnar Myrdal's "An American Dilemma" was cited as a basis for the Supreme Court's anti-segregation decision, reforming social scientists have felt themselves approaching, at last, the high estate they have long claimed for themselves.

Certainly their realm has grown mushroomlike in this century. Scarcely any American now eludes its influence: "Social studies" is a required course in nearly every public school. Teacher-training is heavily laden with social-science indoctrination, at the expense of the humanities and the natural sciences. For the past two decades, the big foundations have poured hundreds of millions of dollars into the social sciences. And, recently, the Federal Government began to subsidize social-science research.

Still, the social scientists' standing is insecure. They are split into warring camps, the basis of their authority remains in question, and there lingers a certain public reluctance to grant them the respect they covet. If a professor declares roundly, "I speak as a social scientist," some other professor may mutter, "That stuff isn't science—it's only scientism."

Among themselves, indeed, the social scientists are divided and vague as to any definition of their discipline. It is "the science of society," of course; and Auguste Comte expected sociology to be the master science, all branches of learning merging upward into it. But in America, the disciplines of economics and politics already were established before sociology made its appearance; and so, often, the sociologist is forced either to deal with marginal activities or to indulge in grand generalizations about society. For the typical college student, sociology consists of "introductory sociology"— mostly talk about in-groups and out-groups—"marriage and the family" and "social problems."

---

*Kirk, Russell: Is social science scientific? New York Times, June 25, 1961. Copyright 1961 by The New York Times Company. Used by permission.

The serious sociologist, nevertheless, aspires much higher. He asserts that his discipline is, or ought to be, as truly scientific as are the natural sciences. He claims that he, like the natural scientist, describes, predicts and controls phenomena; he lays down "laws" of behavior; he is the engineer and the architect of a new, rational social order.

His opinion polls, his analyses of out-groups, his indices of prejudice, his statistical computations of popular choice (and nowadays he is intoxicated with the computing machines), all are intended to convert mankind into a predictable and controllable species.

He may advocate, for instance, with Dr. Stuart C. Dodd, director of the Washington Public Opinion Laboratory, "Project Aimscales"—a plan to ascertain exactly, through a labyrinthine system of preference polls, "America's current inventory of national goals," and to improve those goals.

"Aimscales of the future," Mr. Dodd writes, "will be able to measure with increasing precision the sizes of the itemed target ends, and subtarget means thereto; their costs in terms of man-hours of effort, money, alternatives displaced, or other appropriate terms; their scheduling in regard to any needed regional differentials or adjustments for diverse conditions; and the all-important attitudinal dimensions of the citizens and their leaders." Such is the language and the objective of the social scientist par excellence.

Philosophically, the representative social scientist is an empiricist of the positivist variety; emotionally, he is often a secular evangelist. Yet despite his increasing influence in many quarters, he is not quite so confident as Comte was that the future belongs to him and his science. Jacques Barzun suggests that the term "behavioral sciences" is supplanting the older term "social sciences" because of the sociologist's "desperate conviction that man does *not* behave and should be made to with the help of science."

About three years ago, a youngish instructor in sociology declared to me, somewhat defiantly, "I really believe that we can teach everybody the scientific approach."

A touch of shrillness in his "really" suggested that even this zealot was experiencing doubts. For today's humanitarian social scientist is discouraged by one hard fact: only in totalitarian states have positivistic doctrines of social reconstruction on "scientific" lines been applied thoroughly. So, he is forced back upon studies in "democratic behavior patterns;" but if "democracy" is his ideal, how can he ever attain the status of priest-scientist that Comte ordained?

Thus, the aims of social science remain in dispute: whether this discipline is meant to give coherence and fresh meaning to older disciplines; whether it is intended to work toward a terrestrial paradise; or whether it ought to rest content with recording group behavior.

Is this branch of study, strictly speaking, a science at all? Pitirim Sorokin, perhaps the best-known of American sociologists, maintains that it is indeed a science—but a science which requires something more than the empirical method for its basis, and which ought to recognize and respect knowledge already possessed by the several intellectual disciplines, including the sociological discipline itself.

Undeniably, much of what has passed for social science has been mere scientism, or pseudo-science. Loosely employed, the word "science" means simply any orderly and reputable study, on systematic principles.

But the social scientists have not been satisfied with so general a claim to the laurels of science: many of them have asserted that their discipline must be, or perhaps already is, as exact and regular a science as physics, or chemistry, or botony, or geology. (Some, indeed, have used the term "social physics.") Envying the natural sciences, they have sought to emulate the methods of their natural-science colleagues, and to assert parallel claims of certitude in prediction and control.

"The nemesis of such simulacra," Sorokin writes, "is sterility and error—and this nemesis is already walking abroad among the contemporary psychosocial sciences. In spite of our narcissistic self-admiration, of the enormous energy and funds spent in pseudomathematical and statistical research, its achievements have been singularly modest, its sterility unexpectedly notable, and its fallacies surprisingly numerous."

One consequence of this common social-scientist passion for imitating the outward forms of natural science is the development of an amazing jargon, incomprehensible even to nineteen-twentieths of the body of university graduates and, one suspects, often unclear to most sociologists themselves.

This "scientific" vocabulary of the sociologist, to which every professor feels free to add at will (by way of establishing his claim to "originality") resembles the deliberate obscurity of the learned Marxist—an opaqueness intended to convert the vulgar through awe of erudition.

The medical word "synergy," for instance, redefined to convey the meaning of "the sum total of energy which any group can command and expend," obscures rather than enlightens. The word "valence" is borrowed from physics and converted to mean "attraction in society"—which is not at all like its natural-science meaning and is severed from its linguistic root.

Even a popular and comparatively lucid sociological writer like David Riesman twists terms to suit his passing purpose and, perhaps, to impress his general readership—using the word "anomic," for example, to mean being cut off from the tone and temper of a society, which is a borrowing from Durkheim's *anomique,* the masterless man.

In an age which requires the restoration of clarity and of reasonable persuasion, this pedantry in terminology is a sorry tendency. Genuine science does not need to cloak itself in convoluted verbiage.

More serious than this debauching of language is what Sorokin calls "quantophrenia," or infatuation with statistical surveys and nose-counting. Because the natural sciences are non-moral—that is, they have to do only with things and animals less than human—the aspiring "behavioral scientist" endeavors to develop a methodology which will be equally indifferent to moral norms—that is, to standards and models for humanity.

For old normative judgments, the social scientist of this persuasion substitutes opinion surveys and numerical compilations. However, as Carlyle wrote, "Statistics is a science which ought to be honorable, the basis of many most important sciences; but . . . a wise head is requisite for carrying it on. Conclusive facts are inseparable from inconclusive except by a head that already understands and knows."

So there have sprung up the immense behavioral research centers, most notably the Center for Advanced Study in the Behavioral Sciences, at Stanford University, almost a Mecca for this persuasion. The University of Michigan has a whole series of such institutions, supported by very large sums from foundations and government—the Center for Research on Conflict Resolution, the Research Center for Group Dynamics, the Survey Research Center.

C. Wright Mills, a radical gadfly among sociologists, suggests that very often the research assistants in behavioral institutes are chosen from among the second-rate: "I have seldom seen one of these young men" he writes, "once he is well caught up, in a condition of genuine intellectual puzzlement."

Deficient in imagination, they mistake fact accumulation for wisdom. The ancient Greeks had one word, philodoxer, for the lover of opinion, and another word, philosopher, for the lover of wisdom; and they knew that these two are a world apart. Much modern opinion-and-behavior investigations is only philodoxy.

Such behaviorists often ignore theory and history in favor of the currents of the year or the decade: awareness of the drift is all. One young behavioral professor said to me recently, when the name of a distinguished historian of ideas was mentioned, "How does he think he knows all this? Did he make a survey?" Resentment of unusual imagination and obsession with nose-counting are the behaviorist's form of anti-intellectualism.

Absurdities result. One behavioristic study, cited by Barzun and Graff in their "Modern Researcher," came to the solemn conclusion that "if in a given society an aunt resides with or near the mother, and assists in giving care to the child, the latter will regard her as a mother; less so, or not so, if the aunt lives at a distance."

Thus do some sociologists establish, as brilliant new dis-coveries, on scientific principles, the tiny secrets of the bassinet.

Another expensive survey, financed by the Federal Office of Education, proposed to analyze "succorance and playmirth" — that is, seeking of comfort and companionship in fun — among small children. The researchers came to the enlighten-ing conclusion, after much statistics juggling, that little boys like to play with little boys, and little girls with little girls.

And the absurdities can grow into serious errors about men and communities. If a behavioral researcher acting from the assumptions of nineteenth-century positivism investigates religious beliefs, he is likely to discover exactly what he ex-pected to find: that religious convictions are unscientific, irrational, absurd and perhaps dangerous. He is against pre-judice — but, unaware of his own prejudices. Because he has been deliberately cut off from theological, humane and his-torical disciplines, he may mistake his petty, private rationality for self-evident truth.

Of if the behavioral scientist assumes that political con-servatives are ignorant bigots, he usually finds by his opinion surveys that the conservative folk he interviewed were just that. Ignorant and bigoted folk give ignorant and bigoted answers; ergo, ignorant and bigoted folk are conservatives.

In reality, one can understand the significance of such a term as "conservative" only by painstaking historical and political studies, but too many behavioral researchers confound their unconscious prejudices with complete objectivity.

As Raymond Aron — the most widely read of living French sociologists — remarked recently, the typical American sociol-ogist tends to be "liberal," in part because "many stem from semi-marginal groups: first-generation Americans, Jews, and natives of central Europe are more common among American sociologists than Back-Bay Bostonians."

And although the complete behaviorist may deny the existence of "value-judgments" and normative understandings, never-theless he does not escape, in his researches, the influence of his own value-judgments, even though they are unwittingly held as vague sentiments or animosities.

In his introduction to "The Human Meaning of the Social Sciences," one well-known behaviorist, Daniel Lerner, declares that the social sciences have shown modern man that "there are no more eternal mysteries, . . . there are no more eternal verities"; man is revealed as "plastic, variable, and amenable to reshaping." And the energetic social scientist intends to set to work promptly at that reshaping, free from authority, prescription and value-judgments.

The trouble with this view of social studies and their purpose is that to act without any norms except vague humanitarian sentiments may bring a nation into grave peril. It may injure the institutions which shelter community and freedom at home, and lead to the gravest of mistakes in foreign policy — in the administration of a foreign-aid program in Afghanistan or Laos, for instance.

For the social scientist is not really dealing with things soulless or inanimate or abstract, as does the natural scientist. The sociologist's subject, embarrassing though it may be to the eager reformer, is man, living and erratic man, in complex humanity.

Human beings are the least controllable, verifiable, law-obeying and predictable of subjects. If man were predictable, indeed, he would cease to be truly human. Andrew Hacker, of Cornell University, therefore writes forebodingly about "the spectre of predictable man" — the man of the future whose coming so many behaviorists view complacently, the man of "Brave New World."

Now, of course, there can be ascertained certain general rules concerning human behavior in community; indeed, a large body of literature on the subject has long been available — though often ignored by the novelty-seeking behavioral scientist. But the more important part of this literature is not "scientific" in the strict modern sense. This knowledge is the work of poets, theologians, political theorists, moralists, jurists and men of imagination generally.

One may learn a great deal about the first principles of human nature from Dante or Samuel Johnson; but this is not the sort of knowledge that fits into the calculations of the astronomer or the engineer. Plato and Cicero, Montesquieu and Burke are the sources of much wisdom concerning the civil social order; but they are not "scientists" in the sense of the natural sciences.

Even when one finds a philosopher like David Hume, severely logical and methodical, the zealot for "social science" must be dismayed by Hume's conclusion that rational accounting for morals and politics is simply impossible.

In fine, I think that the behavioral scientist has been the

victim of illusion when he has attempted to solve all the ills
to which the community is heir by the application of the techniques of physics and chemistry and biology.

"It is this false analogy with mechanics and mathematics,"
Prof. S. Herbert Frankel of Oxford says, "that accounts for the
facile belief that the problem involved in living and working
together in a community is similar to the problem of finding, by
abstract thought or local deduction, the 'unknown' factor in
an equation. In the realm of organic life there is, and can be, no
final solution — other than death itself... Those who arro-
gantly write solutions upon their political banners . . . offend
the very nature of all social evolution, which rests on the slow
unfolding of institutions, laws, and habit-patterns of thought
and action." Amen to that.

By deliberately cutting himself off from tradition and theory,
by ignoring theology and ethics and humane letters, the average social scientist of our generation has deprived himself of
the principal instruments for understanding human behavior —
or for effecting any enduring improvement of society, let alone
the "solution" of human striving which he often seeks.

If a scientist at all, he has become a scientist without reliable
means for measuring and weighing. Infatuated with the empirical method, the doctrinaire social scientist omits from his
calculations the higher and more enduring elements in human
behavior.

As Sorokin argues, modern social science desperately needs
reinvigoration of social theory and observation through the
employment of reason and the recognition of poets' and
philosophers' genius. Only by a return to the true sources of
wisdom — which in part are intuitive — can the critic of society
find standards by which to measure our present discontents
and to propose remedies.

Neither the utopian sociologist of the old positivistic breed
nor the survey-taking behaviorist of our time is prepared to
confront the Gorgon's head of twentieth-century social disintegration. What social studies need more than anything else, I
suspect, is the recovery of norms: a restoration of normative
disciplines, a return to the knowledge of standards for human
personality and for the just order. Some imaginative sociologists — one may cite as an example Robert A. Nisbet, in his
book "The Quest for Community" — already have turned that
way.

Imagination, in the long run, rules the world — not scientific
research, and still less scientistic sham. It is pointless, and at
heart unscientific, to survey the shifting opinions of the hour
unless one recognizes standard in opinion — that is, sources of
truth. And it is pointless to ape the natural sciences when one
has to deal with whimsical and impatient and irrational mankind.

So I venture to suggest that we professors of social disciplines might do well if we talked less about the claims of social science and more about the realities of social art. Modern society, in many ways sick, needs, not the shortsighted manipulations of the research technician, but the artist's touch.

SOME QUESTIONS POSED BY THE ARTICLE

1. Is all education indoctrination?

2. How much social science do prospective teachers study?

3. Is security of one's position gained only when there is no opposition? What does one mean by security?

4. If social science is a vague term, what about the term "academic discipline"?

5. When is something "truly scientific"?

6. What is a scientific "law" — probability or certainty?

7. Is it possible to study mankind without being accused of trying to convert mankind?

8. Is Aguste Comte the only social science theorist? (two centuries ago?)

9. Are the "aims" of social science only admitted to be a form of social evangelism?

10. If one does not understand a term does it necessarily have to be considered jargon?

11. Can one study values and norms scientifically?

12. How does wisdom differ from the accumulation of facts?

13. Why are social scientists so threatening as to be viewed as conspiratorial?

14. Is sociology the same as social studies as the same as social science as the same as behavioral science?

15. Is the fact that man is erratic, at times irrational, and often complex make it impossible to study man?

16. If one does not study man with observation, record keeping, statistics, and so forth, how *does* one study man?

17. Is Absolute Certainty the only possible "end" a scholar might have in mind?

18. Is it necessary that a social scientist ignore theology, ethics, history, literature, and so forth?

19. How does one "understand" human behavior?

20. We need a "recovery of norms" — a restoration of "normative disciplines." What norms? Whose norms? Disciplines at what time and whose?

21. Is scientific theory devoid of imagination?

A SOCIOLOGIST'S REBUTTAL*

The Time Magazine of June 25 carried an article by Russell Kirk entitled "Is Social Science Scientific?" In it he contended that:

(1) Claims by sociologists that their discipline is a science like the natural sciences are highly doubtful. Much of sociology is "mere scientism or pseudo-science."

(2) Sociology cannot be a science like the natural sciences because, whereas they deal with "things soulless or inanimate or abstract," sociology deals with "living and erratic man."

(3) A foolish aping of the outward forms of natural science has led many social scientists into an infatuation with jargon and meaningless statistics.

(4) It has fostered in them the dangerous notion that they are the engineers and architects of a "new, rational social order" in which converted mankind will be "predictable and controllable."

Mr. Kirk concluded that a true knowledge of man remains the province of "poets, theologians, political theorists, moralists, jurists and men of imagination generally."

In the following reply, Robert K. Merton, Professor of Sociology at Columbia University and a leading figure in the social sciences, states the sociologist's position.

Once again the season of the anti-sociologists is upon us. The academic year has ended and professors are ready to turn from talking to writing. A self-selected few will dust off and publish yet again the litany that fiercely imprecates sociology and all its works. This year, the avowed conservative professor of political science, Russell Kirk, got in first. His version will serve to exhibit the curious admixture of illogic and sentiment that makes up the creed and canons of anti-sociology.

Some sociologists find these assaults tiresome. To me, they have the peculiar charm of testifying to the need for the very kind of sociological inquiry they caricature. For each jaded version reads as though it were written by a sociologist-*manque.* Each purports to describe the behavior of sociologists, to explain that behavior and, even more ambitiously, to describe and explain the responses to it.

With practiced ease, for example, Mr. Kirk reviews the work of thousands of social scientists and promulgates the first canon that "the representative" specimen is an "empiricist of the positivist variety; emotionally, he is often a secular evangelist." Had Mr. Kirk allowed himself to profit from the introductory course in sociology he so deplores, he might have learned of the danger of creating out of his private impressions a stereotype of the aims and behavior of large numbers of people, all the while pretending to have caught hold of the representative reality. But amateur sociologizing has no place for disciplined inquiry. Rather, it assumes that statements become authoritative simply by being put into the black and white magic of print.

The second canon declares the absurdity and impiety of statistics dealing with the behavior of men in society. For nothing significant about man's behavior can be counted. If it could be counted, it would be immoral to do so. Everyone knows that no good can come of it.

To support this canon, Mr. Kirk cites Carlyle, who knew little about the primitive statistical methods of his own day and nothing, obviously, about the mathematical bases of modern statistics. As further proof, he quotes the attack by the sociologist Pitirim A. Sorokin on "quantophrenia" or an uncritical devotion to faulty statistics. Unlike myself, Mr. Kirk has not had the benefit of having been Professor Sorokin's student, and so does not know, apparently, that Sorokin used vast arrays of social statistics in every one of his major works and, in "Social and Cultural Dynamics" states that "quantitative judgments . . . in verbal form" are inevitable in any substantial work of history.

No doubt it is more inviting to assume statistics of human behavior. The amateur sociologist will explain, for example, why it is that we have such high rates of mental illness in what Mr. Kirk feels free to describe as our age of "twentieth-century social disintegration." But while the amateur sociologist explains *why* this is so, the disciplined sociologist proceeds first to find out whether it really *is* so. Only through painstaking analysis of the statistics of mental illness — as in the work of Herbert Goldhamer and Andrew Marshall — do we find that we had best postpone our ready-to-hand explanations, if only because it now seems probable that the rate of confinement for mental illness is no higher today than it was during the past century.

Turning up like death and taxes, the third canon of the anti-sociologists declares the sociologists to be both perpetrators and victims of jargon. Here, the anti-sociologist knows himself to be on altogether safe ground, for just about everyone can be counted on to be "against jargon" in the same penetrating sense that President Coolidge's minister declared himself against sin.

Perhaps it is time to distinguish between jargon and that essential of all disciplined thought, technical language. Technical language is a more precise and condensed form of thought and communication than colloquial language. It is designed to fix definite meanings in which each word has ideally only one denotation and is deliberately deprived of connotation. Jargon, in contrast, is a muddled and wordy imitation of technical language.

The mere unfamiliarity or unesthetic quality of language is no criterion. Jargon and technical language sound alike to someone untrained in the discipline where the language is employed.

All this is only prologue to the pair of canons central to the anti-sociologists' creed. Briefly put, these hold, first that sociological truths cannot be discovered, for there are no detectable uniformities in human behavior, since man is incorrigibly unpredictable. And second, that sociologists constitute a danger to society, for they provide the knowledge through which men can be molded to fit a new and obnoxious social order. I need not burlesque the logic of the anti-sociologists, for they have preceded me here. I need only review it.

It would seem clear that, if there are no discoverable uniformities about man in society, there can be no sociological knowledge employed to regiment him. Should anti-sociologists admit that there are such uniformities, they can scarcely argue that these uniformities can be discovered by the defective sociology of today, with its inapplicable statistics, its tattered jargon, and its total misunderstanding of human nature.

Forced to acknowledge that there are discoverable uniformities in social life and that modern sociology, for all its limitations, discovers some of them, would they then propose to exorcise this knowledge for fear that it might be used to violate civilized values? On this last line of retreat, the anti-sociologists would join forces with the anti-intellectuals and totalitarian regimenters of thought they ostensibly combat. They would declare themselves guardians of us all, alone able to distinguish dangerous from undangerous knowledge.

The remaining canons of the anti-sociologist are transparently trivial. Criticism among sociologists, for example, is described by the anti-sociologists in the militant metaphors of "warring camps" and "internecine warfare." Perhaps they should pause before advocating monolithic agreement on intellectual issues. It would be a curious reading of the history of thought to suggest that the absence of disagreement testifies to a developing discipline.

As for the anti-sociologists' canon that gives them alone access to the recorded wisdom of the past—from Plato to Montesquieu and Burke—this need only be stated to refute itself.

Since the anti-sociologists impose their grotesque versions of the methods of sociological inquiry upon a public too busy to look for themselves, a few words should be said about those methods. Social scientists believe it no longer sufficient to describe the behavior, attitudes, values and social relations obtaining in a complex society simply on the basis of a large but scattered array of documents, both public and private, and on educated guesses about what people are thinking and feeling. Studies of the historical past, of course, have no alternative. But in the study of present-day societies, these procedures are giving way to systematic, though far from perfected, methods.

One such method is the "sample survey," which sounds out the practices and attitudes of a group selected as representative of the larger population from which they are drawn. This type of survey is now part of the intellectual landscape. However, the "opinion polls" in the popular press do not begin to reproduce the analytical uses to which such surveys are put by academic sociologists.

Furthermore, it is with this instrument as with the rest: the most devastating criticisms of its misuse have come, not from the anti-sociologists who know about it only through casual inspection, but from the professional sociologists who are prepared to study their sometimes disappointing experience with it. For they, at least the best of them, know that, whatever the worth of one or another tool of inquiry, it is the questions put into the inquiry that determine the significance of the results. If the questions are trivial, then the answers will be trivial.

For sociology as for most other scientific disciplines, the electronic computer has emerged as a new resource. Contrary to the imagery of the anti-sociologists, this machine is not the universal mind of our day. It must be told what to do. But, as with most technical creations, the computer has a capacity for deflecting men from the pursuit of purposes that genuinely matter. It tempts its tenders to cast all manner of raw data into its maw and wait for the thoroughly digested product that will itself be senseless if the thought of its managers is without sense. The potential victims, by their professional training, are best qualified to recognize and to counter this danger.

With or without the computer, today's sociology makes no attempt to substitute science for ethics and esthetics or to displace humanism with scientism. Every responsible sociologist, and there are not a few, knows that his knowledge is no substitute for artistic thought.

The thinking humanist, for his part, recognizes that the social scientist who knows his business seeks only to provide an understanding of certain, not all, aspects of the behavior of men and the organization of human society. The intellectual gulf between humanist and social scientist has begun to be bridged. The late Gilbert Murray, critic and classical scholar, said that sociology is "destined to bear abundant and ever-increasing fruit." The political journalist Richard Rovere, has observed that "those of us who have been educated in the twentieth century habitually think in sociological terms, whether or not we have had any training in sociology."

After all this, it is only natural to ask: what is going on in sociology and what does it all amount to? It would be foolish to answer this question by staking out the boundaries of sociology, as though it were a piece of real estate. That is not the character of intellectual property. But we can, in this short space, at least hint at the answer.

In the large, sociology is engaged in finding out how man's behavior and fate are affected, if not minutely governed, by his place within particular kinds, and changing kinds, of social structure and of culture. This means that sociology moves across a wide, varied and, to the layman, often bewildering range of topics and problems.

In doing so, one of its principal functions is to subject popular beliefs about man and his works to responsible investigation. As I have implied, the sociologist asks about many of these beliefs, "Is it really so?" The popular assumption, for example, that the rate of social mobility in America has recently declined has been put in question by systematically assembled data.

The alleged breakdown of the American family, with obsequies read regularly over the remains by those who should know better, has been found to be specious; thorough analyses of data on divorce and death find American marriages remain-intact more often now than they once did. Or, to tackle one last widespread assumption, people who reject orthodox religious beliefs are not more apt to engage in crime than people who hold fast to such beliefs.

Some of the findings of sociology take a considerable time to enter the public domain. For more than a generation, sociologists have found that complex organizations of widely different kinds—economic, political, military, educational—exhibit the same tendencies. These tendencies make for the "bureaucratic man," who is shaped by organizationally induced pressures to conform to the rules even when this means that conformity gets in the way of doing the job effectively. How far this is inevitable remains to be seen, and inquiries are now under way to find out how these tendencies can be counteracted.

Basic to sociology is the premise that, in the course of social interaction, men create new conditions that were not part of their intent. Short-run rationality often produces long-run irrationality. Public health measures may go awry; financial incentives may lead to a decline rather than an increase in production; intensified punishment may aggravate rather than curb crime. Growing recognition of this has become one of the sources of an enlarged use of sociological research in such fields as medicine and public health, social work, law, education, the ministry, architecture and city planning, business, organized labor and agriculture.

Yet it must be added that sociologists, perhaps better than the anti-sociologists, know they are just beginning to acquire the knowledge needed to cope with the many social ills man has the inveterate capacity to contract.

We sociologists need to be saved from the anti-sociologists only in respect to the exaggerated claims they make for our prowess and accomplishments. It is they, not we, who say that "sociology is a power in the land." It is they, not we, who make the absurd claim that sociology has the power and the intent to turn men into robots and to construct a new social order. The men and women at work in sociological inquiry have more modest and less sadistic hopes. Like their colleagues in other scholarly and scientific disciplines, they recognize that this "very new science of an ancient subject" has still a long way to go. And undisturbed by the cannonades of the anti-sociologists, they are methodically proceeding on their way.

SOME QUESTIONS POSED BY THE ARTICLE

1. Is it absurd or improper to apply the products of previous investigation (statistics/computers/etc.) as tools in trying to gain additional knowledge about man's behavior?

2. What's the difference between saying "why" this is so and trying to determine if the thing is, in fact, so?

3. Is much of social science aimed at *testing* previously held views?

4. If technical terms try to deliberately deprive of connotation, does it assume that connotations are "given" and not "brought"? Can the scientists (educators) control this factor?

5. Are there detectable uniformities in human behavior?

6. If man's nature is unchangeable, why do people fear those who are accused of trying to change it?

7. Who are the guardians of all who determine what knowledge is dangerous and that which is safe? What do we mean by the term anti-intellectual?

8. When we talk of scientific study one assumes a systematic approach—always looking for more improved tools. What are the alternatives to such an approach?

9. Why does the author say that it is the *questions* put into inquiry that determine the significance of the results?

10. If one can't substitute science for ethics, upon what are ethics based?

11. If one were to study "bureaucratic man" in any type of organization, how would one entertain the variables?

12. How can short run rationality often lead to long run irrationality?

13. Who (what kind of people) are intent upon making knowledge claims and then projecting them (claims) upon those who are feared?

A PROBLEM AND A PROMISE

In looking at human experience and trying to determine what parts of that experience one chooses to teach, one is plagued with the need to differentiate between what is and what one wishes to be. Hamlet's soliloquy notes the psychological dimensions involved.

Robert Redfield suggests the promises implicit in the social sciences through indicating some of the social uses of the social sciences. This also has implications for content selection.

INTERLUDE: HAMLET'S SOLILOQUY*

To be, or not to be—that is not a question but a tautology. I am not interested in empty statements. I want to know the truth of a synthetic statement: I want to know whether I shall be. Which means whether I shall have the courage to avenge my father.

Why do I need courage? It is true, my mother's husband, the king, is a powerful man and I shall risk my life. But if I can make it plain to everybody that he murdered my father, everybody will be on my side. If I can make it plain to everybody. It is so plain to me.

Why is it plain? I have good evidence. The ghost was very conclusive in his arguments. But he is only a ghost. Does he exist? I could not very well ask him. Maybe I dreamed him. But there is other evidence. The man had a motive to kill my father. What a chance to become king of Denmark! And the hurry with which my mother married him. My father had always been a healthy man. It's a good piece of indirect evidence.

But that's it: nothing but indirect evidence. Am I allowed to believe what is only probable? Here is the point where I lack courage. It is not that I am afraid of the present king. I am afraid of doing something on the basis of a mere probability. The logician tells me that a probability has no meaning for an individual case. How then can I act in this case? That is what happens when you ask the logician. But what if I should start thinking after the deed and find out I should not have done it?

Is the logician so bad? He tells me that if something is probable I am allowed to make a posit and act as though it were true. In doing so I shall be right in the greater number of cases. But shall I be right in *this* case?

---

*Reichenbach, Hans: The Rise of Scientific Philosophy. Originally published by the University of California Press, 1962; reprinted by permission of the Regents of the University of California.

No answer. The logician says: act. You will be right in the greater number of cases.

I see a way out. I shall make the evidence more conclusive. It is really a good idea: that show I shall put on. It will be a crucial experiment. If they murdered him they will be unable to hide their emotions. That is good psychology. If the test is positive I shall know the whole story for certain. See what I mean? There are more things in heaven and earth than are dreamt of in your philosophy, my dear logician.

I shall know it for certain? I see your ironical smile. There is no certainty. The probability will be increased and my posit will have a higher rating. I can count on a greater percentage of correct results. That is all I can reach. I can't get away from making a posit. I want certainty, but all the logician has for me is the advice to make posits.

There I am, the eternal Hamlet. What does it help me to ask the logician, if all he tells me is to make posits. His advice confirms my doubt rather than giving me the courage I need for my action. Logic is not for me. One has to have more courage than Hamlet to be always guided by logic.

THE SOCIAL USES OF SOCIAL SCIENCE*

The social uses of medicine and the press are generally known. The social uses of the social sciences are not recognized—science itself is not understood. The nature of a social science includes a group of disciplines which describe human nature, human activity, and human institutions. The group of disciplines is considered to be a science because it is concerned with what is, not with what ought to be; it is concerned with objectivity; it attempts systematically to formulate its findings.

History is not included in this category. History is a collection of preserved and considered experience; the social sciences are analytical and their uses pivot on the attempt to understand a social problem and/or the description of the general characteristics of some class of social phenomena.

Why have a social science? Because it is useful; it aids in getting things done which society wants done—much of what is learned can be applied; it aids in the decision-making process. But there is more. The social sciences differ from, say physics, and their social use is not exhausted when one notes the practical application. Social science "has other important social uses in the testing and development of social values."

The plainest values with which social science is concerned are those basic to science: objectivity, honesty, accuracy, and humility before the facts. These are virtues which every moral citizen may embrace. But we have no guarantee that our free society will allow the extension of the scientific attitude into the study of social problems—tradition, sentiment, and inviolable attitudes often protect certain areas from rational examination.

---

*Redfield, Robert: The social uses of social science. University of Colorado Bulletin, Vol. XLVII, May 24, 1947.

The subject matter of social science is not morally indifferent. "It is morally significant." Social science is the test case of the vitality of the values previously mentioned. It is related to freedom of the modern mind. Social science is a relatively new instrument for getting specific things done and for the clarification and development of values. It does not preach values or ethics but clarifies choices and checks inconsistencies, tests values, and raises questions of cost. Social science hears the call for freedom and says, "Okay, you believe in the right to examine freely and criticize openly, to reach conclusions from tested evidence. Then you must endure the pain of examination and the testing of customs and institutions you hold dear." Social science tells us that mankind has passed the time when it took its ethical convictions from the past without doubt. Now we must think, investigate, and consider the means and ends of life.

Social science does not have to be sold—only explained. The explanation should make clear that social science is not only a box of tools but a light. It provides categories that help people understand themselves. It helps define the world of human relations and makes clear to us our place in a social cosmos. The social scientist finds a science that is not indifferent. It demands a responsible use of human intelligence and is a proving ground of values.

THE TEACHER AND THE SOCIAL SCIENTIST

The social studies teacher and the social scientist meet on a street corner. They discuss as they walk down the street under a hazy, polluted sky—past people working, eating, striking, laughing; past store windows with various styles of dress; past public transportation vehicles, traffic snarls, pickets, newspaper boys, "X" movies, trash cans, and trash; past a policeman responding to a burglar alarm, a preacher arguing the return to the fold, and a booth manned by a citizen asking protest against the war.

Tchr.: What should I teach in social studies?

S.S.: It is obvious that you do not know me very well. Do I wear a collar or have a crystal ball? How do I know what you *should* do. It is a "nonsense" question. You want me to respond that you OUGHT to do such and such. I won't get caught in such a trap. I have seen what a burden you teachers of social studies have imposed on my history colleagues. It is no game for me! I am descriptive, not prescriptive. When *you* decide what you want to do, then maybe I can help you accomplish your ends.

Tchr.: (ANGRILY) I knew better than to come to you. You and your kind are suspect anyway. Nobody would allow you near a public school! Even Congress saw fit to accuse you of undermining the moral, social, economic, and political fabric of society—of leading us to some form of collectivism![15]

S.S.: I simply provide data that is open to being tested. What is done with the data is not of my doing as a social scientist. Is it the wine that causes drunkeness? Do away with the wine. Do away with women, or with men, if you don't want adultery.[16] Besides, students haven't been trained to use data. Neither have adults for that matter.

Tchr.: I suppose you have no concern for morality, goodness, and truth?

S.S.: On the contrary. I plead guilty to any accusation pointed at my having a value system. It is the heart of what I do. I and my colleagues have our commandments. Granted, they number several less than yours. It will be hard for you to understand, but we cherish complete truthfulness, we try to avoid making wild and unsupported claims, we are committed to support scientific inquiry and opinion, and we are committed to fully communicate and make "public" our findings and our methods.[17] But...(with resignation) ...you fear truth, fact, and openness. This is what you find suspect. I'll grant you, the uncommon *is* usually suspect.

Tchr.: I resent your implying that I am in favor of untruth, blowing one's horn, thinking, and not being above board in my dealings with fellow humans. Yet...

S.S.: Yet, you are anxious about me. You are afraid not of the grapes but of the wine. At least you are honest. But there is a big difference between saying "you are wrong" and "I don't *like* what you say."

Tchr.: I remember reading about President Barnard of Columbia, who was a scientist. He said that he would rather live in a simple ignorance and die in pleasant dreams even if though they were false.[18]

S.S.: That is a real statement of ethics! An educator is supposed to influence others. Was he willing to give the "others" a choice of whether they wanted to live with truth or illusion?

Tchr.: It is not quite so clean a division as you would have me believe. One can embrace parts of your "way" without having to love all of it.

S.S.: To be semi-open is to regard the humanized man as being less capable than the first examples of *Homo sapiens*: to deny the value of development along rational lines and to deny human qualities that have been the essence of the human adventure.[19] Have you thought through your position, or are you just so inclined?

Tchr.: O.K. No games. Since the rise of scientific thought there has been a widespread and rising contempt for tolerance and peace. Science has taken away the traditional guides to human thought and action. You have brought us a way of life less than human.

S.S.: Interesting. Humanities, including religion and ethics, have been the basis of education for centuries. We have noted no decline in the ferocity of men. Scientific "ways" have never been in the social saddle—why blame science for your human failures?[20]

Tchr.: I suppose you blame the clergy and the educators?

S.S.: Cause and effect are elusive. But you educators *have* intensified the quest for absolute certainty by providing an education which conditions the child to regard doubt as sin and confidence as a "religious command."[21]

Tchr.: Well, I won't speak for others, but as for myself, I'll take what man's intelligence has produced—the automobile, the telephone, the radio, frozen food, but I *am* a bit doubtful when you move into human behavior. The truth is, it is more secure having some authority, direction. Most of us want certainty, power, assertiveness, competition, status, prestige. The freedom we talk about is really a freedom to follow. Truth that supports our personal conclusions is the only truth that sets us personally free.

S.S.: As a teacher of social studies, is *this* what you honor and prize? Is *this* the choice *you* make for others. Change the place and situation and you could teach for *any* totalitarian system!

Tchr.: You confuse me. For heaven's sake, what *is* the nature of this science of which you speak?

S.S.: You educators *should* be interested. It is a method of learning and not a system of ready-made beliefs. And I thought this is what education was all about. A false premise, no doubt. At any rate, the method called "science" has two main objectives: to enable man to *do* and to *know*.[22]

Tchr.: So do religion and speculative philosophy.

S.S.: True. The difference rests in what the scientist *does*. He explores nature and human experience. He "discovers" order. Order doesn't just expose itself, nor is it amenable to common sense — you don't point a finger or camera at it. It must be discovered. Actually, it must be *created*. What bombards us is mere disorder. We are trying to create order in our home.[23]

Tchr.: I still don't see a major difference.

S.S.: When one has order and has related objects and experience, he can predict. The prediction depends on its success, in turn, on the validity of the order and relationships. Prediction built on wishful thinking is a fragile and risky business. What is observed is recorded. The map of the exploration is laid out for others to check.

Tchr.: In a sense, all education is based on prediction. I hadn't quite thought of it in this manner. We predict what a person needs to know, the world he will live in, the challenges to survival—.

S.S.: Right. Our lives are built on the ability to predict. Especially our social lives and activities. But you have another stake in scientific activity.

Tchr.: Another stake?

S.S.: How can you possibly harmonize teaching with the knowledge explosion? At an increasing rate, we have more and more fragments and pieces of disorder. Keeping the old curriculum and merely adding on becomes a fool's paradise. But given a method to bring things together, to "generalize," can help to simplify the enormous task you face.

Tchr.: You mean I can reduce complexity to simplicity? Is this what science is all about?

S.S.: Would that it were! Contrary to common sense, this is *not* that kind of reduction. All it does is make a complex situation more understandable — while remaining aware of the complexity. Whitehead asked science to seek simplicity and to distrust it. He should have said to the social scientists, seek complexity and order it.[24]

Tchr.: You know, I feel a little silly, but I still don't see how science and its method of doing and knowing differs from that activity followed by any scholar in any field. Aren't all scholars interested in bringing "order" and "understanding" to the human experience.

S.S.: The key is the method. I should say the key relates to the methods used to bring order, to generalize, to predict. There's the difference as found between a Pontiff and a journeyman. The Pontiff knows that science cannot determine absolute truth about reality— can't give an ultimate order. If it is needed by people, it is up for grabs. He uses a meta (above) physical "method"—and he'll use whatever findings of science support his order. He is persuasive. He simplifies and his court of appeal is NOT to the world of experience. The journeyman is content with probabilities and with an "order" that can be tested in experience.[25]

Tchr.: I suppose the journeyman would view most social studies education as simply a parade of Pontiffs?

S.S.: Some would. The social scientist explores human experience. He brings order to human behavior. If he can bring order (not impose it), he can predict. If he can predict, it opens up opportunities to choose more effectively. If one can choose more effectively, he has greater chances to control and to create his life. It opens the door to move human experience from random chance to a range of probability. In a sense, it is a liberation movement.

Tchr.: This is a real threat. It challenges the traditional concept of what it means to be human. It moves away from a concept of a constant human nature—one independent of knowledge, situation, time—a nature governed by the same laws that governed the world of Bacon and Newton. It moves us out of a mechanistic world.

S.S.: Yes. The Newtonian world-view has been modified. Why not the view of the individual and the view of human nature? The social scientist knows that man is dependent upon his concepts of order and the symbols he uses to put labels on such concepts. Man was born without an elaborate instinctive pattern of adjustment, and without some empirical rationality, human life would be impossible.[26]

Tchr.: But it seems so cold and objective. I may be hung up, but the whole effort seems somehow to counter what it means to be a human being.

S.S.: I can't satisfy learned psychological needs. As a social scientist, however, I can take them into account in human behavior. Any value system in today's world must take scientific discoveries into account. Biology informs us of patterns of basic needs. You may see a moral question involved in whether or not a society assists in satisfying these needs. All science can do is to provide another source of potential information to be used in human concerns and in approaching human problems. It appeals to experience rather than authority and tradition.[27] Don't expect too much of it. Instead of saying to humans "You OUGHT to want "A," and thus you should do "B," it says, "If you want "A"—then maybe I can help. But there is no guarantee.

Tchr.: You are arguing that science is a human activity and is no less humane than other sources of knowledge—even *more* humane, according to you. But what can you do for me as a social studies teacher?

S.S.: Your question has been modified. Good. I have two things: (1) a method or approach, and (2) some findings that have emerged from the use of the approach. Both may prove of help—if you want to make use of them.

Tchr.: Let's start with the method. What is it? Give me something to latch on to.

S.S.: Science is *reasonable*. It is willing to analyze and question basic premises—even those things that common sense seems to have confirmed. Science is *rational*; there are rules for relating phenomena into mental organization. Being *reasonable* and *rational* support one another. One can start with a false or invalid premise and still have internal logical consistency. And science is *empirical*. Everything has to stand the test of "public" accessibility to testing. It is committed to a "sense" world.[28] It is *generalizing* and *repetitive*. It relates, orders, and allows the conditions for prediction. One crucial thing: The ordering of relationships into sets of ideas or concepts takes into account more than one unique incident. And it does assume simple cause-effect relationships.

Tchr.: And your "products" of this method? your findings?

S.S.: The essence of knowledge is generalizing.[21] Fire can be produced by rubbing certain wood in certain ways under certain conditions. Generalizing is moving from one individual experience to many. When one has generalized, he has explained.

Tchr.: But to communicate, one must use language. And you folks have so much jargon.

S.S.: I can understand why an educator is sensitive to jargon. Language manipulation is crucial. It is hard to take static words and have them refer to dynamic relationships. Language form and grammar work with thought. To have new thoughts creates the· need for different descriptive language. Jargon isn't always a grand conspiracy to delude the nonfraternal members of the species. Terminology may, in fact, be an indication of the dimensions of the struggle going on.

Tchr.: New terms are to be expected?

S.S.: Why not? Where do you find concepts for contradiction, ambivalence, inconsistencies?[29] Language might prove a major concern in the area of social studies. So often symbols become barriers to effective thinking and action.

Tchr.: Is this social science the antithesis to humanities?

S.S.: No, not at all. Some argue that science and the history and philosophy of science form the basis of a new humanities.[30] It inquires into human culture—into the story of man. It relates past with present. It embraces human dignity and human values. It is concerned with human cooperation, human decision making. It abhors prejudice and wild, unsubstantiated claims. What could be more vital to a humanities program? And it knows that no concept grasps all the facts about any phenomena and that evidence is always selective.[31] Science and the humanities—mutually supportive, complementary, in dialogue about human experience.

Tchr.: With your methods and findings, we could build a relevant and exciting program. But my clients demand a guarantee that you refuse to give. Now, I find that neither history nor social science offers a guarantee.

S.S.: Apparently you have done your job well in the past. If you dare use my services, I ask that you don't imply to the students that I am more than I am. Let them see me as human, let them work with my value system—it is commited to means, not ends. Let them see that cheating is not sharing ideas with others but rather short-cutting and hiding one's methods. And let them know that there is nothing sacred about my findings—they are NOT the final word. They beg to be modified, challenged, changed. Don't present me as cold and sterile. I am as alive as human thought and behavior! And don't make me an either/or with history. Use us both. It is not either social sciences or history: it is social science with history; history with social science. My disciplines shouldn't frighten people. I made them in order to help study. They are no more sacred than are my findings. I am willing to help. My family background is "public" if one chooses to look. To be sure, we have our skeletons and our charlatans. And like history, we have our family squabbles. Why not?

Tchr.: A line from Amy Lowell keeps coming back to me: "Christ, what are patterns for?"

S.S.: That is *your* issue. *You* have to make choices. You have to predict. What evidence will you choose to use as you decide for and with other people? The teaching act is premised upon prediction. Prediction is premised upon generalizable relationships. And these relationships are forged with sound methods. In short, my teacher friend, you are to provide a partial answer to Amy Lowell.

Tchr.: You *are* complex!

S.S.: Am I understandable?

Tchr.: I think so . . . there is much to do.

S.S.: There always has been.

Tchr.: I will meet with you again. I have several questions: what generalized concepts can we draw from human experience? What concepts may prove of most use? How does one learn to use your methods? How . . .

APPLIED EXAMPLES

Applied examples attempt to move into teaching/learning situations and to apply some of the issues as they have been approached with students.

The inclusion of the following materials suggests that students can also wrestle with some of the issues faced by the professional educator. The materials can be viewed as an introduction to science, as assessment of factors involved in human study, and/or as ways to motivate skill development on the part of the student. Hopefully the selected student materials indicate that there *are* ways of differentiating between history and social science *without* negating either's potential role.

In looking at the *focus ideas,* what strategy would you develop to "test" them in order to validate, qualify, or completely challenge the ideas? (In what way might you *use* history? For example, does the play *use* history and, if so, to what purpose?)

FOCUS IDEAS

1. Findings in "pure" science have implications for the way man views himself, his world, his values. In a sense, it may help him to know himself.

2. To challenge one idea is to challenge the consistency of many other related ideas. For example: To say that the sun was not perfect and that the earth was NOT the unique center of the universe is to challenge what ideas about man?

3. Some people resist any new information that might challenge the ideas they already hold. People may be bright, intelligent, shrewd, and cunning, but this in no way guarantees a *willingness* to seek out truth.

4. Ideas have consequences. The ideas that people accept sometimes keep them from even looking at new and different ideas.

5. There is no guarantee that science will lead to a *certain* end or truth.

6. Giving reasons (telling *why*) is a different activity from describing what is. Sometimes people only want to look for descriptions that support the already held reasons.

7. Some people believe that only "certain" people should seek truth and that the little people should just do their work and accept what others (the "certain" people) tell them.

8. Bacon: "The more absurd and incredible any divine mystery is, the greater honor we do to God in believing it."

9. Man uses his senses (seeing, hearing, touching, smelling, and tasting) to receive information about his environments. He has created instruments to help him to gain even more information. The information is *given meaning* when man organizes, arranges, and relates the informations with one another and with his previously held ideas or "organizations."

10. People usually hold attitudes which are similar to those of others in the groups to which they belong. They would rather be "right" with the group than change their attitudes.

WAYS OF LOOKING AT SCIENCE*

The whole world seems to be living in an age of science and the products of science. Leaders in countries where abundant natural resources have not been used for years agree that they

---

*Adapted from Dart, Francis E., and Pradhan, Panna Lai: Cross cultural teaching of science. Science, February 10, 1967.

have to turn to science if they are going to take care of the problems of their people.

The United States aids a large number of countries around the world. Some of this aid involves trying to help people to understand and to use science.

A question which comes to mind is: How do people *learn* to understand and to use science? If we say that science is a way of looking at the world and is a way of knowing how to put what is seen to use in solving problems, is it possible that some people have different ways of looking at the world? If so, would this make it hard for them to understand science?

Some scientists decided to study some people who might have a different way looking at the world.

They went to Nepal and tried to find out what school children (nine to fourteen years old) thought about nature and what caused nature to behave the way it sometimes does.

What kinds of questions could they ask in order to find out what they wanted to know? They decided to ask:

What causes it to rain?

Where does rain water come from?

What do most people think about rain?

What causes earthquakes?

How can you get new knowledge about the world?

Should human beings try to influence the rain?

How did you learn about such things as rain and earthquakes?

How do you find out if what you have learned is true?

Besides asking such questions, the scientists were also curious about the *kind* of thinking students did. For example, if someone asked you for directions about how to get to a certain place you might draw them a map. It is possible that you might put things on the map which other people might think are not important. The scientists also asked the students from Nepal to draw a map.

If the students from Nepal answered the questions and drew maps, what would the scientists know? Could the scientists look at the information and say, "These people will have a difficult time in understanding science"? Would it be more helpful if the scientists took a group of American students (who supposedly live in a world of science and scientific products) and asked them the same questions and asked them to draw a map? Would *comparing* what they found in Nepal and in the United States help the scientists to better understand how different people look at their world?

The scientists thought it would. They worked with a group of elementary students (ages nine through 12) in Hawaii as well as with the students from Nepal.

The scientists were not concerned if the answers the students gave were "correct." They wanted to know how school children from Nepal and Hawaii explained their world.

What did the scientists find out?
The school children from Nepal said:
>   Earthquakes: "The earth is supported on the back of a fish. When the fish grows tired it shifts the weight, and this shakes the earth."
>   *and*
>   "There is fire at the center of the earth. It seeks to escape and sometimes cracks the earth, causing an earthquake."

Another group of students from Nepal said:
>   "The earth is supported by four elephants. When one of them shifts the weight to another shoulder an earthquake results."
>   *and*
>   "There are fire and molten metal inside the earth which try to escape. They may crack or move the rock of the earth, causing an earthquake."
>   Rain: "The deities break vessels of water in the sky, causing rain."
>   *and*
>   "The sun evaporates water from the sea, producing vapor which is cooled by the mountains to make clouds and rain."
>   Lightning: "Lightning comes from the bangles of Indra's dancers."
>   *and*
>   "Lightning comes from the collision of clouds."

The scientists were told that it rained only in the summer season "because we need the rain then. In the winter we do not need rain." They were also told by the same group of students that "It rains in the summer because the sun is hotter then and causes more evaporation."

It seems that the students from Nepal hold *two different views* of how and why nature works at the same time. They seem to explain the same thing in two different ways. What about the students in Hawaii?

The students in the Honolulu school did not hold the two views. They seemed to accept that lightning is caused when clouds collide; that the heat evaporates and "lifts" water up; that parts of the earth "shift," thus causing earthquakes. The students from Hawaii said that nature would not respond to magic. They said that you used science to control nature.

The Nepalese students said that their knowledge about nature came from "books" and from "old people." They were asked how the old people got their knowledge or how knowledge got into the books. It was handed down from older people or came from other books. Where did the knowledge come from in the first place? A number of the Nepalese students said that knowledge had always been known. One student said that perhaps it came from someone accidentally observing nature. The Nepalese students said that new knowledge was not to be expected. Knowledge has always been known, they said, and is passed down from teacher to student. A student should accept what he is told. The student in the Nepalese school should memorize what is known.

The scientists felt that drawing a map helps to indicate how people think. A map is not a "real" thing: in a sense, it is a model for something else. How one draws a map and what one puts on the map can tell how the person puts a number of different things together in order to explain something.

The students from Nepal would draw a map which included a picture of their house and their school. The two would be connected on the map. Actually, the two buildings were NOT on the same street and were separated by many landmarks.

The teacher using the study started by asking his own class some of the questions asked in the study: What causes rain? How did you learn about such things as rain and earthquakes? How can you find out if what you have learned is true? How can you obtain more knowledge.

After reading the article, a number of issues emerged:

Do the ideas one has influence *how* one thinks and what one does?

What's the difference between saying, "It rains because we need rain," and "It rains because the sun is hotter and causes more evaporation"?

What happens if one does not expect "new" knowledge? How would this influence how one behaves? What one learns?

And a *transfer:*

How does one's idea about history influence how he thinks?

Is there a difference between saying something happened because it was right and saying something happened because of these specific things?

What happens if one thinks history is the unfolding of a predetermined plan and leads eventually to progress? or that history runs in cycles? repeats itself?

What seems to be the difference between the following maps?

Map 1. (15 year old student from Nepal)

Map 2. (11 year old student from Hawaii)

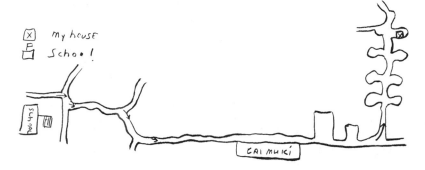

If history is a "map" of where man has been, what different kinds of maps might one draw, depending on his view of history?

STEP IN MODERN SCIENCE

Galileo Galilei was born in 1564. He is considered to be one of the founders of modern science. He wrote books on science and in 1610 he published a book called "The Starry Messenger," which caused great excitement. He wrote of the heavens in a new way. Up until this time information about the heavens had been gained by observing with the naked eye. Galileo had an instrument to help the eye see better—the telescope.

Galileo lived at a time when people did not believe that the way one learned was by experimenting and testing observations. What Galileo observed was not what other people believed to be true. He found that the earth was moving and not standing still. He said that the earth was not *unique* but a great deal like other heavenly bodies. He also said that the sun was not "perfect" but had spots and was changing. In essence, he was saying that what man had believed up until this time was not true!

Galileo was attacked for having such ideas. He was told not to meddle with things that had been settled once and for all.

Galileo's ideas are not the most important contribution he made. His greatest contribution may be the way he went about studying. He said that to study something was not to just accept what others said. A student should observe, draw conclusions, and test his conclusions — always being ready to change if new information challenges a previous conclusion.

He also made another contribution: He helped us realize that sometimes people will not change even if they are given information and told how to test it for themselves.

Questions

Galileo not only challenged the old theory about the earth being the center of the universe, but challenged an old way of "knowing." What were the old ways?

To believe that the earth was the center of the universe — unique and pivotal — and to believe that the sun was perfect might lead to what conclusions about man on earth — his purpose, his way of knowing, and what man thought of the individual and his social organization?

If one challenged the above theory of the earth and sun and claimed the earth to be a star among many stars in an infinite universe, how might it change the conclusions man has drawn about himself? Why was Galileo thought to be dangerous?

Why is it said that it is harder to change peoples' attitudes than to split the atom?

Galileo

The following play, modified from Bertolt Brecht's effort, if used with students, raises these issues: Does one simply accept the findings of previous studies and then screen all new information in terms of what seems to support the old findings, or does one observe and follow his "senses" to form new findings? What human behaviors are at work when humans study themselves and their environments?

Galileo's Friend:	Are you out of your mind? Do you know what you are involved in? You want to go shouting to the whole world that the earth is a star and not the center of the universe!
Galileo:	Yes—I want the world to know. Why shouldn't it? Why shouldn't it know that the whole vast universe does not revolve around our tiny earth? Friend, the truth is so obvious.
Friend:	But people who have said this before you have been punished—some even put to death. If you have believed this truth you talk about, why have you not spoken out before now?
Galileo:	Because I could not *prove* it.
Friend:	And you think that being able to prove something makes a difference?
Galileo:	Look, my friend. I believe in people and I believe in their common sense. If I did not believe in people I would not bother to get out of bed in the morning.
Friend:	As your friend, I shall tell you something. I do not believe that people have common sense. I have worked among them for forty years and I have observed them. Show them a circus or fill them with terror and they will run from their homes. But tell them one sensible truth. Give them seven reasons for its truth and they will laugh in your face.
Galileo:	That is not true!
Friend:	Be careful, Galileo, you confuse their being shrewd and cunning with their willingness to look for truth.
Galileo:	Not really. I know that they love to fool each other at the market place. But I see an old woman give her mule an extra bundle of hay when she knows he has hard work to do; I see a sailor who knows that a storm is coming and who takes pains to put his ship in shape; I see a child protect himself when it is raining. People reason. I cannot imagine someone seeing a stone fall and then saying that it did not. People will react to proof. Thinking is one of the greatest pleasures of the human race.
Friend:	Ah, Galileo—there is a big difference between seeing a stone fall and asking people to accept something they see as proof that what they have believed for a long time is not true. Rather than accept this, they will deny what they see with their own eyes.

Galileo: You have very little faith. I shall seize them by their necks and drag them before the telescope. Even the scholars! I ask only that they believe their own eyes.

Friend: It is a night of disaster when a man sees the truth. There are hours of tears when he expects others to accept what he sees. I love science, Galileo, but I love you more. I plead with you—forget what you have learned.

SCENE II. (Before the telescope)

Galileo: (Pointing to the telescope) would you gentlemen care to look and observe that of which I speak?

Scholar 1: Thank you for the opportunity. But before we spend the time looking through your tube might we not first debate if it is possible for planets to exist?

Scholar 2: By all means. This is the scholarly way to do things.

Galileo: I thought that it would be a simple matter to look through the tube and convince yourself that planets do, in fact, exist.

Scholar 1: Galileo, the books which report the findings of ancient scholars tell us that it is impossible that such should exist.

Galileo: I have read the old scholars. I know what they say.

Scholar 2: Of course, my first interest is to decide if planets are necessary. *Aristotelis divini universum . . .*

Galileo: (Looking at his friend who is standing in the back of the room) Please do not speak in Latin. My friend does not understand Latin.

Scholar 2: Is it important that he understand us? I thought he just ground your lens. I thought he worked for you.

Galileo: We work together. He, too, is a scholar.

Scholar 1: Well, we shall honor your wish, Galileo. It is your house. But, in speaking the common language we will lose much of our elegance.

Galileo: Gentlemen, will you please observe the impossible and unnecessary stars through my telescope.

Scholar 1: My response to you, Galileo, is that your telescope which shows something which cannot exist must not be reliable.

Scholar 2: Perhaps if Galileo would give us the reasons why he thinks planets can exist. . . .

Galileo: Reasons? Just look! Just look through the telescope and you will see them.

Scholar 1: I am afraid of exciting you further, Galileo, but I must say that perhaps what is in your telescope is not in the heavens.

Galileo: I don't understand what you are saying.

Scholar 2: He is saying that perhaps you painted the stars on the lens.

Galileo: (Looking at his friend with dismay). You accuse me of being dishonest? (In anger) Will you look through the telescope or not?

Scholar 2:	Every school book tells us that they cannot exist.
Friend:	Then, we need new school books!
Scholar 1:	Suppose—and mind you I say "suppose"—you are right, Galileo. All our ancient scholars will be dragged through the mud.
Galileo:	I suggest that it is not the purpose of science to ask where the truth may lead us.
Scholar 1:	*Your* kind of truth might lead us to absolutely anything!
Galileo:	Let us not defend and protect dying teachings.
Friend:	You scholars should be the first to lead the attack against teachings which are not correct.
Galileo:	I have lived among the people—with people who work at building and making things. These people taught me. They taught me a new way of doing things. They could not read, but they used their senses, their five senses, in most cases regardless of where the evidence might lead them.
Scholar 2:	Come now . . .
Galileo:	Yes, it is true. They were a lot like the mariners who left the shore without knowing what other shores they might reach—if any. They followed a high curiosity which leads to greatness.
Scholar 1:	I suggest that Galileo and his friend stay among the people or go to sea.
Galileo:	Gentlemen, all I ask is that you look through the telescope.
Scholar 2:	(Addressing himself to Scholar 1) Come. We must give examinations to our students. We have wasted enough time with all this foolishness. It will be refreshing to return to a classroom where people think.

(The scholars leave. Galileo is once again alone with his friend. The silence is broken by the friend)

Friend:	I won't say that I told you. People will not look at the world as it is. They see it as they want it to be. There is a big difference.
Galileo:	I don't understand. All I did was ask them to look. And even those who should know better could not be bothered. I don't understand.

The teacher may point out that Galileo's biggest problem seemed to be a nonscientific one: that of convincing the scholars to change their view of the world so their views would be in line, or consistent with, new information.

Students should be asked to develop, as a class, strategies they would use in trying to get a new idea across. They may be asked to anticipate obstacles, to determine what they would have to know about the person or persons they were trying to influence. If they had been Galileo's public relations man, what would they have suggested?

SYNTHESIS AND PROLOGUE

The materials at the conclusion of Chapter 4 have shown various learning experiences prepared for students at different grade levels. The experiences involved working with science as a "way of knowing" and, indirectly, with its influence on man. The materials are part of the social studies area.

Since the turn of the century, the social studies area has remained fairly well rooted to a historical approach. There have been efforts to make some substantial modifications and one can assess the efforts by reading *Social Education*, the journal of the National Council for the Social Studies. Projects in anthropology, sociology, political science and economics, to name a few, are slowly making inroads, but they encounter some of the problems raised in the chapter.

We have noted history through the eyes of history and some historians and have noted that to turn to the historian and to ask him, "What *should* we teach?" is untenable and unfair. If we view the teacher as a teacher of the *use* of social studies rather than a teacher of social studies, we start encountering the various content "disciplines" of the social studies in a different way—a way that underscores the need to have a thought-out rationale.

The same situation is faced in trying to assess what the social sciences have to offer. If the teacher's functioning differs in ends and means from a scholar's functioning, then it is difficult to abdicate certain basic decisions the profession and the teacher have to make. Making these decisions may help us in determining *how* to use the subject areas in our *own* efforts. Ends and means have an odd habit of influencing one another: new ends, new means; new means, new ends.

We have also noted that each content area has some findings available for use. The findings vary in kind, and if we plan to use the findings, we do well to assess the kinds of concepts available and the possible uses open to us.

Chapter 5 will deal with concepts and their implication for teachers of the use of the social studies.

As a lead in—a health teacher asked what concepts she should be teaching in her senior high school "personal health" course. One student helped to narrow down the problem. "You come up with the concepts, but I'm interested in only one thing: no misconceptions."

Point well made.

REFERENCES

1. Collingwood, R. G.: The IDEA of History. New York, Oxford University Press, 1957.
2. Wesley, Edgar Bruce: Let's absolish history courses. Phi Delta Kappan, September, 1967.
3. Metcalf, Lawrence E.: Some guidelines for changing social studies education. Social Education, April, 1963.
4. Fuller, R. Buckminster: Planetary planning. The American Scholar, Winter, 1970–71.
5. Barker, Ernest: Church, State, and Education. Ann Arbor, University of Michigan Press, 1957.
6. Smith, Page: The Historian and History, New York, Vintage Books, Inc., 1966.
7. Geyl, Pieter: Debates with Historians. Cleveland, World Publishing Co., 1958.
8. Commager, Henry Steele: Should historians write contemporary history? Saturday Review, February 12, 1966.
9. Commager, Henry Steele: The Nature and the Study of History. Columbus, Ohio, Charles E. Merrill, Inc., 1965. (Social Science Seminar Series)
10. Becker, Carl L.: What are historical facts? Quoted from Hans Meyerhoff (ed.): The Philosophy of History in our Time. New York, Doubleday Anchor, 1959.
11. Crowl, John A.: History in crisis, some declare; Others disagree. Chronicle of Higher Education, January 11, 1971.
12. Hunt, Erling M.: Changing perspectives in social studies. In Perspectives. Boston, Houghton-Mifflin Co., 1962.
13. Marin, Peter: The open truth and fiery vehemence of youth. In The Movement Toward a New America. New York, Knopf-Pilgrim Press, 1970.
14. Massialas, Byron G.: Teaching history as inquiry. In Engle, Shirley (ed.): New Perspective in World History, NCSS Yearbook, 1964.
15. Darley, John G.: The Nature of the Social Sciences. Minneapolis, Minnesota. Social Science Research Center, Graduate School, University Press, 1955.
16. Chrysotom, St. John: Quoted in Black, Max: Critical Thinking. New York, Prentice-Hall, Inc., 1946.
17. Glass, Bentley: The ethical basis of science. Science, December 3, 1965.
18. Lundberg, George A.: The postulates of science and their implications for sociology. In Natanson, Maurice (ed.): Philosophy of the Social Sciences. New York, Random House, 1963.
19. Aron, Raymond: Rationality of modern society. Bulletin of the Atomic Scientists, January, 1964.
20. Frank, Philipp: Modern Science and Its Philosophy. New York, Collier Books, 1961.
21. Reichenbach, Hans: The Rise of Scientific Philosophy. Berkeley, University of California Press, 1962.
22. Taylor, F. Sherwood: Science and Scientific Thoughts. New York, W. W. Norton and Company, 1963.

23. Bronowski, J.: Science and Human Values. Harper Torch, 1956.
24. Geertz, Clifford: The impact of the concept of culture on the concept of man. Bulletin of Atomic Scientists, April, 1966.
25. Ayer, A. J.: Polemic, March, 1947.
26. Barber, Bernard: Science and the Social Order. New York, Collier Books, 1962.
27. Fellows, Erwin W.: Science in a time of moral confusion. *In* Readings in Social Policy, Dubuque, Iowa, W. C. Brown Co., 1954.
28. Lazarfeld, Paul: The American Soldier. Public Opinion Quarterly, Fall, 1949.
29. Schrag, Peter: The end of a great tradition. Saturday Review, Feb. 15, 1969.
30. Sarton, George: Referred to in Kranzberg, Melvin: On understanding our time: The history of science. Teachers College Record, April, 1963.
31. McCorquodale, Marjorie K.: Poets and Scientists. Bulletin of Atomic Scientists, November, 1965.

"This is step No. 1 in our goodwill program."

(By Joseph Farris. Copyright 1971 Saturday Review, Inc.)

5

CONCEPT DEVELOPMENT

"Precept upon precept..."

Experience is ultimate because it confronts us with a continuous ultimatum. For a man to by-pass experience in the pursuit of truth is to make himself God, for only He can say, "Let there be!" and there is.... However selfless the love of truth for its own sake may be, the self, to satisfy its needs, needs knowledge of what to do. And appropriate action on things depends on experience of them; only empirical knowledge provides a basis for successful action.

ABRAHAM KAPLAN, *The Conduct of Inquiry*

RESEARCH IN DETERMINING METHOD*

TEN CONTRASTS BETWEEN OLD AND NEW METHODS OF TEACHING SOCIAL STUDIES

A review of recent course of study bulletins in the field of social studies reveals these ten contrasts with past procedures; some apply to other subjects as well as to the social studies.

1. Carefully selected content vs. encyclopedic materials
2. Vivid oral presentation vs. book teaching
3. Study materials vs. memorizing
4. Discussion and work periods vs. recitations
5. Pupil initiative vs. explicit teacher directions
6. Pupil incentive vs. meeting school requirements
7. Learning where and how to find facts vs. learning all the facts
8. Correlation of subject matter vs. water-tight compartments
9. Vivid, dramatic idea of time, space, and events vs. dull, disconnected facts

---

*Research Bulletin, National Education Association, Vol. VI, No. 1, January, 1928.

10. Basis for interpretation of
    present life   vs. lack of discovery of relation of
                                        cause and effect

On the back cover of the 1928 Research Bulletin is the following quotation from John Dewey:

> By law and punishment, by social agitation and discussion, society can regulate and form itself in a more or less haphazard or chance way. But through education society can formulate its own purposes, can organize its own means and resources, and thus shape itself with definiteness and economy.

It is discouraging to say the least. Since 1928 a preponderance of subsequent research has been conducted, codified, and reported — most of it in some way affirming what the Research Bulletin reported over 40 years ago. Having information may be similar to a nation's having all the natural elements at its disposal to become an industrialized state, but not having the desire or awareness or ability to tap the potential. When do research and information — natural elements — become resources? When they are put to use?

In 1928 we were informed that the "new" methods would put emphasis upon selection, student involvement, student needs, using information, relating and connecting facts, and that the purpose of all these "new" methods would be a basis for interpreting the present situation in which the student in society stood. Sound familiar?

Today, we can go into many public schools, into a domain called social studies, and find encyclopedic materials, hefty textbooks expanded to encompass the encyclopedic, memorization of facts, teacher-directed classes, classroom evaluation based on the learning of facts, disconnected subject matter, and very little stress on associations and relationships. We also find teachers surviving to the extent that they do such things. They are evaluated and tenured; and outside the school walls we find problems with law and punishment, social agitation, and haphazard ways of organizing means and resources in order to approach purposes of chance and power.

The old seems to have managed to incorporate the *language* of the new, which reminds us that the word is not the thing. Language often obliterates the thing.

What seems to get in the way?

Let's use a little of past experience to see if we can't identify some of the things that might have contributed to placing impediments in the way of the "new" teaching and learning. Let's *use* a little history.

Francis Bacon (1561–1626) attacked the medieval methods he felt worked to limit man. In the attack he seemed to assume that much of learning included *un*-learning—a point that we teachers of the use of social studies might be wise to assess. Bacon had to uproot "false notions" and "prejudices" in order to lay bare the problem. The mind was (is?) possessed by "idols" and these "idols" he attempted to make public.

IDOLS OF THE TRIBE

The human understanding is of its own nature prone to suppose the existence of more order and regularity in the world than it finds....What a man had rather were true he more readily believes. Therefore he rejects difficult things from impatience of research; sober things, because they narrow hope; the deeper things of nature, from superstition; the light of experience, from arrogance and pride, lest his mind should seem to be occupied with things mean and transitory; things not commonly believed, out of deference to the opinion of the vulgar.

Human nature:
   Assumes order
   Gets an idea and then looks for support
   Believes what it would *like* to believe
   Is impatient—wants quick answers
   Wants certainty, and thinking gives rise to doubt
   Equates transitory with meaningless
   Would rather go along with the crowd than be different

IDOLS OF THE CAVE

These take their rise in the peculiar constitution, mental or bodily, of each individual; and also in education, habit, and accident.

Living cave:
   Man is born into different experiences
   The individual through circumstance, education,
   and social environment learns habits; these
   become his unthinking presuppositions

IDOLS OF THE MARKET PLACE

The most troublesome of all: idols which have crept into the understanding through the alliance of words and names. For men believe that their reason governs words; but it is also true that words react on the understanding—words stand in the way and resist change. The idols imposed by words on the understanding are of two kinds: They are either names of things which do not exist—names which result from fantastic suppositions and to which nothing in reality corresponds.

Words:
   Simple commands can be understood but not words
   dealing with ideas
   Resist thinking and change: we "name" what we do not
   understand; it becomes real; we react as though "real"

IDOLS OF THE THEATRE

   Not innate, nor do they steal into understanding secretly, but are plainly impressed and received into the mind from the play-books of philosophical systems and perverted rules of demonstration. The corruption of philosophy by superstition and an admixture of theology is far more widely spread, and does great harm, whether to entire systems or to their parts.
   Theater:
   World views accepted
   Discounts evidence for its existence
   Deductively seduces
   Harms individuals and groups (cultures, nations)

   1. What was going on in the world which Bacon shared? What did he observe that may have fed his "idols"?
   2. Are the "idols" still at work? What *specific* examples of the four "idols" can we identify in our own situation? How might these impede teaching/learning?
   3. If one were to use Bacon's "idols" with students, what approach might he have used? (How would this differ between elementary and secondary classes?)

STUDENT MATERIALS

   Bacon's characteristics of things that seem to harness man's potential (which he grouped or classified under the Four Idols) seems, in varying degrees, to haunt us today. The unwitting worship of such idols may partially explain what Silberman meant when he wrote:

> What makes change possible is that what is most wrong with the public schools is due not to venality or indifference or stupidity, but to *mindlessness*. ... By and large, teachers, principals, and superintendents are decent, intelligent, and caring people who try to do their best by their lights. If they make a batch of it, and an uncomfortably large number do, it is because it simply never occurs to more than a handful to ask *why* they are doing *what* they are doing — to think *seriously* or *deeply* about the *purposes* or *consequences* of education.[1]

Perhaps this *partially* explains why the reports in the 1928 Research Bulletin appear like a description of wishful thinking on the one hand and the actual somnambulist's somniloquy on the other. We say "partially explains" because we feel that it *does* occur to the educator to ask such questions, but with teaching oftentimes being more a case of physical survival than intellectual engagement, there is an implicit recognition that once one is in the front lines, it is rather absurd to question the point of the war. It takes time to be "mindful," and time is the one major scarce commodity an educator has. Time is also the one major scarce commodity for students as they become actively involved in the "mindless" activities. When one becomes wedded to teaching the encyclopedic world of exploding data, time is the first casualty. It is a wedding in which the bonds are forged of mounting insignificant trivia and activity,...and a sense of the helplessness of the love trap.

Use of Bacon's Four Idols has been made with secondary students as a lead into the Newtonian world view which, in turn, provided a framework for assessing the "self-evident" truths implied by the Declaration of Independence. There are implications for the assumed order in the world of human affairs.

The following sections, How Do You Know?, What Do We Think We Know About Early Man?, and Making Ideas — Making Concepts, have been used with intermediate level students. The materials address some of the questions Bacon addressed, but at a different level of sophistication.

How Do You Know? raises the issue of what kind of evidence one accepts for knowledge, and how what one thinks he knows — his ideas — influences the options he has open. A consideration of superstitions helps to reinforce the problem.

What Do We Think We Know About Early Man? fits in with the organizational structure of the conventional social studies program but allows the student to wrestle with the basis for having ideas; it asks that he transfer the basis to his own world — a world of people, things, words, *and* ideas.

Making Ideas — Making Concepts considers the nature of ideas, how they are *made*, and how we use them in our own lives.

In other words, the students are wrestling with some of the issues that we encounter in trying to determine what concepts might be used in teaching. The use of Bacon's ideas and the intermediate materials suggest that we *can* use the conventional organizational pattern in achieving ends and means other than those implied strictly by the organization. More about this later.

HOW DO YOU KNOW?[2]

For the third time something had gone wrong with the Gemini space craft.

The first time, a small electric box had failed to work.

The second time, the weather was so poor that the people in charge of making decisions decided that it would be difficult to track the space craft once it was launched.

The third time, the launching was stopped at the last second. Nobody knew exactly why.

Scientists had worked for months to get the space craft ready. They had gathered together a great amount of scientific information. They had cooperated in putting the information together. And they had decided on what parts were needed to build and fly the ship.

Over 600 companies had manufactured the needed parts. The parts were put together. They were tested. Everything seemed to work well, and it was believed that the space craft was ready to carry two human beings into space.

But with all this careful work, something went wrong. The count down had moved from 5 to 4 to 3 to 2 to 1,...then a *machine* had detected that something in the craft was not in order. The machine stopped itself and cut off the fuel supply. The craft never left the launching pad.

The machine had caught a problem. The human beings who had made the space craft did not know of the problem until the machine acted to stop the launching.

A television newscaster told the audience which was viewing the scene "live" that the people at Cape Kennedy were disappointed. He said that some of the people were afraid that Gemini was jinxed. It had failed for the third time.

What did he mean when he used the word "jinx"? He probably meant that no matter what the human beings wanted to do, no matter how well the scientists had done their job, no matter how carefully all the parts had been made and put together, something over which man had *no control* refused to allow the space craft to be launched. Some power or force kept the craft from taking off. The newscaster also probably meant that no one could think of a reason for the failure. He probably reached a conclusion that because the scientists could not think of a reason, there was no reason. So, if there was no reason, the space craft must be jinxed?

Suppose that everyone had said that the space craft had been jinxed? Would there have been any sense for anyone to see if he could find the reason for the failure? Suppose the people at Cape Kennedy had said, "We do not know the reason"? Suppose the people at Cape Kennedy said, "We do not know the reason and will not be able to know the reason."

While checking the space craft, the launch crew found that someone had left a small cap, small enough to fit over a person's little finger, in the ship. It was this little cap which had caused the trouble. There was no jinx. There had been a human mistake. On the fourth try, the space ship was launched into orbit without any difficulty.

HOW DID THE SCIENTISTS KNOW THAT THE SPACE CRAFT WAS READY TO BE LAUNCHED?

DID THE SCIENTISTS HAVE ANY DOUBT ABOUT THE FOURTH ATTEMPT'S BEING A SUCCESS?

HOW DID THE NEWSCASTER KNOW THAT THE SPACE CRAFT HAD BEEN JINXED?

IF YOU WERE THE ASTRONAUT, WOULD YOU HAVE MORE CONFIDENCE IN THE SCIENTISTS OR IN THE NEWSCASTER?

Most human beings spend a great deal of their time making decisions about all sorts of things. The decisions may be little things like what color shirt one should wear, or whether to buy a new tube of toothpaste. Or the decision may be a big one like whether one should move to another job, or for whom one should vote for the Presidency of the United States.

Often we are not aware of how we make decisions. Often habit keeps us from thinking too much about what we do. For example, do you always come to school by the same route?

Many times, however, we are aware of the *reasons* for doing what we do. Sometimes the reasons add up to why we do things a certain way. Our decisions, then, can be based on evidence.

IT IS RAINING OUTSIDE. THE LAST TIME IT RAINED I DID NOT WEAR A RAINCOAT OR RUBBERS. I GOT SOAKED TO THE SKIN. TWO DAYS LATER, I CAUGHT A COLD. THE WEATHER REPORT SAID THAT IT WOULD RAIN ALL DAY. I DECIDE TO WEAR A RAINCOAT BECAUSE IT IS RAINING. BUT I ALSO HAVE EVIDENCE THAT SHOWS THAT IF I DO NOT WEAR A RAINCOAT AND RUBBERS, I MAY CATCH A COLD. MIGHT NOT THIS EVIDENCE BE ANOTHER REASON FOR DECIDING TO WEAR A RAINCOAT AND RUBBERS?

Evidence is *continually* being gathered by man to help him to decide on courses of action to take in meeting problems.

For instance, the *evidence* collected by social scientists about criminal behavior is helpful in making *decisions* in dealing with criminals.

In fact, because man has been able to gather new evidence about mental illness, most patients are no longer locked in cells and chained to walls. But this was not always the case!

How one knows, what kind of evidence one has, and what one wants, all add up to how one decides what he will do. Thus, one of the most important questions which human beings ask is: HOW DO I KNOW? Do you think that evidence is important to the answer to this question?

How could you *test* to see if the following beliefs have evidence which would make you think that they are true? What questions would you have to ask, and what would you have to do in order to obtain evidence?

1. Knocking on wood will bring you good luck.

2. Walking under a ladder will bring you bad luck.

3. For over 3000 years it has been believed that the fourth finger of the left hand — the ring finger — is very special. It is believed that this finger has a direct line to the heart. It is believed that this finger possesses magic power — that if food is poisoned, it will sense it right away. Because it has a direct line to the heart and because it has magical powers, wedding rings are put on this finger. (Look around!)

4. Some people believe that if a girl is shelling fresh peas and finds nine peas in one pod, she should hang the empty pod over her door. If she does this, the next man who comes through the door will be her husband.

5. If one touches home base with a bat before he bats in a baseball game, he will get more hits.

6. The number 13 is unlucky. If a person carries a single dollar bill in his wallet, he will have bad luck because the Great Seal on the back has 13 steps on the pyramid; the eagle carries 13 arrows in one talon and a branch with 13 leaves in the other. Its tail has 13 feathers. There are 13 stars above his head. The shield has 13 stripes. (Why all the 13's?)

When you are setting up a way to test the evidence for these superstitions, what would you say if: A person wished for $100, knocked on wood, and the mailman brought the person a check for $100?

What would you say if: A friend of yours walked under a ladder and had paint splattered all over a new sweater?

What would you say if: A person carrying a single one dollar bill in her purse received some bad news?

How would you answer someone who gives you *one* example of a superstition's being true?

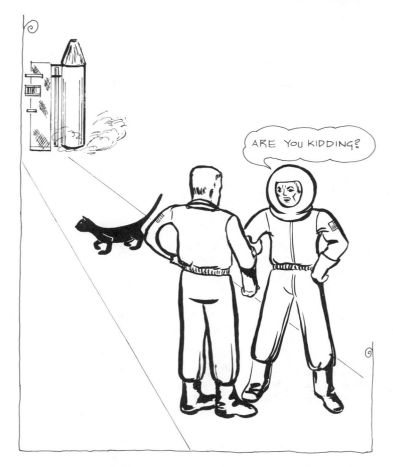

The kind of evidence one has for knowing something to be true is important. In the United States over $20,000,000,000 is spent each year by people who believe in superstitions. They ask that fortune tellers or star readers (astrologers) give them solutions to their problems.

What is the difference between "knowing" through superstition and "knowing" through FACTS? What is a fact?

WHAT DO WE THINK WE KNOW ABOUT EARLY MAN?[3]

FOCUS IDEAS

1. Human beings appear to take their experiences and information and organize what they "know" into large ideas.

2. The large ideas one has usually go beyond just the experiences and information one has.

3. Large ideas are usually based on a small part of all information available.

4. Large ideas can become a trap if human beings don't realize that the ideas can be changed when new information or new experiences make one question if an idea is sound.

Suppose you notice an object flying in the sky. Suppose the object is called a "bird." Suppose the bird is black.

Then you see a few more birds. They are also black in color. More birds fly around you a few days later, and you notice that they, too, are black.

Suppose that these are the only birds you have ever seen. Now someone asks you what you know about birds. You might say, "Ah, yes, birds are black creatures that fly."

By saying this about birds, what have you done? You have taken the *only* information you have. You have made this information into an idea about all birds. You then made a broad or *general* statement about *all* birds. ("Ah, yes, birds are black creatures that fly.")

Of course, you haven't seen *every* bird that ever existed.

Most of us make general statements about many things. And most of us know that general statements will have to be changed as we get new information. Sometimes it is easy to forget that we do not know *all* there is to know.

We make general statements about ourselves, others, and people who lived at other times. From the information we have about early man, we make some general statements about what we *think* we know. The general statements may have to be changed as we learn more about early man.

What do we think we know?

1. We think that early man lived in small groups. We think the groups moved around looking for food.

2. We think that these small groups of people did not have much contact with other small groups. Each group had to take care of itself.

3. We think that each person in a small group had close contact with all the people in the group. They knew each other very well. They knew who was sick, who was well, who was strong, who worked hard, and how efficiently people did what they were supposed to do.

4. We think that each person in each small group was

called upon to do many things. Each person did not become an expert in one thing. If he wanted to survive, he had to do many things well enough to satisfy his needs.

5. We think that a person in a small group was respected or earned leadership because of what he could do. He was not "given" respect but "earned" the respect of others.

6. We think that early man looked at all of nature around him—the trees, rivers, animals, sun and rain—and believed that all these things were like man himself. For example, trees could have anger, the sun could weep tears in sorrow.

7. We think that one of the reasons the small groups of early man survived and "paved the way" for the people living today is that the people learned to work together and learned to cooperate. Problems could be better solved by working together.

From the information which we have, we say that this is the way early man lived. We look at the information and make general statements.

We get our information by looking at paintings on cave walls. We uncover old campfire remains. We discover different types of tools. We discover an animal grave which seems to show that many people were involved in killing the animals.

This kind of information becomes our clue to an idea about the way early man lived.

TEACHING/LEARNING GUIDE

Questions

What kinds of *clues* do we have about the way modern man lives?

What kinds of general statements could you make about the way man lives today? For example, could you say that modern man moves about in small groups looking for food? Could you say that modern man gets to know the people about him as well as early man did? What people today are "modern" people?

When you try to make statements about modern man, what information or clues do you use?

Why does it become difficult to make general statements

about modern man? Why does it become difficult to make general statements about anything?

When we make generalizations about early man and modern man or about ourselves, how do we know we are right? And what difference does it make whether we are right?

Activities

1. Suppose you are a visitor from outer space. You have landed in a room that looks just like your classroom. You have never been on Earth before. You have never seen an Earth creature. Everything is "new" and different. You are afraid of what you don't know. You don't want to leave the room, but you want to learn as much about Earth as you can. You look about the room for clues. You just take for granted (assume) that the classroom is a home for Earth creatures.

List all the "clues" you find in the room.

For example: Thirty chairs
Two pictures on the wall

List all the "clues" you find missing from a home as you know a home.

For example: No beds
No food

Take the list of clues you found and the clues you expected to find but did not, and list some ideas about the way you think Earth creatures live. Let yourself "go" and have fun.

For example: The clock on the wall has only twelve figures.
Earth creatures have a 12 hour day.

The size of the chairs makes you think that Earth creatures are small. They live in groups of 30. Leadership is determined by size (the big chair?)

2. After you have come up with all the ideas you can from the "clues" and have made large ideas, what would you have to *do* if you wanted to see if your ideas were correct?

3. *Think!* If you really came from outer space, would you compare what you found with the ideas you have about your *own* planet and way of life? Would this make a difference about the kinds of clues you would seek?

4. Try to find pictures of some of the clues you have which help you to build ideas you have about early man. Can you find different ideas in the *same* clues?

Objectives

1. You should be able to list at least five ideas about the way we think early man lived.
2. You should be able to identify at least two clues which helped us to conceive the ideas about early man.
3. You should be able to give two reasons why the ideas may not be accurate.
4. You should be able to list at least five ideas you have about "modern" man, give the clues you used to achieve the ideas, and be able to tell how you could "test" the ideas to see if they are accurate.
5. You should be able to tell what you mean when you use the words "modern" man. Is modern man all the people living in the world today? Is modern man only *some* of the people living in the world today?

MAKING IDEAS – MAKING CONCEPTS[1]

When we make a general statement we are trying to put an idea into words. Why is making a general statement about an idea important to each of us? Or, to ask this question in a different way, what do ideas do for us?

Ideas can help us to *organize* many different things we see, hear, or experience.

Instead of talking about each separate bird which is black in color, we organize what we have seen and then talk about *birds* instead of just a number of separate birds.

Instead of talking about just *one* early man who lived in *one* place a long time ago, we talk about "early man" – we organize what we see, hear, or learn into a general idea or concept about many early men and how they lived in many places.

We don't do this just in books.

You and I have general concepts or ideas about many things. We have general concepts about such things as school, food, friends, clothing, fun, sadness, parents, teachers, policemen, television, science.

A concept is an organization. It is built from many parts. A concept is NOT the type of organization you can see or touch. It is a *mental* organization. And this mental organization does work for us! Concepts are tools which we use.

For example:
On Monday of this week there may have been dark clouds in the sky and it may have rained.

On Tuesday there were dark clouds and it rained.
The same thing happened on Wednesday.

You wake up on Thursday morning and look out your window. There are dark clouds. You think to yourself: When there are dark clouds, it rains. Today there are dark clouds. Therefore, it will rain. Because of your ideas, you decide to wear a raincoat to school. You have *predicted* (said before) what will happen. And you make plans for what you think will happen.

DAY → CLOUD → RAIN → WET → RAINWEAR
DAY → CLOUD → SUN → DRY → RAINWEAR

You have an idea that it will rain. This idea may have influenced what kind of clothing you selected to wear. An idea can be important because it influences the way we behave.

How is your idea about rain—your prediction—a mental organization of parts?

Let's take a look at this mental organization we call concept?

Will it rain for sure? It may not rain but you have formed an idea that it will rain. And your idea influences what you will wear to school.

If ideas are like a mental organization and if ideas influence how you and I behave, ideas become very important. You can imagine what might happen if a person had an idea that red traffic lights meant to "go" and an idea that green traffic lights meant to "stop"!

If ideas are so important to us, it would seem that you and I should be quite careful to know how we get our ideas. We should be quite careful in trying to figure out if our ideas are right.

You would be surprised at how often we do not know how we get our ideas!

If we are going to study ourselves, one of the things we will want to study is how we achieve our ideas; then, how these ideas influence us.

DO NOT EAT HARD AND GREEN APPLES

Let's see if we can figure out different ways by which people get their ideas. Study the following situations carefully and see if you and your classmates can figure the way which might best help Sam to make a decision.

Situation One: Sam wants to eat a nice, sweet apple. He dreams that he is sitting under a large apple tree. The tree bends with the wind and whispers to Sam: "Do not eat hard and green apples because they are sour."

Situation Two: Sam wants to eat a nice, sweet apple. He visits an old man who, everyone says, has a great deal of wisdom. The old man has lived for many years. He has heard and seen many things. Sam thinks that the old man must be wise. The old man tells Sam: "Don't eat hard and green apples. They are sour. I ate one and got sick."

I TRIED ONE ONCE

Situation Three: Sam wants to eat a nice, sweet apple. He tells his friends that he wants an apple. His friends tell Sam: "Everyone knows that hard and green apples are sour. If you want a sweet apple, don't eat a hard and green one!"

EVERYONE KNOWS

Situation Four: Sam wants to eat a nice, sweet apple. He goes into a grocery store. The grocer tells Sam to try some apples in order that he may select a sweet one. Sam picks up a hard and green apple. He bites into it. It is sour. He takes an-

AH···

other hard and green apple and bites into it. The second apple is also sour.

The grocer comes over to Sam and offers Sam a third apple. Sam looks the apple over. It is hard and green. Sam says: "No thank you. I believe that it is sour."

In Situation One, Sam got his idea from a dream. In Situation Two, Sam got his idea from another person who had made *his* own idea from tasting *one* apple. In Situation Three, Sam got his idea from the people around him. In Situation Four, what did Sam do?

1. Sam tasted one hard and green apple. It was sour.

2. Sam tasted a second hard and green apple. It was sour.

3. Sam formed an idea. He put the parts together and formed an idea: Hard and green apples are sour.

The grocer offered him a third apple. Sam looked at the apple. He observed that this apple was hard and green. Sam thought:

1. All hard and green apples are sour.

2. This apple the grocer is offering me is hard and green.

3. Therefore, this apple must be sour.

4. I do not want a sour apple.

5. I will not take it.

What *parts* did Sam put together in his mental organization or idea: Did his idea influence what he decided to do?

When we study about ourselves and when we study about other people, we will hear many ideas. We will want to know how these ideas came about. We will want to know if they seem to be correct.

We can just accept ideas without worrying about whether they are sound. If we do this, we are saying that we do not really care about ourselves and what we do.

Or we can try to figure out a way of studying ideas so that we can see how and why ideas are organized and whether the ideas seem right. If we do this, we are saying that ideas *are* important and that you and I *do* care about ourselves and how we behave.

"KINDS" OF CONCEPTS... AND EVIDENCE

What are the differences among the following statements?

Statement	Source
1. The Battle of Hastings was fought in 1066.	Secondary text
2. The people of the Americas want to be good neighbors to all the world.	Elementary text
3. Our government is called a democracy because it is carried on for the benefit of many, not just for a few.	Elementary text
4. Conflict	Social studies project
5. Through the socialization process man learns approved ways of behaving in a variety of societies.	Secondary text
6. Man's use of his land is seldom the result of any single physical factor. Land use depends upon an interplay of phenomena, physical and cultural.	Secondary text
7. "Be a good citizen."	Elementary teacher to his students
8. "Anybody who does not believe in God is not a good American."	Junior high school teacher to her students

Which of the above are statements of fact? Which lend themselves to being supported with empirical data? Which lend themselves to being "tested" — to the gathering of data which supports or deny the statement? Which ones are commands — to be accepted? Which ones reflect value judgments? Which ones are verbal definitions? Although most of the statements appear in declarative or imperative form, which ones attempt to *generalize* about more than one situation?

Given the world situation as *you* view it today, can you place in rank order, the statements (as given) which would be most helpful in assessing some of the variables at work in the situation? In other words, if you have to select *one* of the statements to use in teaching, which one would it be and why?

Given on the top of page 150 is a collection of "concepts" as they appear in social studies programs. *Neglecting the specific content* of each concept, classify the concepts into four major categories according to the characteristics of the concept.

If you had to pick one category to use as an *initial* base for selecting concepts to use in teaching, which one would you select? Can you analyze the implications of your choice?

You may have noticed that the conventional "fact" is included under the term "concept" and is presented as one form of concept. This is done on purpose. Let us explain why.

Concepts

IF THERE IS A
CHANGE IN ONE THING
THEN THERE IS
CHANGE IN MANY THINGS . . .

OPEN HOUSING
IS GOOD

POWER

THE DECLARATION
OF INDEPENDENCE
WAS WRITTEN IN 1776

RIGHT WINS OUT
IN THE END

IF CHANGE TAKES PLACE
IN AN ORGANIZATION THEN
THERE IS AN INCREASE IN
INTERPERSONAL
COMMUNICATION

THE PROGRESSIVE
MOVEMENT WAS
EXPERIMENTAL

LONGITUDE

DEMOCRATIC
CITIZENSHIP

CAESAR CROSSED
THE RUBICON

FACTS AND CONCEPTS

While on the staff of a school system, we were asked to work
with an in-service program which focused on conceptual teaching.
Naive and unsophisticated, we agreed out of a "feeling" that a conceptual approach to content and teaching made more sense than
concentrating on countless piles of discrete and unrelated data.
But feeling isn't enough. Nor is the desire to be helpful. As you will
see, we found the "term" concept very elusive among the literature.
It apparently meant all things to all people; the mathematician, the
physicist, the linguist, and the man on the street and in the classroom agreed on a sound but not on objects of reference. To say the
least, it was mass confusion. In the social studies area, teachers
told us that they were academically oriented and thus taught
"facts" and not "concepts." In the middle of the eight-week in-
carceration called in-service, one administrator became so upset
that he passed out to his staff the following as a tool to be used in
fighting against the "anti-intellectual" push to teach concepts.

The Use and Abuse of the Cept*
Q. What is a cept?
A. A cept is the smallest convenient unit of knowledge.
Q. Give an example of a cept.
A. I just did.

---

*Reprinted by permission from TIME, The Weekly Newsmaga-
zine; copyright Time Inc., 1965.

In their pursuit of academic excellence, the better liberal-arts teachers insist that their students read the original writings of the world's great thinkers and then take essay tests for comprehension of ideas rather than multiple-choice quizzes for recall of facts. This strains both the study time of the student and the grading time of the teacher—but neither has ever been shy about seeking shortcuts. And, sometimes openly, sometimes secretively, a shortcut device known as the "cept" is creeping across U.S. college campuses.

The term springs for the widespread use of the cept at Princeton University, which boasts of the small, conversational classes that it calls "precepts." The cept is jokingly defined as "half a concept"—meaning that it is more than a fact but less than a philosophy, more than an epigram but less than an axiom, more than a thesis but less than a synthesis. The Princeton student has it made if he can spot these prized nuggets in rapid reading or sporadic attendance at lectures, spin them out glibly during a precept and, above all weave them dazzlingly into an exam essay.

Handy Grading. To the cept-savvy student, cepts leap right out of the pages. In a politics course, he would readily note as a cept, "Revolutions are caused by rising expectations"; in philosophy, "To be is to perceive to be perceived"; in economics, "Calvinism caused capitalism"; in religion, "Capitalism caused Calvinism."

Some professors openly encourage ceptsmanship, stress the cept in their lectures, argue that students who retain the cepts acquire an understanding that goes beyond a rote knowledge of who said what. These teachers may also delight in the cept as a handy way of rating the quality of a student's essay in quantitative terms. They merely scan the essay, underline the cepts, assign a numerical value to each, and total them up. Other teachers never admit they are even aware of cepts—but tacitly use them anyway in grading. Superlative ceptsmanship amounts to a canny duel between teacher and student.

The leading expert on cepts is Princeton Senior Ed Tenner, a Phi Beta Kappa who devised the "smallest convenient unit of knowledge" definition. He reports, after much research, that Princeton courses average, per lecture, 8.8 cepts in philosophy, 5.2 in American history, 4.6 in literature, a mere 1.5 in art. A student may emerge from a course with as many as 250 cepts in his notebook. Hopefully, a few rare "kilocepts" and "multicepts"—cepts so basic they can be applied in many courses and to almost any historical period—may turn up among them, although Tenner has been able to identify only 17 kilocepts during his four years at Princeton. Examples: "A determinist creed induces not fatalism, but the will to assist in the accomplishment of some irresistible density"; "Obscure third-rate thinkers are historically more important than great thinkers."

Superficial Felicity. The student who can sprinkle some real comprehension over his cepts has an unbeatable essay. The difficulty with this is that it requires the student to read rather than browse through the assigned books, and to attend lectures rather than crib the cept notes of a conscientious friend. And doing all of the assigned work leads to a dangerous temptation: The student may answer an exam question with original thoughts, not cepts. To the cept-conscious prof, this is evidence that the student is trying to cover up his loafing and his failure to learn his cepts.

Princeton's philosophy department recently was concerned enough about the potential evils of ceptsmanship to hold a meeting on how to stop its spread. And even Ceptsman Tenner, when not in a whimsical mood, gets a bit worried: "The ceptsman too often thinks he knows more than he does because of his superficial felicity. We may be getting a generation of illiberal liberal-arts majors who think of ideas as symbols to be manipulated rather than as important issues to be serious about."

There are many techniques used to keep us from arriving at Dewey's 1928 conclusion, and this was one. The levity, the thrusts in the jargon "jungle," the implied "authority" from Princeton, all led to a serious breech between those involved in the in-service effort. Neither side understood the article's relevance to the issue at hand, but this didn't daunt us. We fought on: "facts" vs. "concepts"; the intellectually honest vs. the academic charlatans. It got so bad that unsigned poison-pen letters arrived wishing us an early demise and expressing sympathy for our families, who deserved to be protected from the likes of us who would rob children of their facts.

At one bleak session, a department chairman somberly informed the group that if there were a choice between facts or concepts, he would leave the teaching profession. It was tempting!

He was asked to give an example of one of his facts. It was, "Ceasar crossed the Rubicon in 49 B.C."

It so happened that one of the instructors was familiar with Carl Becker's *What Are Historical Facts?*[5] and used it with the group. Becker asked, "What *is* the historical fact?" and stressed the "is" over "was" — the fact that we are living now makes us interested in the Magna Charta, if at all, for what it is and not for what it was. This is an interesting distinction. But he took the fact of Ceasar, the Rubicon, and 49 B.C. — a "simple fact." But, he asks, Is it this simple? He didn't cross the river alone. He had an army. The Rubicon was a small river. How long to cross and how many acts, words, thoughts of how many people went into the effort? There must be "a thousand and one lesser 'facts' going into this one 'simple' fact." The fact is not simple. *The statement about the fact is simple:* "a simple generalization of a thousand and one facts." The term "concept," if one finds need to seek out origins, refers to learning by "gathering together." Thus, the fight over "facts" *or* "concepts" appears rather ludicrous. All teaching involves concepts—especially *statements* about concepts. There are different kinds of concepts serving different functions and denoting both different things gathered *and* different ways of gathering. The issue boils down to what kinds of concepts one keeps gathering, how concepts relate one with another, and to what use we intend to put concepts. (Exercises in the appendix focus on such issues.)

Mr. Secretary

The use of analogies can be dangerous. One uses analogy to point out similarities; unfortunately, the use may imply similarities which do not, in fact, exist. Knowing this, let's use an analogy to point up some of the problems a teacher faces in organizing a system for the selection and use of concepts. Instead of discussing students in a classroom, let's suppose we are in a position of having separate office communications which must be filed in such a way as to allow the most efficient and effective retrieval and use.

Organization . . . of Sorts

In the particular office there are approximately 100 pieces of communications per day which have to be filed. You are new to the job and notice that no filing system has yet been established. Thousands of communications are just piled up and are of no use to anyone in the present state of affairs.

The boss asks that you establish a filing system—and he emphasizes the term "system"—an organized, systematic method of relating diverse communications so that retrieval and use can be facilitated.

You notice that the communications bear people's names. They are dated. Some come from big companies and some from small independent outfits. Some are invoices and some receipts. Some refer to people. Others to things. Some are first inquiries, whereas others assume past information.

The information—types, kinds, intensity, timing, personnel, etc.—is overwhelming. What kind of a "system" does the boss want? *He* doesn't know. That's why he is paying you. Make your own!

OK! There are two major functions and they are related. No matter what situation comes up, you are going to have to be able to retrieve the needed information quickly. You need to do this in order to efficiently and effectively use the information in new and unanticipated situations. Granted, some will be routine, but this then is relatively easy. It's the possible new situations that will require some thought.

You are going to have to classify and categorize. This means that the classification and categorization will depend upon the analysis and synthesis you make of the predicted situations. The broad categories exist to help to relate different kinds of information and subcategories of information. Your system will depend (and be tested) on the intended use to be made. With a change in the situation, there may be need for different organizational categories.

Now use the analogy. Suppose you want your own filing system to use in your situations. How would you go about organizing your experiences in order to have them become functional tools for you?

In a way, the office problem is not dissimilar from the issues involved in selecting what concepts to use in teaching — concepts that are functional, that give access to related information, that can be used as tools in screening new experience and seeing in what ways past experiences can or cannot relate to the situation at hand.

U–N AND G–R CONCEPTS

One of the main differences we note in the kinds of concepts we can use in teaching the use of social studies is that some are: UNIQUE AND NONREPETITIVE (U–N); for example, The Declaration of Independence was written in 1776. In *varying degrees,* some are GENERALIZABLE AND REPETITIVE (G–R); for example, "Conflict situations arise or occur in the context of interdependency."

Some are PRESCRIPTIVE AND NORMATIVE STATEMENTS, and others are DESCRIPTIVE AND EMPIRICAL STATEMENTS.

The more highly generalizable and repetitive a concept is and the more empirically based the relationships in the concept, the more functional the concept becomes as a tool. It should be pointed out that unique and nonrepetitive concepts are NOT dismissed; rather they serve vital but different functions. A generalizable and repetitive concept is a gathering together of unique and non-repetitive concepts into patterns of relationships and associations. A generalizable and repetitive concept needs the unique and non-repetitive concept for support. A unique and nonrepetitive concept, however, does not need the generalizable and repetitive "organization."

Statement: The Battle of Hastings ("A") occurred in 1066 ("B").

This is a U–N concept: "A," "B." It is Unique and Nonrepetitive and, as given, has no statement of relationship other than placement in time.

Statement: George III's attitude and behavior ("A") precipitated the Revolutionary War ("B").

This is a U–N concept: "A" caused "B." It is Unique and Nonrepetitive and, as given, has a causal relationship indicated. (It may or may not be valid).

Statement: Executions of convicted murderers ("A") deter murders ("B").

This is a G–R concept: "A" influences "B" and is not restricted to *one* murderer in *one* situation. It is generalized, repetitive, and states the relationship. It can be tested for its validity.

For the teachers of the use of social studies, the differentiation between kinds of concepts as well as the qualities a particular concept maintains, is of *vital* importance.

The historian's rigorous inquiry is directed not at establishing G–R concepts but at discovering U–N concepts. Historians use concepts from the social sciences as tools in their own inquiry, and the social sciences use the "facts" of history. The two functioning inquiries are mutually supporting. *Our hang-ups come when our expectations demand that the historian produce G—R concepts and that the social scientist produce U–N concepts.* It is this unnecessary type of demand that turns teachers and students into bitter cynics in regard to scholarship and learning in the areas of history and social science. This credibility gap can be lessened if teachers let the students "in on" the different kinds of statements about human experience and the limits of inquiry as well as the promises.

As Abraham Kaplan says, no matter how good our intentions, wishful thinking will not feed a starving man nor will saying, "Let there be!" make it so. We go to school on experience, and we must take this into consideration in determining what and how to teach.

The G–R and U–N concepts can be viewed as a continuum moving from the general to the specific in usage or from the specific to the general.

To know the difference between the following statements and to be aware of what the differences imply about how we use such statements in our teaching is an important step:

Statement One: Given these conditions (a,b,c, . . .), then it is probable (p) that a riot (q-qualified) will take place.

Statement Two: Given these conditions . . . *in the United States* then (p) a riot (q) will take place.

Statement Three: Given these conditions . . . *in urban U.S.A.,* then (p) a riot (q) will take place.

Statement Four: Given these conditions . . . *in Los Angeles,* then (p) a riot (q) will take place.

Statement Five: This condition existed and a riot took place in Watts.

Statement one is a general statement of probability within a universal context: Given these conditions anywhere, they are sufficient to cause a riot. Probably. Statement two narrows the relationships, as do statements three and four. Statement five is unique and nonrepetitive, but necessary if we are going to test the validity of any of the previously mentioned statements.

Bruner argues that learning serves man in two ways:[6] There can be a *specific* application of learning to a highly similar situation; there can be a nonspecific transfer of principles or general ideas which recognize subsequent problems as being special modifications of the learned principle or general idea. Statement one, if valid, would be the most generalizable and thus the most useable statement of concept for student transfer. *In teaching* the use of such a statement of concept one would have to use the other four remaining statements. If one rests his case solely on statement five, there is no need to utilize the other four statements.

SOURCES OF CONCEPTS

The teachers of the use of social studies should focus their teaching efforts on findings or concepts that are:

1. Empirically based: This allows a way to test the concepts with certain kinds of data and methodology.

2. Generalizable: The finding or concept includes more than one incident; the more inclusive, the more potential for transfer use.

Where can one locate such concepts? Does a teacher make them up and then hope that they have some validity? No. It is here that the teachers may make a valid request of the scholars in supportive disciplines to make available their most generalizable findings. You will find that the more generalizable the findings, the less likely they are to be anchored within discernible confines of one discipline.

Below is a list of findings taken from a number of disciplines supportive to the social studies area. Each finding is considered to be "major"; that is, highly generalizable and repetitive under universal conditions. See if you can identify the discipline source. (Does it make any difference for the teacher's use?)

Discipline

1. Continuous change has been a universal condition of human society. _____

2. A society exists in the minds of its members and occurs only when there is interaction among members. _____

3. Each culture tends to view its physical habitat differently—a society's value system, goals organization, and level of technology determine which elements of the land are prized and utilized. _____

4. Practically all significant differences in human behavior (and among human populations) are understandable as learned cultural patterns rather than as biologically inherited characteristics. _____

5. The larger the society, the more an individual must rely upon group membership; uniting with others increases the self and the chances to "move" in decision making. _____

6. The study of human experience allows man the possibility of a wider range of choices. The study offers no immutable laws, givens, or inevitables upon which to make decisions. _____

7. Man is a flexible and "becoming" creature. Through the experiences he encounters he learns a complex of roles, understandings, and expectations. _____

8. Man moves from isolated and self-sufficient communities to a growing interdependence: more trade,

migration, diffusion of ideas and practices, and the importance of relative location and situation. _____

9. Every cultural system is an interconnected series of ideas and patterns for behavior in which changes in one aspect generally lead to changes in other segments of the system. _____

10. As a minimum condition for its existence, a society establishes authoritative institutions that can make decisions which are binding on all the people, provide for resolution of dissent, and effectively enforce basic rules. _____

How practical is all this? After all, most teachers in the social studies area inherit a "set" of materials—usually a single test—and are expected to "cover" them. Where do the generalizable and repetitive concepts come in? It is possible to take a chapter in any standard text and dissect it into U–N concepts and G–R concepts and to determine what data a particular chapter includes; that is, maps, charts, and so on. Suppose, in one chapter you find:

A group of people (X) existed in a geographic area. (U–N concept)

and

The group (X) moved as a group to a new geographic area. (U–N concept)

and

There was a shortage of food in the former location (U–N concept)

and

Whenever there is a shortage of food for a period of time, people tend to migrate. (G–R concept)

Now the G–R concept states that such a relationship exists. You can pose this G–R concept in the form of a hypothesis: *If* there is a shortage of food for a period of time, *then* people tend to migrate. You analyze with the students the hypothesis: What constitutes a shortage? How long a period of time? *What* people tend to migrate? Migrate to what kind of area? In short, you identify the generalizable and repetitive concept as such and analyze it in question form so that conditions become part of it. Then, using it as a base and *as a tool* for inquiry, you TEST its validity within the chapter and with the U–N concepts included in the chapter. More information will be needed and comparative studies will need to be undertaken as part of the test. In this way, you are still working with a G–R concept which is transferable (in qualified form), and are helping in the transfer by using the U–N concepts in the chapter to be "covered." There are many ways to use a text.

We are suggesting that a primary teaching method is not necessarily the students' "discovery" of relationships as much as a TESTING of relationships in order to discover other relationships.

A concept is part of the real world, so why not make it "public" and then test it through experience to see if it holds up, under what conditions it appears to hold up, and what variables are at work within the concept?

At this point we are primarily concerned with what considerations are basic to concept selection. The considerations *are practical* even in a conventional program. IF the teacher recognizes the functions served by various kinds of concepts.

Some readers will be claiming at this point that our emphasis is on the cognitive—the intellectual—aspects of teaching. We do not make the assumption that cognitive and affective are split into two opposing camps. If one wishes to emphasize the affective area of human activity, there are concepts or findings which stem from studies of such behavior. (See the chapter on Rationale and the findings listed under the "user" of knowledge.) It is assumed that a teacher stressing the affective aspects of human behavior has a rationale *and* has a conceptual base for that rationale. And it is assumed that there is *some* cognitive activity going on when teaching about affective activity. The differentiation of kinds of concepts is still valid and still functional. It is the teacher's determination of the *use* of such concepts that may differ, depending upon the goals he has in mind.

THE WORD IS NOT THE THING
(or STATIC TERMS FOR DYNAMIC PROCESSES?)

You have probably noticed that we did not offer a precise definition of the term "concept" and you have probably gathered that the term "concept" has been used a number of different ways by different people working on different programs. Our failure to define was intentional. A former student suggested that, because the term carries so many different "cargoes," it might be best to involve people in wrestling with the issues rather than with a term. We have tried this.

It is said that if one wanted to take the "l" out of the world, one would end up with the "wor d." Now we are back to Bacon's idols . . . and to our own dilemma. Becker writes that the "historical fact is not the past event, but a symbol"; sometimes we end up studying word symbols and signs more than the "thing." Learning sometimes ends up being merely the memorization of sounds. Dictionary definitions are useful and may be the last word—but they are *not* the concept.

To say that 3X equals 2Y plus 1 is to give a statement of relationships. It is not "learned" at this point. Only when it can be used does one know the functional relationships for which the statement stands. To know the statement is not necessarily to know the concept. To know the grammatical structure of a particular sentence is not necessarily to understand the sentence.

We have noted that a highly transferable G–R concept is composed of a relatively large number of "facts," of U–N concepts. The greater number of U–N concepts in a particular relationship and under specified conditions, the greater chance (probability) of the relationship being maintained in similar conditions. Thus, the G–R concept becomes a tool with which to control, to predict, and to make decisions. It is a tool which can be used to help to test itself in order to form new G–R concepts when new "facts"

suggest modification. *A G–R concept is NOT a closed, finished, completed precept to become idolized;* rather, it is a tentative but fairly stable foothold that permits more learning—*even at its own expense.*

The possibility of transfer to a variety of new situations and to modification "transforms the human organism from a creature that adapts to a changing environment by trial and error to one that adapts by seeming hypothesis and insight."[7]

"Concepts" are "entities formed by the mind" and denoted by terms,[8] are "general notions" made up of complex characters and can be traced to the Latin "conceptus" or conceiving,[9] are "anybody's oyster."[10] Anybody's oyster: philosophers have looked for the pearls for centuries, psychologists pry, and educators appear to ignore or to devour!

Call them what we may, ideas, principles, schemes, findings, concepts stand for *methods with content,* not just products. They stand for processes with products which feedback to the processes and then to products; a systematic way of cataloging and patterning experience in order to "control" more experience which, in turn, is cataloged and patterned. Never final. Never finished. Never complete.

Call them what we may, they stem from and interact with human *experience.* They are always abstracted from this experience and thus are never complete. They are attempts to mentally organize experiences involving acting, reacting, influencing, being influenced, and so forth, and this is an organization that infers meaning—through its classifying, cataloging, and patterning. They are a concert of associations, connections, junctures. And they are *given* labels to facilitate more effective and efficient use.

They have relevancy to the degree to which the vicarious experiences and the abstractions of such experiences allow a transfer to the world as it is—to the "situation."

Notice that the labels are given last—as a way of cataloging. It should be significant for teachers that a person need not verbalize and use labels *before* he is in the act of conceptualizing—of organizing and giving meaning to experiences. Education has a tendency to label *first* and then hope that subsequent experience may, in fact, make the label functional; this is an approach that is just the opposite of creating relevant meaning out of experience.

We use the pictorial diagram on page 162 with public school students. It is oversimplified but tries to illustrate the conceptualizing processes and how the "products" or organization of meaning influences subsequent processes with products.

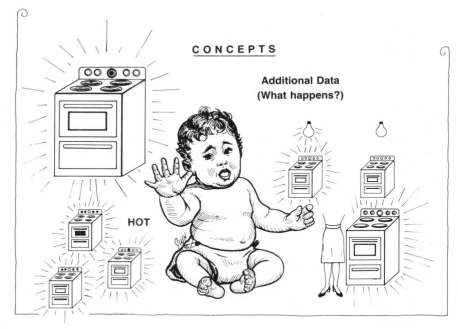

CONCEPTS

Additional Data
(What happens?)

HOT

The baby doesn't have the labels for experience as yet. He crawls into a room we call a "kitchen" and goes to an object we call a "stove" and touches it. He relates himself with the stove and finds the experience unpleasant. This may happen once or a number of times, but the child will relate the experiences (conceptualize) and his behavior will become modified by his concept. With additional data the concept may be modified and qualified. The label for the concept comes, in this case, after the relationship has been formed. In school we sometimes worry more about the label than the experience.

John B. Carroll, in an extremely sensitive and articulate article appearing in the Harvard Educational Review, argues that there are three components to the [thing] we cluster under the term: words or physical entities, meanings in terms of verbal relationships, and the cataloged experience which may or may not relate to the language used.[10] Facts don't always speak for themselves.

WHAT DO CONCEPTS DO?

If we recognize that definitions are sometimes limiting if used in the old sense ("ice is ice" sort of thing), then in our approach to concept selection and use, it might be wise to modify the question from "What are concepts?" to "What do concepts do?"

Assuming that:

Concepts are *not* an unchanging commodity.

Concepts combine processes with product.

Concepts are involved in abstracting relationships into patterns.

Concepts are tools to assist in continual learning.

Concepts are concerned with patterns of relationships and, thus, stand ready and willing to be challenged by additional *empirical* data—even if seeding their own demise.

Assuming this, what specifically do concepts do for us?

The primary function may be to lend some credence to the old axiom that one "must learn how to learn"; an axiom that became a symbol, much like the three gold balls over a door.

Inquiry starts not with isolated facts but rather in a conception, " . . . a deliberate construction of the mind. On this conception all else depends. It tells us what facts to look for in the research. It tells us what meaning to assign these facts."[11] We don't start any inquiry from scratch; we don't know the facts we ought to seek until we have some screen, some conception which acts as a guide to inquiry. Part of this inquiry may well be the testing of a concept which the individual puts into a "conception."

Again, recognizing that a primary function of teaching is helping others to learn, take a look at what has been used with students to help them analyze the functions of concepts (see illustration on page 164).

The key idea (concept) we try to raise with the students is that concepts are very much a part of the real world, as real in consequence as "that tree outside the window" and as much a "fact" as the Magna Charta.

The use and kinds of concepts provide a base for selection and instructional use. It also helps the teacher to articulate what kinds of help are needed from the supporting disciplines and academic scholars.

If the students can be taught to become cognizant of the "things" called concepts—the processes used in concept formation, the varieties, and the possible functions—the teacher's task then moves from the vague to the particular. The expectations of the teacher and student become realistic.

Teaching now takes on a different dimension. Instead of focusing on one thing or idea at a time—clarifying and memorizing—and then going on, the teaching process becomes one of "focusing on points of contact and connection among things and ideas clarifying of each thing on the other and how each connection modifies the factors in the connection—portraying not things in themselves but as parts of patterns."[11] This is seen as a drama, with actors mutually influencing, feeding back, changing, and is applicable to other "actors" in similar "plots." However, the script

WHAT DO CONCEPTS *DO*?

(*Not* - What are concepts?)

		VERBAL
1. Organize experience (data)		ALL RED-HEADS HAVE A QUICK TEMPER
2. Screen new experience (data)		AH! RED-HEAD! SHE HAS A TEMPER
3. Modify and reorganize (data)		NOT *ALL* RED-HEADS
4. Determine reactions (behavior)	?	RESERVE JUDGMENT
5. Act as analytic tools (skills)	(example)	COGNITION OF *LOGICAL* BASE

is created as it is acted and is dependent upon the actors and their interaction, just as the actors are partially dependent upon the script. There is no final "act."

Instead of precept upon precept—orders upon orders—one finds concept with concept, order*ing* with order*ing*.

CONCEPTS USED AT DIFFERENT GRADE LEVELS*

Can you determine if a concept is U–N or G–R?
Can you determine a flow to the generalizability of the concepts?

KINDERGARTEN A person lives in many "worlds" and each world—the family, school, friends—asks that one behave in certain ways.

Each world in which a person lives gives something to the person and the person gives some thing to the world.

---

*Selected "concepts" taken from various grade levels in an actual social studies curriculum.

Almost every world includes people, things, words, and ideas.

FIRST GRADE   Human beings are changing all the time, but most of the changes are hard to see.

When human beings live and work together, they figure out a way to understand each other and to share ideas with one another.

People *learn* different ways to satisfy their needs.

SECOND GRADE   A change in one thing usually brings about changes in many things.

Usually *many* things cause some one thing to happen.

People can use their intelligence to change the use they make of nature.

THIRD GRADE   When *organizing* human activity (community) it is necessary that many "parts" come together in a way which will help to achieve goals.

Dividing the work to be done among a number of "specialists" tends to make man more and more dependent upon what others do, and others more dependent upon what an individual does.

The choices one makes in his activities relate to what other people have done and will do.

FOURTH GRADE   The human being inherits certain potentials. Most of his behavior is learned as his social environment interacts with his individual potential.

A study of man's habits can contribute to predicting man's behavior.

The child coming into the world in a specific place in the world is born into a situation which has certain beliefs and approved ways of acting. Much of what the child learns depends upon this framework.

FIFTH GRADE   The solving of one problem usually creates new situations and new problems.

Social change builds on what is, and usually part of the "old" becomes part of the "new."

Some factors change more readily than do others and tensions develop between the old and the new.

SIXTH GRADE A stereotype is often a misleading generalization into which one attempts to classify specific parts.

Man's ideas about the universe and his place in it are usually reflected by the types of political, economic, and social organization that evolve.

The consequences of wars are difficult to appraise, as both the victor and the conquered are faced with new situations, new problems, and different ways of meeting their situations and problems.

JUNIOR HIGH
SCHOOL Jefferson's basic premise was that man is capable of shaping his experience and that the experience, in turn, would shape man.

SENIOR HIGH
SCHOOL Half the poor in the United States live in metropolitan urban centers in ghettos. Sixty per cent of the Negro poor are under 21.

SYNTHESIS AND PROLOGUE

In a world of concepts and conceptual teaching, a "concept" of concept is elusive. It is an abstraction: an abstraction from experience, *certain* aspects of which are *related* into "meaning." It is a form of mental organization. When one becomes aware of the organization and what it *does* for a human being, cognition helps to *do* a number of things: to organize, to obtain more information, to screen new experience, to develop "meanings," to predict, and to evaluate. Concepts have consequences. Concepts are "real" in that they influence behavior.

We have tried to make a "concept" of concept less elusive. This seems necessary if one is concerned with conceptual thinking and conceptual teaching. There are different kinds of concepts: some are empirically based and some are not; some are unique and nonrepetitive, while others are generalizable and repetitive in varying degrees. If one is concerned with the teaching the *use* of concepts, the distinction between U–N and G–R concepts should prove helpful. Which ones are more likely to be trans-fered or used in "real" life situations?

The old hangup over facts vs. concepts has been considered. Facts are U–N concepts and are necessary for deriving and testing G–R concepts. G–R concepts are transferable, which means they can be used in many situations. It is not a case of "either-or." A teacher can use a conceptual approach even within the frame-work of a conventionally organized curriculum!

If we are to teach the *use* of concepts in a systematic way, the term "use" suggests the need to have ways of obtaining and using information. These ways require methods and skills for working on and with data from vicarious and first-hand experience. The next chapter focuses upon how one functions with using expe-rience, upon the tools related to conceptual teaching.

Warning: Skills are *not* mechanical and nonintellectual commodities. They are not simply putting nuts on bolts.

We thank Mr. Kaplan (*The Conduct of Inquiry*) for the follow-ing:

"Some fool has put the head of this nail on the wrong end."

"It's for the opposite wall."

"Turn it around."

REFERENCES

1. Silberman, Charles E.: Crisis in the Classroom. New York, Random House, 1970.
2. Mallan, John T.: *How Do You Know?* Cleveland, *Focus Texts*, Educational Dynamics, 1970.
3. Mallan, John T.: What Do We Think We Know About Early Man? Cleveland, Focus Texts, Educational Dynamics, 1970.
4. Mallan, John T.: Making Ideas – Making Concepts. Cleveland, Focus Texts, Educational Dynamics, 1970.
5. Becker, Carl L.: The Western Political Quarterly, September, 1955. Quoted in Meyerhoff, Hans (ed.): *The Philosophy of History in Our Time.* New York, Doubleday, 1959.
6. Bruner, Jerome S.: The Process of Education. Cambridge, Harvard University Press, 1960.
7. Klausmeier, Herbert J.: Learning and Human Abilities: Educational Psychology. New York, Harper and Row, 1961.
8. Bunge, Mario: Intuition and Science, Spectrum. Englewood Cliffs, N. J., Prentice-Hall, 1962.
9. *The American College Dictionary.* New York, Random House, 1969.
10. Carroll, John B.: Words, meanings and concepts. Harvard Educational Review, Spring, 1964.
11. Schwab, Joseph J.: The concept of the structure of a discipline. The Educational Record, July, 1962.

"Wait! I've changed my mind!"

(By Dennis Renault. Copyright 1966 Saturday Review, Inc.)

6

SKILL DEVELOPMENT

"And tools to work with all..."

The recording of facts is one of the tasks of science, one of the steps toward truth; but it is not the whole of science. There are one-story intellects, two-story intellects, and three-story intellects with skylights. All fact collectors who have no aims beyond their facts are one story men. Two-story men compare, reason, and generalize, using the labors of the fact collectors as well as their own. Three-story men idealize, imagine, and predict. Their best illumination comes from above, through the skylight."

JUSTICE O.W. HOLMES

SOURCES OF DATA, OR SKILLS?

The thing that keeps us diverging—diverging from relating concepts *with* methods (as we sometimes reinforce in teacher training)—and from separating classroom from living situations is that we sometimes confuse the *source of data* (maps, charts, readings, television) with concepts and with the methods of *using* data to form and to test concepts. Because the *sources* take different forms, we assume that the methods of using the varied data are *also* dissimilar and unique. This leads to a dysfunctional separation and to misconceptions on the part of the student. It also leads to dissipation of energy on the part of the teacher.

If you ask a craftsman what he means when he refers to a colleague as a *skilled* craftsman, he is likely to respond to the question in the following manner:

> He knows what to do and can do it well. He knows what the
> finished thing should look like or how it should work. He can
> *follow* a design or blueprint and yet make modifications which
> fit but which improve what he's trying to do. He knows his
> tools—he knows what they can and *cannot* do and he knows
> what he has to do with them in order to make them effective.
> He knows *when* to use them, and he constantly "reads" his

169

work and modifies his approach. He knows the material he is working with—what it can and cannot do when he is working with it: the limits within which he can work effectively. He makes decisions all the time: what to do, how to do it, when to change; he predicts—but knows why. He's skilled because he "puts it all together." He's not a dreamer. He's realistic—about himself, his tools, his ends, his material, his time. This comes through experience.

If you ask a teacher what he means when he says that a student is skillful, he might respond to the question in the following manner:

He can read well—fast and comprehensively. He is skilled in oral and written expression. He reasons well and can handle maps and critical thinking. He shows effectiveness in research. He's respected and gets along well with others. He's curious and is not afraid to pursue his curiosity.

To argue by analogy can be inconclusive if one is trying to clarify a situation. But we *can* raise some questions:

In what ways are the skilled craftsman and the skilled student the same? In what ways are they different? Do they both read? reason? obtain data? Do both work on materials? Do both use feedback? Are both aware of their tools? what to use, when to use, when to adapt the tools to the situation? Are both aware of the limitations of the materials, the tools, and themselves? Do both have specific purposes within a larger purpose, and do both see how the parts relate with one another and the whole? Do both have a finished product?

Are both involved in decision making? in prediction? in self-correction?

What about the tools? The craftsman has physical entities as tools and he has conceptualized their use. The student has abstractions or mental abilities, and these become *tools* when he has *conceptualized* what to do, how to do, and when to do certain kinds of mental manipulation on the materials with which he is working.

If our purpose is, simply, to have students develop the ability to repeat, upon cue, certain verbal statements, then the problems involved with skill development are relatively easy to assess. If learning is directed toward a student's being able to come to terms with a barrage of data, to seek relationships, to conceptualize, to test, and to transfer—if our ends are in terms of reasonable and rational *use* of experience to come to terms of more experience—the discussion of skills becomes vital.

As we have seen with concepts, a collection of U–N concepts or facts is not enough. Few would argue with this. The questions then emerge: How does one operate upon the barrage of data he encounters? How does one make functional sense out of experience? What does one *do* when working with U–N and G–R concepts? If the concepts that one brings to new experiences have consequences, one can have some assurance that the techniques used to derive and to test such concepts are of basic importance.

Skill teaching can be just a part of the tribal teaching ritual, or it can be a vital aspect of teaching and learning.

We don't know very much about the "system" called human functioning. It is probable that the bio-social-chemical variables at work in the system will be increasingly understood and duplicated; life is being created in a test tube and memory is being transferred through the use of chemicals. Learning theory is not isolated in the psychologist's domain.

When it comes to thinking and learning, we often pretend to have more at our disposal than actually is. This suggests that perhaps our educational approach is based on an erroneous premise: that we teach thinking. *Perhaps what we should be doing is teaching the norms one uses in testing the products of functioning (thinking, learning, acting) and, in so doing, assure more effective functioning.*

Let's not get hung-up on the cliché of having to teach youngsters "how to think." Youngsters think or function prior to their entering the portals of the school.

Before entering school:

Does a youngster have problems or questions?

Does a youngster try to resolve his concerns in one way or another?

Does a youngster look for reasons?

Does he look for sources of help—information, suggestions?

Does a youngster classify his experiences and draw upon his conceptualizations of past experience?

Does he become frustrated?

Does he observe what's going on around him?

Does he predict? note causal relationships?

Does he have general ideas about himself? his behavior?

Does he "de-code" messages?

Does he communicate?

The youngster may not be especially effective or efficient; he may rely on trial and error methods. He may not be skillful. But he *is* at work trying to make some sense out of himself and the world with which he interacts. He may not even be able to verbalize or to bring to the conscious level what he is doing or why he is doing it. But he *is* "thinking" and he *is* functioning.

He hasn't been formally taught to do this.

He is doing all this without having a mind full of other people's facts. He is somehow getting facts, using them, getting more, putting them together—acting, reacting, making all sorts of decisions.

Perhaps one of the key functions of the teacher is to *assume* the above, and then to try to bring ways of monitoring methods to the cognitive level so that a student can evaluate, judge, and improve. Shattering as it may seem, a youngster does not come to us with an empty mind.

All of us, while awake, are in constant interaction with our environments.[1] We are engaged in a process of give and take, of doing something to or influencing objects, people, ideas, words, and situations. And we are constant recipients of influence: impressions, vicarious experience, thoughts—all sorts of stimuli that we somehow bring sense to and fit into a conceptual scheme called self.

John Dewey, in the initial introduction to *How We Think* (1910), commented that the schools were troubled with a multiplication of studies and materials and that the teacher's task was made more difficult by his having to deal with individualized instruction. In this morass of magnitude he saw the need for some "clew" to unity—some principle that synthesized if not simplified the dimensions of the teaching effort. This principle was seen in an attitude and habit of mind in which there was a desire and ability to put skills to work on experiencing.

Skills, therefore, become methods and techniques of monitoring and controlling the nature of the interaction. Instead of reacting, man acts purposefully. Instead of reacting in "blind imitation of past performance," man can bring his intelligence and intellect to the act of experiencing.[2]

You don't hold your own by merely standing on guard, G.B. Shaw reminded us. You have to attack, and this may mean getting well "hammered" in the process—and being *aware*, cognizant, of the attack strategy *and* the hammering as the mutual influencing takes place.

What then does this mean to the teacher of the use of social studies?

You probably have some doubt about the generalized nature of skills—especially if you've glanced at the literature related to social studies skills. You find reference to "work-study" skills such as reading, outlining, using maps, using charts; "thinking skills" such as critical thinking, problem solving, decision making; "group-process" skills; "social-living" skills such as acting responsibly, cooperation, etc.[3] And you'll find "value" skills, "attitudinal" skills, "citizenship" skills, ad infinitum.

Are there skills unique to social studies education? We would argue "no." The social studies area may provide a different focus to the objects, people, ideas, words, and situations, and perhaps provide different *forms* of data, but the *skills used to monitor the interaction* of that data are the same as in *any* experience — in school *and* out. Skills are built for transfer and can provide the synthesizing principle of which Dewey spoke!

These are functioning skills and not merely social studies skills. The social studies as a "subject" area simply provides various opportunities and settings in which to put the generalized and transferable skills to work.

If skills are methods and techniques of working on the interaction of an individual and his environments — on experiencing — we find the individual interacting with a number of *sources* of data: people, objects, situations, ideas, words. The data come in different forms and styles.

Actually, when we talk about skills we are talking about a "field" *communication* process: the methods and techniques that go into creating, sharing, and influencing in terms of *meaning*. The form of meaning exchange may take a number of forms: i.e., a symbol such as a flag, a cross, or in the case of Walden Two, a lollipop; maps; charts; statistical tabulations; television; cartoons; readings; talk — formal and informal. Some of the forms allow immediate feedback and two-way modifying, whereas others influence without being open to mutual modification. But *all* the variables, including the individual in the process of experiencing, can be monitored. Methods and techniques can be applied to this broadly conceived communication process.

Of course, one realizes that one's senses and conceptual framework allow the influencing to take place. For example, a large portion of our input in experiencing comes from *listening* and *observing;* to a lesser degree, except in school, from reading.

If we recognize the G–R nature of skills, we are saying that there are *concepts* related to such things as *listening* and *observing* which, if brought to the cognitive level and if used as part of the subject matter in the classroom, can assist the student in developing methods and techniques of monitoring *and* modifying experience, that is, in assisting the student to be skillful in working on his experience. For example, the behavioral sciences have a number of findings which can be used in skill development, such as factors that impede or facilitate listening, factors at work in screening what is heard, the affective factors at work, how listening is modified when listening *and* viewing as opposed to just listening. There is a wealth of information about the importance of listening and about its influence in daily functioning, on the job, and so forth.

The same is true of observation.

There is a tendency to think of concepts as being related solely to a certain kind of subject matter: geography, economics, sociology, political science, anthropology, and history. We recognize that a G–R concept takes on discrete human experience and moves up through various levels of transferability to a number of similar human experiences—from one, to some, to many, to all. But there is sometimes a failure to recognize that the use of social studies includes findings from psychology, social psychology, biology, chemistry, and so forth. Some of these findings are inclusive and transferable at the process or skill areas.

The skill comes in when one puts it all together *conceptually* and then finds *use* in monitoring and improving one's behavior in terms of the situation.

To view skills as pedestrian, as something distinct from and separate from content and intellectual activity, limits our view and our use of data. It also limits the development of functional skills. Instead of thinking of a set of discrete skills—work-study, critical thinking, interpersonal, social, etc.—it might prove beneficial for both teachers and students if we considered the area as *one* major SKILL, that is, a method for functioning. To be sure, there would be subskills, but always viewed as interacting, interdependent, and part of a whole.

SKILL MODELS

It is difficult to break from a "preset" which views skills as distinct and separate activities. A superintendent requested of a consultant that some specific models for *separate* skills be established. For example, a model for teaching observation—one that would be clean and neat, and which a teacher could "plug in" at various grade levels. The fact of life is that skills are not "clean and neat," and it is the relationship among techniques that provide a SKILL method. Observation may, for example, be an *entrance point,* a *focus of interest,* but this does *not* imply that observation can be approached without a coordinated and integrated relationship among a variety of activities: questioning, reasoning, perceptual screens, hypothesizing, generalizing, testing, semantics, and so on.

To ask for a model of how one teaches separate skills presupposes a host of concepts about learning and functioning. It is like saying that a man intent upon purchasing a gift for his boss is an economic man — involved in a strictly economic activity. The fact that he considers such things as taste, proper amount to spend, what people will say, anticipated response by the boss (and his secretary and wife), proper store, overt and covert functions of the gift, his *own* priorities and values, and so forth, makes the economic man perhaps focusing upon an economic exchange, but with a host of political, social, and psychological variables at work. To artificially construct a simplification is not to reduce complexity to simplicity when it comes to actual functioning.

Parsons and Shaftel make some lucid comments on how models may become "straight jackets."[4] In an extremely helpful look at some of the basic issues, the authors saw two types of models being offered and felt that both types "may inhibit rather than facilitate the development of thinking skills." One type, the *categorical,* is a schematic means of presenting the *results* of inquiry at the conclusion of a process. The other type, *strategic,* sometimes implies a series of discrete cognitive operations which may, in fact, lead to an artificial — dysfunctional — approach to the processes. The models may be theoretically helpful but cannot be "plugged in" as neat recipes for use in classroom situations. In a sense, the superintendent was asking for a categorical-strategic skills model which was fixed and static. If teachers use such prescribed practices with students, there may be a ready-made set of categories which work to limit functioning (thinking/acting), and this runs counter to the basic reasons for working with skill development.

Trying to train students in skill development out of context of the "whole" is analogous to a pianist exercising the pressing of the foot pedal without any reference to synchronizing his hands on the keyboard, the visual input from the music sheet, or the auditory feedback.[5] Reading *Power Golf,* having a set of clubs, and having a nice warm-up swing do not make for golfing skill until all factors are put together in an actual situation (the test, as always, is what one is able to do) in a total situation, fraught with dynamics.

QUEENIE   By Phil Interlandi

"What do I do now? I'm sick and tired of thinking!"

If Dewey saw "skill" teaching as the synthesizing and simplifying principle for teachers back in 1910, why haven't the teachers of the use of social studies understood this? With the exception of perhaps the preschool and primary levels, most social studies classrooms still pivot on U–N concept input, have little concern for evidence and empirical issues, and stress U–N output. When G–R concepts are dealt with they often appear as categorical and closed. Thus, the concept of content appears to preclude skill development as method and to substitute gadgets and gimmicks and situational techniques for skills.

If one views data to be used in deriving and/or testing G–R concepts and if one views skills as the METHOD of functioning with experience so one can monitor and improve the functioning then the "principle" of what Dewey wrote may, in fact, give sound direction to teaching as well as to learning.

Teaching has been going on since the beginning of man's awareness of himself. Probably social studies teaching is the granddaddy of all if man looks first at survival and then at the quality of that survival. We can assume a tradition, but with tradition comes myths. Following are some of those myths which must be dispelled.

S-M-O-S-E: SKILLFUL MYTHS OF SKILL EVASION

MYTH 1. SOCIAL STUDIES IS REALLY A COURSE IN APPLIED READING

We are told that it is "impossible for a student to be deficient in skills and to excel in social studies."[6] It is interesting that research supporting this view stems from "The Relationship Between Reading Skills and Selected Areas of Sixth Grade Achievement."[7] Social studies skills are often subsumed by the broad area of "reading." If a youngster can't read well, he is doomed in many social studies courses.

This might not prove too much of a detriment if social studies teachers were prepared to teach reading and if they had a grasp of the intricate subskills at work in any reading effort. For example, in *The Getting Ready to Read Workbook*,[8] used in kindergartens and primary schools, the teacher is informed that the workbook covers: patterns, cause-effect relationships, recognition of likenesses and differences, classification, perception, inferences, interpretation, language development. In other words, reading subsumes a host of functional cognitions that feed one another in developing the ability "to read." But in the social studies, if a youngster can't read, he fails or is "carried" because he doesn't make a fuss about having his time wasted. Most social studies teachers don't break down, or reduce, reading into the subareas in order to help the youngster. If he can't read, he can't get the data. If he can't get the data, he can't pass. It is not unlike a football coach's claiming that if a candidate can't tackle, block, run the hundred in 9.8, and doesn't *already* know all the intricacies of the plays, he shouldn't have any hopes of making the team.

One of the authors used to coach football along with teaching senior high school social studies. He had a fullback who was bright, perceptive, and who caught on to things without any trouble — on the football field. But the student was in a "slow" social studies class. It didn't make sense. When questioned, the boy told the "coach" (not the teacher) that he couldn't read. His sister would read the textbook assignments to him. On the field he watched, listened, and learned. In the classroom, he watched, listened, and failed.

We are not disputing the need to learn how to read.

We *are* questioning whether a youngster has to be able to read in order to learn.

Whether we like it or not, people obtain their data input in *many* different ways and are NOT limited by whether they can decode the structure of written symbols. They listen, observe, and think. If concepts are formed from data, and data comes from a number of sources other than those committed to a print form, and if concepts can be learned and *tested* through other than just reading—then, what we have is simply *one* of many sources of data now readily available to the student. This brings us into media and into some of the *same* subskills subsumed in reading skill but now applied to sources of experience other than print.

The myth is powerful.

To many teachers, the "real" academic material is perceived as that which appears in the textbook or in another form that demands an adequate reading ability. If concepts and skills were perceived as being of more importance than the form of the source, social studies teaching could conceivably bow to the twentieth century.

On one occasion some teachers working in a volunteer federally funded program were asked why children had to learn to read. The response? "To get through school." (The reason for going to school and for taking seriously the experiences the school provides is simply to get through school?)

In approaching this myth, it might be well to be informed about what the reading people have to say. In so doing we may come across such things as causal relationships, classifications, inferences, and we may find that the printed form of data, important as it is, is NOT the only source of data and NOT the only arena for skill development.

MYTH 2: THINKING IS A NEATLY STRUCTURED, STEP-BY-STEP ACTIVITY

As in Bacon's Idols of the Tribe, humans assume more order than there is. So it is with thinking processes. We go along in a contented manner until something gets out of balance, doesn't fit, raises some concern, and we have a "feeling" that the situation is indeterminate. "Mind leaps forward with possible solution."

This is the first of five aspects or phases of reflective thought according to Dewey.[1] The second aspect is a move from generalized perplexity to a formulation of the problem or to a question to be answered. From here we move to formulating hypotheses which act to guide observations and to assist in collecting information; then to reasoning, conceptualizing, making inferences; and, finally, to testing either in the imagination or in overt action.

Five *phases* of reflective thought; it is easy to move from "phases" to "stages." It is even easier to assume stages are in set, sequential *steps*. Ross and Van Den Haag stated that examination of empirical methods of science yields "a general pattern of scientific inquiry, which can be described as a progression through five stages."[9] This may be interpreted as meaning five steps.

The view of skills and "critical thinking" as being cold, analytic, sterile, and mechanistic—almost suprahuman—comes from an image of scientists "moving coolly, methodically, and unerringly to the results they report may stem from the etiquette that governs the writing of scientific papers. This etiquette . . . requires them [papers] to be works of vast expurgation, stripping the complex events and behaviors that culminated in the report of everything except their cognitive substance."[10] This is interesting. We judge the process by the form used to report research findings. It is methodical, exact, structured, and consistent. We tend to assume that the report implies inquiry processes.

Dewey warned about the trap. "The five phases . . . do not follow one another in set order," he wrote. The process is an ebb and flow—each move leading to refinement, each yield of data leading to subproblems, new questions, need for more data, different hypotheses. The five phases were only "traits" and, in practice, could telescope. "No set rule can be laid down on such matters."[1]

If one views thinking as a functioning system and *not* as a static, linear progression of sequenced steps, the whole idea of skill now becomes a creative and related effort to understand, monitor, and modify human experience. Skill, then, is the method or process, the creative effort which takes the raw material of experience, works on it, and produces concepts which, in turn, feed continued creation. The aspects or phases Dewey offered are simply monitoring checks.

This is significant for the entire teaching strategy. Several years ago when the social studies movement began to move away from the conventional deductive approach, there seemed to be an extreme move of the pendulum to pure induction, as though this were the "scientific" way. We would work from the particular to the general. We would "discover"; the students would "discover." And the students did just that! They discovered that selected and determined data, plus set and determined strategies, led them to discover what someone else had decided they should discover. It sometimes became kind of a seducto-deducto "game" under the guise of inductive reasoning. What some of us naively assumed to be the "scientific way" just wasn't so. Scientists were human and applied their skill in a whole arena of deductive-hypothetical-inductive activities. What scientists had, however, was not a set of ways of inquiring or discovering *but rather a set of norms for checking the validity of processes, both along the way and after the trip.* Scientific reports, as they appear in journals, give little help in grasping the anguish, fear, doubt, mistakes, excitement, error, accomplishment, self-correcting moves, work, cooperation, discarded data, competition, and pride, or how each of the variables has influenced the collection and use of the data. The reports usually tell how to verify whether the recorded concepts, findings, and principles are empirically verifiable. To judge the *nature* of the effort by the product can be a trap in the pursuit of effective teaching.

MYTH 3. SKILLS ARE TAUGHT AS SEPARATE AND DISTINCT FUNCTIONS

If one sees thinking as a series of sequential steps, it appears to logically follow that *specific* aspects or subskills involved in each step can also be assumed to be separate and sequential. This reasoning is compounded when one mistakes *distinct* forms of data sources for the use of *distinct* techniques for understanding and relating the data found in the specific source.

Thus, we find such skills as "map skills." Just as we found that "reading" is a label applied to a whole host of interrelated activities, so we find that map skills call for the same activities *but* applied to a different form of presentation.

Consider the maps on pages 182 and 183. Take the charts that are on pages 183 and 184. You will notice that *both* the maps and the charts deal with related data but present the data in different forms. The data in a map are presented in other than strictly written form. The data have been selected *and* the form of presentation has been selected. When using the maps and/or the charts, what activities are put to work?

Must there be some identified *purpose* in using data presented in such a form? Does one have to articulate *questions* which will guide in data determination, selection, and use? Is there a need for some *criterion* which allows one to differentiate between *relevant* and *irrelevant* data, or does one use all the data included? Is it necessary to *classify* data, to seek out *patterns*, to use *inductive* and *deductive* reasoning? Does one make *inferences*? When one uses the forms, is one *observing*? What about *hypotheses* in regard to relationships among the data? Are there abstract *symbols*? Is one able to *evaluate* and *check* the data as well as the implications suggested by the use of a specific form? What new *questions, hypotheses,* need for *additional data* arise? In what ways can one *record* the data and concepts so they can be used?

Are these same types of activities at work when one uses a book? a motion picture? attends a local city council meeting? sees a slide? a picture? a lecture? a classroom discussion?

The tendency to leap to simplistic conclusions about student skill development is exemplified by the following: An elementary principal from an inner-city school was upset because his primary school pupils "didn't even have the skill of telling time." We have a tendency to take this skill as rather routine and automatic, and even simplistic. Our habits allow us to move fast. What time is it? A quick look at a watch, and we say 3:45. But what did we have to know (be able to do) in order to know the proper words or symbols?

We had to know something about part-whole relationships.
We had to know something about numbers and sequence.
We had to know something about fractions.
We had to have a functional vocabulary, and know a host of signs and symbols.
We had to know something about relating data into patterns.
We had to know something about transfer.
We had to somehow come to terms with a man-made and highly abstract system.

So the simple skill we call telling time is really not so simple, not *a* skill but many conceptualizations and activities in interaction. The *product* of this field of effort is put into a verbal form which describes highly abstract relationships—it is 3:45.

We are suggesting that skill labels—work-study skills, critical thinking skills, decision-making skills, research skills, affective skills, survival skills, interpersonal skills, social skills, map skills—can and do impede effective teaching. Only when we *reduce* the labels to activities and *reduce* cognitions subsumed under each label do we find common types of activities used to manipulate and monitor and improve human experience.

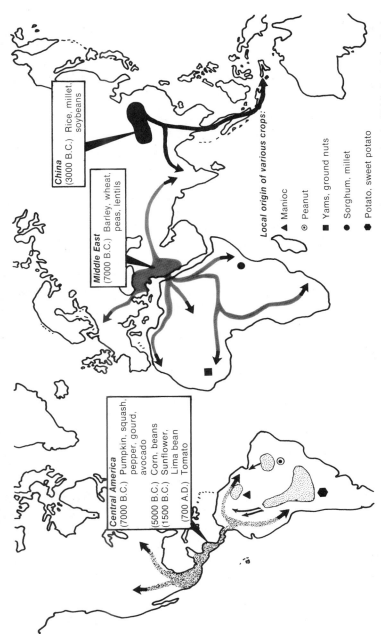

China (3000 B.C.) Rice, millet, soybeans

Middle East (7000 B.C.) Barley, wheat, peas, lentils

Local origin of various crops:

▲ Manioc
⊙ Peanut
■ Yams, ground nuts
● Sorghum, millet
⬟ Potato, sweet potato

Central America (7000 B.C.) Pumpkin, squash, pepper, gourd, avocado
(5000 B.C.) Corn, beans
(1500 B.C.) Sunflower, Lima bean
(700 A.D.) Tomato

Agriculture probably developed simultaneously but separately, starting about 7000 B.C., in Central America and in the Middle East. Its beginnings in China are considerably more recent — about 3000 B.C.

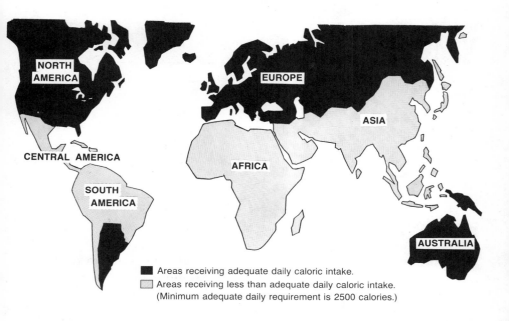

Areas receiving adequate daily caloric intake.

Areas receiving less than adequate daily caloric intake.
(Minimum adequate daily requirement is 2500 calories.)

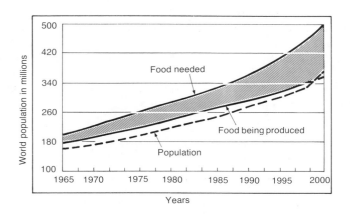

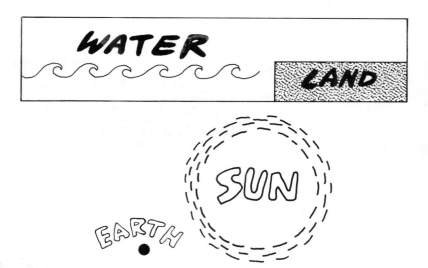

The *same* activities are pursued kindergarten through twelfth grade, but at different levels of sophistication. They may not always be at the awareness level and, thus, not under control, but they *are* at work. With some trepidation we argue that the activities are natural to human experience. And the *same* activities are at work *regardless* of the subject matter—a particular subject or course gives focus to different kinds of data and different forms of data presentation. For example, one may work in an analytic and relatively closed system of manipulating data such as mathematics *or* may work in a synthetic and relatively open system such as social studies. He will still perform the same activities, but with different purposes and different data and different materials.

You ask, What does this mean to me in *my* classroom? Fair enough. You have all sorts of data sources appearing in all sorts of forms: books, reading materials, charts, graphs, statistical tables,

POPULATION DISTRIBUTION

• = Population Location

motion pictures, almanacs, slides, pictures, tapes, lectures, people, situations. All these sources exist to provide you and your students with data. There is utter chaos unless one knows *what* he is trying to do with the data and *how* he can work with it. In a sense, the student faces, at a different level, the same problem the teacher encounters. When processing experience, one is facilitated by having an awareness of what he is about to do and why he is doing it, as well as a method or conceptual scheme to help him check on whether he is doing what he says he is doing and on whether he is doing it well. In other words, a person who is aware of the activities he is engaged in, and who is able to monitor these activities, becomes more effective in using his experience.

We have seen that conceptualizing is a crucial part of the process and that concepts serve to help him in developing skills or in functioning. These, in turn, help to shape new concepts. And these, in turn, help in effective functioning—a reciprocating and mutually influencing system—dynamic, creative, total.

ISSUES

In teaching skills, we face two main issues:

1. To have students become aware of the *conceptual base* involved in monitoring and improving the use of experience.
2. To have students be able to *use* the cognitions as a "system."

For example:

Concept: There are different kinds of evidence a person may accept in believing a statement.

Concept: Some statements have no evidence other than just "feeling" something to be so.

Concept: Evidence that can be seen, heard, and tested by more than one person is more likely to be accurate.

Concept: The different sources of information that support each other make the evidence more likely to be accurate.

These concepts are of a G–R variety but are applied to different kinds of data sources and to different levels of confidence in the sources. These are skill concepts.

One approach in using skill concepts is to give students G–R concepts such as the above. However, these are not simply to be accepted but rather to be tested. Students are then given an exercise such as the following:

> Which of the following statements would you not likely believe? Mark an "M" next to the one you would most believe and an "L" next to the one you would least believe.
> 1. A classmate says that he has a hunch that it is raining in England right now.
> 2. It is raining in England right now because the newspaper said that the English needed rain or there would be a crop failure.
> 3. A classmate says it is raining in England right now because he just finished talking on the phone with his cousin in England.
> 4. The Telestar satellite is telecasting live pictures of it raining in England, and everyone in the class can see it.

In one situation the students responded by "testing" the given concepts in the given situation *and* by assessing their *own* reasons for accepting and/or rejecting certain kinds of evidence. All sorts of things emerged in the class discussion: the importance of the word "now"; the possibility that the "hunch" classmate had a pretty good record of past hunches being right; who cares if it's raining in England?; there had to be some faith that the Telestar was, in fact, showing live pictures—and how *long* did it take to transmit; the teacher threw in the possibility of confusing the words "reigning" with "raining" in the telephone conversation; and so on.

Students were then asked to observe and record, when the four different concepts seemed to be working in their own classroom situation. At this point the teacher had approached skills through G–R concepts and asked that the concepts be tested. There was an *initial* reinforcement (the students already had a "feel" for evaluating data) through conceptualizing. One of the monitoring devices used in the class then became: How do you value your data? These feed into concepts about fact/opinion, probability, reasoning, generalizing, and so forth.

One can approach with students the cognition of what one is doing through such exercises. What about viewing such concepts about evidence in terms of a reciprocating system?

At the elementary level, a teacher posed the following concepts:

> Concept: When one gets some information, he usually forms a conclusion or some conclusions.

Concept: More data may raise some questions, which allows one to obtain even more data.

Concept: The additional data may change the first conclusions and give rise to new questions.

The class was given a situation in which there had been an automobile accident. A friend of one of the occupants in a car involved in the accident explained how a teen-age driver had run a stop sign and piled into his friend's car. (The teen-age driver was presumed to be at fault). A policeman who came upon the scene of the accident after it happened says that the intersection has a four-way stop system and that the two cars collided in the middle of the intersection. (Did the friend stop or did he ignore the sign too?) Photographs taken of the automobile accident immediately after it happened show no signs of either car driver having applied brakes. Damage was at the front end of both cars and was slight. (Did one stop and the other go through? Did both stop and start again? Neither seemed to be going fast or the damage would have been more severe. If the two front ends were damaged, it would seem that neither car had a head-start on the other.) An occupant of one of the cars involved said that both cars had stopped and that each appeared to start up slowly, each driver thinking he had the right of way. (Was the visibility OK?)

Using *just* the concepts from the first experience, the photographs of the cars after the accident might have been the "best" evidence. (Stories get mixed up when coming in second-hand, an occupant of one of the cars might have been excited and might not have noticed things. The policeman could only "guess" what had happened, but his guess might be good because he is trained to look for certain things.) In the second experience, what seems to be happening to one's view of the accident? Different viewpoints, different kinds of evidence, new questions, evidence relating in part with other evidence, and a changed conclusion being that one doesn't "know" what caused the accident or who was at fault.

It isn't a neat, sequential five-step process.

Everything is at work influencing everything else and, thus, itself. What we have is not a recipe so much as a way of checking one's efforts. It is a way of being able to develop self-feedback. It allows for intuitive leaps, divergent thinking, and creativity. The important thing is being aware of what one is doing in the process of conceptualizing. This awareness frees one to meet experience in a responsible, self-correcting manner.

At the secondary level there are a number of possibilities. For example, one could give students the following data:

United States:
1. Population	204,500,000
2. Pop. density	57 per sq. mile
3. Agriculture (% of GNP)	6%
4. Life expectancy	70.5 years
5. % of GNP spent on education	7.1%
6. Urban distribution of population	70%
7. Rural distribution of population	30%

What could students do with this information? Unless there is some purpose in using the data, not very much. They could memorize the information—and give it back. It is possible that the idea of "density" might raise some questions about an abstract average and actual distribution. Life expectancy might lead to some questions about the average of 70.5 years. Is it for males? females? whites? blacks? rich? poor? In other words, the data as they stand may raise some issues in terms of clarifying what the data mean. But there is little opportunity to move into G–R concepts using *only* the data given.

Now add to the data on the United States that of the Soviet Union:

1. Population	241,700,000
2. Population density	27.8 per sq. mile
3. Agriculture (% of GNP)	16.5%
4. Life expectancy	70 years
5. % of GNP spent on education	6%
6. Urban distribution of population	55%
7. Rural distribution of population	45%

The two sets of data can be compared:
The Soviet Union has a larger total population
Life expectancies are about the same in both countries.
The Soviet Union is more "agricultural" than the U.S.
The Soviet Union spends less % GNP on education than does the U.S.

The limited data might give rise to some possible relationships. Could it be that "the more agricultural a nation, the less it will spend on education?"

With the first set of information—the data on the United States—the students are likely to mull around and ask, "So what?" or ask the teacher what they should do.

In adding the second set of data, some *comparative* functions arise and allow even the most fugitive hypotheses related to G–R concepts. These lead to the need for more data, but in obtaining the information certain kinds of questions have more value than do others. For example, the question, "Do the Soviet citizens like their government?" is not going to be of as much help as a question seeking more data dealing with the initial hypotheses: i.e., more comparative data on rural distribution of the population, percentage of GNP spent on education, population density of other countries, and so forth.

More data are solicited.

Japan has a population of 103,500,000 people. The population density is 716 per square mile; agriculture accounts for 12% of the GNP; life expectancy is 71 years; the amount of GNP spent on education is 5.8%, and population distribution is 68% urban, 32% rural.

Can we say that the more agricultural, the less percentage of the GNP is spent on education? Can we say that the greater a nation's population density, the more likely we are to find agricultural activity? What can we say, if anything? What happens if we add data from India? from Greece? from Poland? from Argentina?

New data raise new questions. New questions show the need for more data. This raises the question of pinpointing our purpose. Can we develop *any* G–R concepts in terms of industrialized nations? nations whose economy pivots on agriculture? Similarities, differences, variables, conditions, . . . testing . . . data . . . concepts . . . data . . . testing . . .

In all this activity the students can monitor their efforts and strategy in terms of purpose and purpose modification, questions, data sources and data collection, relevant and irrelevant data, reasoning, terminology, conceptualizing with qualifications, and so forth.

In looking at the "functioning system" in which the influencing variables are at work in decision-making, one senior high school class used Robert Kennedy's *Thirteen Days: A Memoir of the Cuban Missile Crisis* as a case study designed to view how decisions are made, how data are used, and how all the variables constantly interact.[11] The teacher posed a number of questions. For example:

In a day of specialization and expertise, what happens to information *before* it is made available to us?

Major decisions involve a whole complex of subdivisions. Are major decisions "made" or do they evolve?

Are decisions ever made with complete information?

Most decisions of major importance have no one simple or obvious solution. How would this temper any dogmatic position?

Perceptions and the urgency of time often play an important role in how decisions are made. In a period of swift change, is it possible to always make decisions with assurance of being "right"?

In the decisions discussed in the book, how did ego needs, perceptions, position of those involved, data, and interpretation touch upon one another and influence the process of evolving a strategy.

Students were asked to chart a "flow" of how the decision-making group functioned. From analyzing the flow, they became more aware of what kinds of things influenced the functioning of sincere, dedicated, intelligent, and informed leaders when face to face with a critical situation.

MYTH 4: ATTITUDES AND VALUES ARE AREAS OF CONCERN DISTINCT AND DIFFERENT FROM SKILL DEVELOPMENT

"The teacher and the student live in a world mad with dichotomies. The teacher is asked to teach the American experience and the values of the founding fathers. If he teaches them so well that students believe them, he is often castigated for being un-American."[12] Part of the "madness" is that the teacher and students are caught in the paradox of a world that demands that certain attitudes, values, and beliefs be accepted through verbal commitments. Yet the same world makes "pay-offs" for behavior which, at times, appear totally inconsistent with the verbal admonitions.

For teachers the paradox is compounded. Often their very entry into the teaching field is de facto acceptance of second-class citizenship and of limited personal *use* of the social studies. They often accept a self-denial of their own *individual* functioning by being excluded from practices implied by the founding fathers' Bill of Rights. Some teachers feel they should not become publicly involved with political issues as "citizens." De Toqueville's "tyranny of the majority" is implemented for a social studies teacher by the expectation that he will be a model for the young—a model in the form of an ideal citizen as deemed so by the majority, a model in the form of being a small imitation of the real thing by those holding contrary views. One looks hard and long to find schools that would dare openly to hire an agnostic or atheist, dare to have in the classroom an outspoken critic of a war, or dare to have on their payroll an advocate of a socialist economy within a cultural-democratic context. One personnel man said of interviewing social studies candidates: "You've got to be careful. These 'parlor pinks' are dangerous. My first question of any candidate is to ask what they think is the biggest problem faced by the United States. If they don't say 'big government,' then I just cut the interview short." He said this as he headed for combat with a small group of senior high school students—"some of the brighter students in the school"—who had formed a protest group!

The school does imply attitudes, values, and beliefs that are perceived as being sound, worthwhile, and absolutely necessary. The teacher of the use of social studies—whether from tradition or professional conviction—is often held responsible for "instilling" these attitudes, values, and beliefs. All are responsible, but some are more responsible than others. (One of the G–R operational concepts for teachers is that much of what man says and does is not reasonable, is often irrational, and is *not* concerned with evidence. Authority is allowed to substitute for reasoning with empirical data. But to let the kids "in on" such a concept and to have them test it against experience is considered heretical, inhuman, and subversive by many educators. We will discuss the issue of surviving within the system in a later chapter.)

What are these attitudes, values, and beliefs? They are seldom differentiated from one another and appear as clustered under: Americanism and patriotism, capitalism, a belief in God, and a commitment to work hard while adhering to the Scout Law. It is an endorsement of being an "individual" (as defined by the majority group) and an internalization of social skills—cooperating, being nice, getting along with others—the Golden Rule.

At the bottom of the clusters are Renaissance assumptions:[13] a belief in the traditional concept of reason—the world is knowable and there are universal principles that hold universally; culture is a unitary concept and not something that changes with time and place; there are "higher" and "lower" cultures but always on a linear scale; we're near the "top."

Several years ago, the NEA *Journal* discussed the issue:

> The difficulties of achieving goals relating to character have long been recognized. In the nineteenth century the school placed its principal reliance on the study of literature to form the citizen. At that time, it was widely believed that practice followed precept. The schoolbooks of that day were replete with patriotic slogans and citations, on the assumption that those who could recite them would be patriots. . . .
>
> But in the twentieth century the experience of the public

school has fully demonstrated that goals sought require considerably more than memorizing of precepts.[14]

Sandwiched in the comments was the statement that "even today there is pressure to teach [the nineteenth century way]."

On occasion, primary school children find their social studies partly in "pledging a legion to one naked (under God) individual with liberty and justice for all." We find the names of Presidents being memorized in sequence along with the phrases, "not one cent for tribute" and "I've just begun to fight." "Four score and seven years ago . . ."—not unlike "The American Eagle," "The Eternity of God," "Indolence and Want of Order," and "The Gambler's Wife" of the *Progressive Fifth Reader* of the 1850's.[15]

Much of social studies teaching deals with language on the assumption that a *statement* is a *sufficient* example for learning.

Man, in his functioning, is a "language-using creature," and "without language, nothing can be taught or learned about the past, nor about things removed from immediate observation . . . without language . . . ."[2]

With language comes logic: the application of rules to the *use* of language and to the *use* of language as applied to experience. Language and logic allow the "monitoring of meaning" through defining, relating, interpreting, explaining, justifying, evaluating, and conceptualizing.

The teacher of the use of social studies knows (and perhaps feels it is vital that his students know) that words are signs in that they point to something else; but a particular kind of signs— symbols—which are NOT direct or causal but rather creations of human convention. If the symbols are arbitrary relationships and we are *aware* of them, as not being reality itself, we can avoid (if we want to) pitfalls to disciplined and rationale discourse.[16] An applied label may be a short cut to thinking, but it may also cut off thinking.

"What distinguishes a rational from the irrational thinker is not the presence or absence of belief but the grounds on which belief is accepted."[16] We note that skills—techniques of monitoring meaning—are not exclusive of concerns with beliefs but *are* inclusive of concerns with evidence.

Thus, when one deals with language and logic as pivotal in functioning, one deals with judgmental acts. One is immersed in a process of evaluating and valuating: in values and valuing. Ennis[17] sees this process involving a number of specific functionings:

Grasping the meaning of a statement.

Judging whether there is ambiguity in a line of reasoning.

Judging whether certain statements contradict each other.

Judging whether a conclusion follows *necessarily*.

Judging whether a statement is specific enough.

Judging whether a statement is actually the application of a certain principle.

Judging whether an observation statement is reliable.

Judging whether an inductive conclusion is warranted.

Judging whether the problem has been identified.

Judging whether something is an assumption.

Judging whether a definition is adequate.

Judging whether a statement made by an alleged authority is acceptable.

In using this we note the dimensions of logic: meanings, words, statements, relationships, classifications, terms, and so forth; and the dimensions of the practical: do our functionings suit our purpose? When we act, do we have evidence and reasons for acting?

To the person satiated with signs and sounds, the *use* of symbols and the cognition of the intellectual processes involved is indeed a threat. The stable world is in jeopardy.

It must be assumed that the *entire* school and entire formal educational effort have some concern with citizenship, patriotism, affective relationships, and creativity. *The teacher of the use of social studies contributes to the total effort. He contributes things unique to his particular field of inquiry—in our case, the use of the findings about human experience.* The G–R concepts are empirical. *They deal with verifiable evidence.* The *processing* of getting, validating, modifying, testing, and using such concepts are rooted in reasonableness, in rationality, and in humility about what one does NOT know. Reasonableness is valued. Rationality is valued. Humility is valued. Concepts concerning self, learning, perceptual development, pressures, interaction variables which influence the individual in social settings and vice-versa, observation, listening, relating cognitive/affective, and so forth, are *all* cognitions that are transferable into situations involving the affective and social concerns. *These concepts are concepts used in processing the self-in-environment* and, in this sense, are integrally related with skills, attitudes and values.

Helping a person to know and to respect himself with others feeds his respect for the community—local, state, national, international—the *human* groupings.

What are human relations skills? Do we mean how to manipulate others toward our ends? or being nice and smiling and optimistic and accepting? Or do we turn to the behavioral sciences and what we think we know about generalized human behavior: fear, anger, change, habits, communication processes, trust, learning, and *test* the findings with an attitude of being willing to modify concepts and behavior if necessary? In human relations skills do we consider the differences between confrontation and encounter in terms of the verified consequences to *self and others,* or working with others with intent at blood-letting and winning at any cost or with a selfish-unselfish stake in the others being the best they can be, which thus allows us to learn and to continue to grow?

When people talk about cooperative skills, interaction skills, affective skills, decision-making skills, and work skills—do they want to play GOD in the classroom? Do they want to divine and decree from a podium *not* hammered and ground out in human experience? The findings in social science and the METHODS social scientists use to put the findings to work are what social studies teachers have to offer. Once this is understood the problem becomes one of educating the public to understand the difference.

When the METHOD—including affective/cognitive functioning—deals with identifying concerns; selecting and gathering data; determining methods of using language; creating from expression; rigorous testing of ideas, an honoring of doubt and being willing to say "I don't know" out of strength and not weakness; predicting in probabilities of sustained relationships rather than absolutes; working in terms of processes and not linear cause-effect sets; working with "structure" (relationships), open and searching for new data and leaving previous "solutions" open to change; and having no secrets, no monopolies, and no pay-offs but rather concepts and methods open to all—[18]when the method includes all these interrelated functionings, attitudes and values are implied *and* are put to work.

What attitudes?

An attitude that doesn't just accept a closed "authority"

An attitude that prompts one to modify his environment, to become involved.

An attitude that is open-minded: towards oneself, others, experience, evidence.

An attitude that seeks evidence and "controls" behavior in terms of prediction.

An attitude that is equally concerned with means and ends.

An attitude that is willing to modify its position with new data.

An attitude which allows people to act without expecting the impossible; all decisions are made from incomplete data.

An attitude which is humble but not passive.

An attitude that allows a person to respect himself (and others) in terms of what he can do and in terms of what it is difficult to do.

An attitude that stresses cooperation and sharing, not because it is the "nice" thing to do but because it allows greater and more diverse options for self and/with others.

An attitude that is committed to life as dynamic and changing.

An attitude that recognizes how human values interact and modify.

An attitude that recognizes his functioning as a human demands a climate—a social organization and political structure which serves human and humane ends.

The attitudes have one value: Human life as a creating, evolving force—a value giving honor to those things that help in the creating and evolving means, and dishonor to those things that arrest and impede human experience.

The attitudes and value apply to people, situations, ideas, and human effort.

When a parent asks that his child be taught Americanism, citizenship, and patriotism, one might ask what attitudes and behaviors beyond the ones listed would the parent include? What does a "good" citizen *do*? And what does he have to *know about* in order to help him to do? How does Americanism differ from humanism as implied by the listed attitudes? Is it an honest pride in trying to create such attitudes within the framework of one nation? Is patriotism "the defense of every abuse, every self-interest, every encrusted position of privilege in the name of love of country—when in fact it is only one of the status quo—that indeed is the lie in the soul...?"[19] Or is it indignation when a climate denies the attitudes to be at work and a love of a value and people committed to that value? What does one *do* when he shows his love? What does one need to know about in order to more effectively *do* in his loving?

There is a difference between educating and indoctrinating. That difference revolves around METHOD — the functioning subsumed in the METHOD, and the attitudes and VALUE implied. The teacher of the use of social studies offers verified and verifiable usable concepts as part *of the materials of the METHOD. The commitment is to reasonable, rational experiencing and if being a citizen, working in groups, being an American, and practicing human relations is part of that experiencing, the offer is consistent and honest.*

MYTH 5: SKILLS CAN'T BE TAUGHT — EITHER YOU HAVE THEM OR YOU DON'T

Let's *test* this concept. What questions do we ask? What data do we seek? What empirical and G–R concepts from our field challenge the myth?

How does one approach the teaching of skills? We realize that skills are *not* taught as separate entities divorced from the influence of other functions. And we realize that skills are contributors to the larger concept of METHOD: ways of operating on data and experience.

In our case THE WHOLE IS GREATER THAN THE SUM OF ITS PARTS because it includes a number of *interacting processes* which go beyond any label for any one activity, i.e., observing, or inductive reasoning.

The objective is NOT necessarily to get rid of all existing thought habits. Many are useful and should be reinforced. But the method allows us to be ready to revise; our ability to function makes us flexible and adaptive creatures who are not trapped into habitual responses. Robert Thouless, in his *How to Think Straight*,[20] comments that unless we use our potential, our brains will degenerate into mere mechanisms.

The same question is raised when we are asked to suppose that, if it were perfectly certain that the life and fortune of each of us would, eventually, depend on our winning or losing a game of chess, would we consider it a primary duty to learn at least the names and moves of the pieces; to have some idea about the strategy, and a decided knowledge about the means of giving and getting out of "check"? Would we look with scorn upon a father who allowed his son to grow up without knowing a pawn from a knight?

It's not a bad comparison. Our life chances do depend, to a degree, upon our knowledge of workable tools, the strategy of how to use them, and our ability not to be "checked" in our pursuits.

We would suggest that we *at least* bring the tools in the over-all "game" to the cognitive level, name them if we have to, and provide some experience in their use in the "give and take" strategy under "game" conditions.

With this in mind, and realizing that the tools we want to sharpen are to be used in monitoring and improving experience, *why not share the tools, terms, and functions with the students so that they can be referred to and used in the strategy, so that they become habits of attitude and function?* We provide "log" tables to students in mathematics, element charts to chemistry students, dictionaries to students in language arts, and income-tax tables to adults; why not a "tool table" or a "strategy sheet" to social studies students? This is for reference for students.

Why not use the conceptual basis for such tools as G–R concepts in strategy? Why not explore the nature of the "piece"— its functions and limitations. We know that each G–R concept has a host of more limited G–R subconcepts and, as they are put to use, more skill and conceptualizing will be needed.

Why not use the given "table" or "sheet" with the concepts to help to determine and to monitor and to *evaluate* strategy?

Initially we might work with students in establishing a reference base for reflecting upon strategy. Let's label this "Amber (Caution) Thoughts": this establishes an initial reference in TERMS OF WHAT WE KNOW WE DON'T KNOW: thus, the caution signals.

"AREAS" OF FUNCTIONING

AMBER (CAUTION) THOUGHTS[21]	IMPORTANCE
1. SO FAR AS I KNOW	This is a reminder of incomplete knowledge and thus helps us to keep our eyes open for more information.
2. UP TO A POINT	We can't fully describe everything. We can to a degree, and this helps us to know we are working with only some characteristics.
3. TO ME	There are other points of view. The judgments we make reflect our own wants and desires. It is dangerous to assume others see it the same way.
4. THE SAME BUT DIFFERENT	A man 1 and man 2 are similar in some ways, different in others.

	Situation 1 and situation 2 may have some things in common but they also are different.
5. TIME	Things change. What was true at one time may no longer be true. There is a need to constantly re-evaluate what might have happened.
6. SITUATION	The same person or thing in a new situation may change behavior as there is interaction with the changes.
7. MY WORLD	Meanings change with time, people, and situations.

What do we have? Under the "Importance" column are G–R concepts. The "Amber Thoughts" column lists words which *cue* us to the more elaborated concepts. The words we call "Cue Concepts." Either we can give the list to students and ask them to set up a strategy for testing the validity of the concepts, or we can provide specific cases to illustrate each concept and ask them to derive the G–R relationship. Either way, the key caution in regard to METHOD has been introduced.

Bruner writes, "A child is able to go beyond the information that has been given to generate additional ideas that either can be checked immediately from experience or can, at least, be used as a basis for formulating reasonable hypotheses. But, over and beyond that . . . success and failure are not reward and punishment but information."[22] Our approach to establishing a tool table or strategy sheet is not to test and evaluate and grade in the conventional sense; rather, it is to help the student to devise a means for obtaining information about himself, for self-evaluation. His successes and failures do not earn gold medals or derision, but are self-monitoring information. We are told that a child is realistic when he can make a sensible, accurate, practical appraisal of the potentialities and limits of objects, situations, people, and himself.[23] And, we might add, of his own strategy.

STRATEGIES FOR TEACHING SKILLS

We have discussed the need for the teaching of skills and how "myths" prevent this from happening. If the myths are not functional, the question is, "How does one go about teaching skills?" Following are five ingredients to be kept in mind in developing strategies for teaching skills.

FRAME OF REFERENCE

One's own frame of reference—his assumptions and pre-dispositions—acts as a screen in approaching a new situation, selecting and using data, and so forth. Being aware of one's own "set" at least keeps some options open and helps to qualify interpretations. For example, in testing the concept that all societies exhibit some means of ranking and judging people, a high school student, himself an integral participant in a subclass society—the school—has viewed and been influenced by the divisions: "collegiates," "jocks," nonacademics, and so forth. Depending upon where he finds himself, his life style is definitely influenced: dating patterns, grades, associates, friends, dress, speech, wheels, roles, expected behavior, school pay-offs—all feed his outlook. He brings to a study of social class structure a set of experiences which influence and perhaps impede his functioning. A teacher discussing "separation of powers" may find different kinds of student presets: one youngster thinks of the coach separating the "men from the boys"; another faces a "separation" of parents at home; another has a friend with a shoulder "separation," and still another student may be involved with black power.

We are by no means suggesting the need for an in-depth psychological study of each student. We *are* suggesting that students need to be made to realize (and we need to realize) that they never enter a new situation empty handed. This realization and the ability to identify what is *brought* to a given situation may lead to more effective functioning.

SPECIFIC PURPOSE

Identification of a *specific* purpose for a particular study or inquiry moves one away from nonsystematic and random experiencing to an awareness level of what specific types of activity might pay off. For example, one might present students with the following data:

a large piece of paper	a piece of cardboard
a ruler	a paintbrush
a pencil	some water colors
a pen	a sketch pad
an eraser	a page of notes
a book	a clip board
	some lined paper

One might ask the students to classify the articles and to place them into categories. Or one might ask, "How many different categories can you evolve from the above list? Can you group according to size, shape, function?" But the teacher must ask, "Why the effort in the first place?"

QUESTIONING

The mere phrasing of a question is an attempt to bring or to suggest more clarity in a statement or situation. A question suggests that certain relationships do exist, could exist, or could not exist. And the question or questions can be used to guide inquiry: asking more specific questions, focusing upon certain kinds of data, the making of tentative hypotheses. Asking questions is not so easy as it sounds.

There are different kinds of functions implied by different kinds of questions. A "who, what, when, and where" barrage of questions posed by a teacher or student is like a bank statement: it is designed to find out what's in the "pot." In social studies classes, such techniques are often only reading checks or recall checks: "What did the general say when he accepted surrender?"; "Name the chief products of Spain"; "When was the Declaration of Independence signed?" Such questions are safe and comfortable and require "the least amount of thinking or understanding."[24]

Obviously, different kinds of questions can be identified. Some questions bring immediate closure and restrict opportunities to be creative and exploratory. Some do not allow responses that give factual information. Some ask for an opinion or a revelation of another person's psychological "set." Others open the door for finding and using data, and some point to a need to operationally define terms in order to communicate.

The following was used with students:

WHAT IS THE DIFFERENCE BETWEEN THE FOLLOWING QUESTIONS ONE MIGHT ASK OF A SOCIAL SCIENTIST?

1. What is the best form of government?
2. How many people of voting age and qualification voted in the last national elections?
3. Are laws good?
4. Why do we have so many homicides?
5. How many murders did we have before legislation out-

lawing murder was passed? How many since? What other factors besides the law might have influenced the data?

6. Is this person a good citizen?
7. What is the purpose of this piece of legislation?
8. Does this piece of legislation have some other purposes?
9. Is the population density of this city greater than it was before mass transit was inaugurated?
10. How does a poor person feel?
11. What things inspire the mayor to be honest and reliable?
12. What would happen if we had a national minimum income?
13. Why are the unemployed so lazy?
14. What are some of the considerations in determining where urban renewal efforts will be initiated?
15. Why does permissive education lead to so much discontent?
16. Why did "X" use "grass"? He knows it is illegal!
17. Why do we suddenly have so much violence on the American scene?
18. Are there any indications that violence has been a part of the American heritage?
19. Does history repeat itself?
20. How do the United States and the Soviet Union compare when it comes to their standards of living?
21. How do you define the "establishment"?

THE TYPE OF QUESTION ASKED SOMETIMES DETERMINES THE TYPE OF ANSWER OR RESPONSE MADE. AN ANSWER OR RESPONSE CAN BE TESTED ONLY IF THERE IS A WAY BY WHICH YOU CAN VERIFY. WHAT QUESTIONS LISTED ABOVE WOULD HAVE TO BE CHANGED IN ORDER TO BE ABLE TO "CHECK" THE RESPONSE? HOW WOULD YOU CHANGE THE QUESTIONS?

RELEVANT AND IRRELEVANT INFORMATION

One must establish some criterion for screening and sifting needed data. Knowing one's frame of reference, purposes, and questions helps to establish a workable criterion.

The following was used with intermediate level students as a way of noting how a criterion is established and why it functions to help to solve problems:

YOU ARE FACED WITH A PROBLEM. THERE IS A
STREAM. YOU ARE ON ONE SIDE AND YOU WANT TO
GET TO THE OTHER SIDE AS SOON AS YOU CAN.
PUT A CHECK MARK NEXT TO THE STATEMENT OF
INFORMATION WHICH WOULD HELP YOU TO SOLVE
YOUR PROBLEM.

1. There is a bridge which has collapsed.
2. The water is too deep to wade across.
3. You can't swim.
4. You are by yourself.
5. The temperature is below freezing.
6. It is a pretty day.
7. There are plans to rebuild the bridge.
8. There is a boat tied to a tree but you don't own the boat.
9. There are wooden planks on the ground.
10. You will eat lunch when you get to the other side.

This is fun to work with. Students are asked to work individually and to record what they feel to be important information
and why? Then they pool their efforts with one another. Frames
of reference are shared: How important is my getting across?
I almost drowned once fooling around water. There's no harm in
taking the boat as long as you don't harm it. Questions were posed:
How wide is the stream? Has the bridge collapsed completely?
Are you expecting anyone else to come along? With new data
coming from the questions and the pertinence of existing data,
the collecting and discarding takes place with reasoning.

This framework can be transferred to such problem areas as
pollution, political campaigning, passing a school bond issue.
Students can be asked to structure a "relevant/irrelevant" model
of their own, using data involved in a particular area of study.
This helps them to analyze and clarify their own thinking processes.

LANGUAGE

Language serves communication functions, is man-made and
culture-given. Language and thought patterns are intricately
woven, and if a person is concerned with meanings, a crucial
awareness of function, source, and use of language is necessary.
Man translates his direct experience into symbols, and the symbols then become influential in his subsequent interacting with
experience. He lives in an "abstracted" world of words.

When a student is asked to classify, relate, generalize, predict—to think—these activities are done in a context actually removed from direct experience. He is asked, most of the time, to do all these things *with* symbols.

The nature of, type of, and use of symbols, conceptually, is necessary to work with logic. Why have rules when there is no way to differentiate players and what they do? How does one officiate such a "game"—other than making random decisions here and there?

When we teach concepts, we usually refer to the teaching of symbols. When we talk about "skill development," it usually refers to the manipulation of symbols. We trust that somehow and sometime the symbols can be translated and used in direct experience.

If we want to let students in on the monitoring of language, its various uses, and in its implications for thought and for logical use, there are a number of approaches that can be used.

There are concepts about the *development* of symbols which can be a specific part of a social studies program—concepts that stress the point that words are *not* the thing they stand for; the map is not the terrain. Mark Twain's story about Adam and Eve naming the animals in the Garden of Eden has been used with primary youngsters. Told as a story, it leads to all sorts of fun questions about language when Eve tells Adam that she wants to name the furry, hopping, long-eared little animal a "rabbit" because it looks like one; or the question, What would happen if we called the "moon" the "sun"? One might explore what could happen on "the day all communication stopped" in order to stress how important symbols are to man and how important it is for man to use them wisely.

In working with symbol cognition and use, there is a natural move into the logical functions of language. The question of classification is raised when one knows that American 1 is not American 2, and this skill allows the student to move into the analysis of collective terms such as American, fascist, human.

Word symbols are the "meat and potatoes" around which the rest of the "meal" we experience fits.

When we suggest bringing to the cognitive level the concepts about language and symbols within the "content" of social studies, we are often told two things: (1) the English and/or language arts department will handle this; or (2) it is too difficult for young children to work with.

The responses are relatively simple. If one relates content with skills, then "skill concepts" cannot be left to someone else. Children, you will recall, are living in a world of developing and using language—of classifying, differentiating, using, and testing symbols in all sorts of learning experiences.

If we expand the concept of content to include methods of working on content, we find countless opportunities to directly confront the area of language.

A group of third grade teachers had worked with stories of the Pilgrims and of Thanksgiving rituals but were concerned that the word "freedom" was used by everyone in a loose way. The following lesson emerged:

> Concept: Freedom involves the range of choices one has in creating his own life.
>
> Concept: Making choices involves thinking about what one values, desires, and wants.
>
> Motivation Case Studies:
>
> > A. You are hungry. You walk into a drugstore. You can have either an ice cream cone or nothing to eat. Although there are 20 flavors of ice cream, you can have only chocolate or vanilla.
> >
> > Question: What does this have to do with freedom? (Responses: In a way, you're free. You have *some* choice.)
> >
> > B. You come into a strange town. You are hungry. You ask someone where a restaurant is. He looks at your skin color and says that you can eat in restaurant "A" or in restaurant "B." But there are 10 other restaurants.
> >
> > Question: What does this have to do with freedom? (Response: It's wrong. But there is *some* freedom. There is a choice.)

The teachers helped the children to note what they had said about freedom: It involved people having choices.

It involved a question of how much (range).

The teachers then reviewed the Thanksgiving story and there was discussion about the use of the word "freedom." A quotation from King James I was distributed (and the class members read it aloud).

"KINGS ARE LIKE GOD. IF YOU THINK OF WHAT GOD CAN DO, YOU CAN THINK OF WHAT A KING CAN DO. FOR EXAMPLE, A KING CAN DO ANYTHING WITH HIS PEOPLE. HE CAN MAKE THEM A SUCCESS OR HE CAN MAKE THEM A FAILURE. HE CAN JUDGE WHETHER OR NOT WHAT PEOPLE DO IS RIGHT. BUT NO PERSON SHALL JUDGE THE KING. A KING'S PEOPLE ARE LIKE CHESS PIECES AND THE KING IS LIKE A CHESS PLAYER. HE DECIDES THE MOVES. HE DECIDES WHAT PEOPLE WILL DO. THE PEOPLE SHOULD SERVE THE KING. NO PERSON IS TO CHANGE THE GOVERN- MENT. THE GOVERNMENT IS THE KING'S RESPONSI- BILITY."

The members of the classes discussed what the quotation meant to them, and what it would be like to live with someone else telling you what to do all the time and not being able to change things. Who said that? James I. Who was he? King of England. Not today. When did he say that?

The teacher writes on the board: James I — — 1609. Who re- members the date when the Pilgrims landed at Plymouth? 1620. Did 1609 come before or after 1620? Oh!

The teacher passes out another quotation from James:

I WILL MAKE THEM DO WHAT I WANT THEM TO DO. IF THEY DO NOT, I WILL MAKE THEM LEAVE THE COUNTRY

The class then has the elements of freedom listed on the board. Also, there is a small sequence time line: 1609......1620. And there are the quotations. A reconstruction of the Pilgrim experience follows and rests on the issue of why the Pilgrims left England to travel to other lands.

A new date is added.

1609 .... 1620 1658

A new quotation is given and read aloud.

NO QUAKER AND NO PERSON WHO IS OPPOSED TO THE ONLY RIGHT WAY TO WORSHIP CAN BE A MEM- BER OF THE COLONY.

Please note the flow.

The lesson pivots on the term "freedom" and the phases of

the lesson are aimed at (1) viewing the term as an activity not as an abstraction, (2) learning that a "meaning" is not absolute, (3) how meaning is related to situations, (4) the use of simple "story" case studies to raise issues, (5) the use of rephrased primary source quotations, (6) the use of a limited sequence time line (before and after), (7) seeing "freedom" related with "authority," and (8) the use of a previously studied "topic" to move into the issue of language.

This particular lesson was taught in a "bright" third grade *and* in a so-called "slow" third grade. In *both* classes the youngsters brought the question of "freedom" to their own community, to problems some of them actually faced.

There are the inclusion words: all, never, everyone, cognition of which leads into inductive and deductive reasoning as well as analysis.

Using the following two statements, what could you do to develop language and symbol awareness?

The Declaration of Independence was written in 1776. It is the best document on democracy ever written. The people received the news of the signing with great joy.

  a. Can the date of signing be verified?
  b. "best" — unfinished word.
  c. What other documents on democracy were written — best in terms of what?
  d. "democracy"?
  e. "The people" — *all* the people?

A wise man once said, "A thing that is worth doing at all is worth doing well." Boys and girls need to learn to do their best at everything they do. Those who learn that are the ones who grow up to do great things for our world.

The problem of language and symbols is not new. Francis Bacon talked of "ill and unfit" words which obstruct understanding and lead to controversy. "For men believe that their reason governs words; but it is also true that words react on the understanding." The awareness of this is crucial for teaching. We can no longer assume that thinking depends on laws of reason and rules of logic held common by all humans. Nor can we assume that all the laws and rules are imprinted by nature into human mental machinery. We can no longer assume that human languages are parallel systems for sharing the inner thoughts grounded in a universal language called logic.[25] Language with thought—thought with language.

Ross and Van Den Haag write of four basic errors in thinking about and using words: failure to recognize that meanings are assigned; failure to realize that words have no innate power to influence things; failure to realize that words may NOT be like their referents; and failure to realize that some words may stand for "things" *not* open to sense experience.[9]

These basic errors can provide some of the background for exploring with students how to be aware of the relationships between language and thought.

Schopenhauer threw out the challenge: "In learning any foreign language, you form new concepts, you discover relationships you didn't realize before, innumerable nuances, similarities, differences enter your mind; you get a rounded view of everything. Which means that you think differently in every language, that learning a language modifies and colors your thinking, corrects and improves your views, and increases your think skill, *since it will more and more detach your ideas from your words.*"[26]

If we assume all language is foreign—including our own—and if we take care in how we learn and use it, it should assist our being able to monitor ourselves.

THINKING RULES

We have a tendency to think of rules as being restricting, as being negative. Theoretically rules exist to help to structure a situation (society, family, bridge club) in which man can effectively and efficiently achieve desirable ends. Rules may apply to simple things like games or to very serious business such as living. Thinking is part of that serious business and there are rules which apply to the use of language, to the use of symbols employed in communication. These rules we call logic or the rules of reasoning.

Most of us use prediction in our daily lives as a means of surviving. We do this habitually, and often fail to realize the importance we actually grant to the rules. The rules we are talking about are not abstract formal logic but, rather, what could be called "living logic."

Living logic is simply trying to make sense out of our experiences in a consistent manner. Assuming the ideas we have influence what we do, and assuming that what one does not know also influences what we do (by narrowing the range of effective options), each human has a vested interest in applying the rules to the best of his ability in order to function effectively.

Logic is a way of relating statements in such a way that other statements can be related. Logic deals with language, with symbols that have already been put into some grammatical order of relationships. The rules of logic work with language.

The two general patterns of working with language are DE-DUCTIVE and INDUCTIVE.

In DEDUCTIVE reasoning we start *not* with observable facts but rather with statements. We start with a premise or first statement and then proceed to reason from this point.

All government officials are corrupt.

John is a government official

Therefore, John is corrupt.

This is *analytical*. And the reasoning is not concerned with "right" or "wrong" but only with the *process* of reasoning which, in this case, is valid. The reasoning is valid, but the conclusion may not, in fact, be true. In DEDUCTIVE REASONING, one can monitor whether the statements follow one another and are consistent. One can also question the initial statement and, in so doing, question the whole line of reasoning. If the initial premise does not hold up, who cares if the reasoning is valid?

Part of logic is identifying the basic premise. We have seen a group of high school seniors subjected to intensive indoctrination techniques in fascist ideology. The seniors constantly tried to attack the internal consistency of the reasoning which, in this case, was immune to this kind of approach. Although they were greatly concerned, the seniors could not defeat the ideology in terms of intellectual components. Not one student, however, questioned the initial premise upon which every other conclusion was built!

Mathematics is an excellent example of an analytical deductive system. Axioms provide the basic premises. These are man-made definitions of relationships and *not* subject to proof. The axioms are "givens" to be accepted. From a few such axioms a whole system of relationships can be deduced—relationships that *necessarily* follow one another. Mathematics becomes a prime example of the use of deductive reasoning: Given a premise, do other statements of relationship necessarily follow according to the internal rules of logic? If one challenges the major premise, an elaborate internal consistency may be of no consequence. We note that one can establish, within a deductive framework, an entire system of valid, related statements *without* having to verify any of the statements with observable phenomena.

INDUCTIVE reasoning, on the other hand, is based NOT upon a generalized premise which embraces subparticulars and subspecifics, but on *observed phenomena*, on empirical data.

Stone A is round.
Stone B is round.
Stone C is round.
All the stones in this area are round.
All stones on this continent are round.
All stones are round.

In this case one took specific U–N concepts and related them into levels of G–R concepts: from one, to some, to many, to a universal "all."

It becomes rather obvious that one never has *all* the observable facts and, thus, any conclusion inferred from using an inductive reasoning process does NOT allow a guarantee that the conclusion will remain true or be true in every case. It is open to change and to modification. To have a universal conclusion is impossible until *every specific case* has been and will be observed.

As we noted earlier, the clear division between deductive reasoning (formal logic and mathematics) and inductive reasoning does not, in fact, exist when we view human thinking/functioning. As with science, human thinking/functioning is a "system" in which both kinds of reasoning are interrelated and mutually influencing.

The processes used by scholars to construct the "bodies of content" we use in school *combine* deductive and inductive reasoning. Observations are noted, worked with inductively and developed at various G–R levels. These G–R concepts are used, and they are tested. In the testing process more facts are observed and related and there are recycling efforts. Our knowledge is cumulative and open to modification and change. A particular U–N concept—a statement about a particular—is valuable in leading to general propositions. Induction makes sense only within principles allowing deductive reasoning: transfer and use.

The use of U–N and development of G–R concepts must be viewed as a total and interrelated system. To present a number of specifics (U–N concepts) and ask the student to take those specifics and form a G–R concept is an inductive process, or what some call "discovery" learning. But to stop there is insufficient. The G–R concept must be tested (deductive) by gathering additional U–N concepts to support the "discovered" concept. To present four historical examples of external threat to a nation which have led to an increased feeling of nationalism in a given country, may lead the student to discover or induce the G–R concept that, "when a nation is threatened externally the threatened nation becomes increasingly nationalistic." This may be validated with additional data, but may also be refuted. Has the Vietnam war increased nationalism in the United States? Indeed, the student may find sufficient data to refute his discovery. This is a deductive process. If we view this systematically it can be seen that the teacher should not be concerned with only inductive or only deductive learning but with both. Regardless of where one starts in the process, the cycle can continue. If the student is *given* a generalization (G–R concept) and asked to find instances to support such a claim, he is being asked to reason deductively. The data he collects, however, may allow him to formulate new generalizations and thus he operates inductively. The process of learning, be it inductive or deductive, is thus necessarily tied to content-data. To talk about whether one is a teacher of "process" or teacher of "content" is simplistic and misses the complexity of the teaching-learning endeavor.

Students should be made aware of the difference between "emotive" and "informational" or cognitive statements. Students should be made aware that some statements allow for testing—some observations would prove it true and some observations might suggest caution. Knowing the difference between strictly analytical statements (closed statements by definition) and empirical statements (open to being verified) allows one to apply significant methods of use. Knowing when a conclusion does not logically follow from the data on hand, or that because something precedes something else it does not mean that one *causes* the other, is important.

The rules of thinking/functioning focus on creating and testing relationships. To conceptualize that common characteristics of parts may not infer the same characteristic to the whole—"the whole is greater than the sum of its parts"—helps in monitoring. To conceptualize that characteristics of the whole may not be the identical characteristic of subsumed parts and to conceptualize *how* concepts are made lead to realistic expectations of how they may effectively be used.[27]

NONWORD SYMBOLS

Increasing amounts of data and concepts are being presented in forms other than printed words. For example, tables of quantified data are materials to be used; there are charts, pictures, graphs, slides, television, and so forth.

The *same* cognitions are applicable to these different forms. The forms allow students to put the cognitions to work and to allow functional transfer of skill concepts from one source form to another.

For example, elementary statistics are frightening to many people. But if we view quantified material as a collection, classification, cataloging, and conceptualizing of numerical facts (U–N concepts in different form), we can note opportunities to apply and to use skill concepts.

Every time a student makes and interprets maps, works with trends in population growth or pollution, migration, industrialization, and so forth, he is using some form of data put into numerical form.

The following is a lesson used with intermediate level students:

Major Concept: Planning one's own behavior depends upon how one is able to anticipate or predict what he believes *will* happen.

Skill Concept: Sometimes information comes to us in numbers. The numbers are "facts" and can be used.

Skill Concept: To predict or to anticipate one must think about what has happened in the past, the knowledge one has, and things that might change what has happened in the past.

Students are initially asked to give examples of how they predict things and how this makes a difference in what they do.

The class is told to assume that it is a planning commission for City "X." They are meeting to plan for the number of schools that the city should have. One member of the "commission" brings in the following information (duplicated and passed out):

Population of City X: 100,000 people.

Population Growth		*Number of Schools*
1960	50,000 people	10 schools
1961	60,000 people	11 schools
1962	62,000 people	11 schools
1963	65,000 people	11 schools
1964	66,000 people	11 schools
1965	70,000 people	12 schools

Population Growth		*Number of Schools*
1966.................75,000 people...................12 schools
1967.................78,000 people...................12 schools
1968.................85,000 people...................12 schools
1969.................90,000 people...................12 schools
1970.................100,000 people..................12 schools

The teacher and the students put the above information into other forms:

1. Chart   100
              90
   Population: 80
              70
              60
              50
   Year: '60 '61 '62 '63 '64 '65 '66 '67 '68 '69 '70
              12
   Schools   11
              10

2. Cartoons depicting the situation (cartoons of overcrowded schools, youngsters on the streets, students not having any knowledge, etc.)

The teacher poses a question: Taking the information we have, do we citizens of City X need more schools?
Response: Resounding "Yes"

The teacher says that *she* really isn't sure, and raises these questions:
What does the information say?
What does the information NOT tell you?
For example, where in the information does it say more children will be going to school?

After raising and discussing these issues, there is a transfer. Suppose the students were the principal of their school. And suppose the principal was told that 100 new people moved into the school district and that she should go out and hire four new teachers. What questions would you want answered before you would hire four new teachers?
(How many of the people were school-age children, what grades would they attend, would some go to parochial school, and so forth.)

A census was being taken at this time, and this was used as a vehicle. What is a census? Why have one? What questions are asked? What is the importance of the answers to the questions?

It was an interesting lesson. When asked to put the data into different form to present to the public, the students drew cartoons dealing *not* with the data but with the "big jump" conclusions. One student challenged the cartoons by asking what if all the people moving into the city were old?

Senior high school students are being confronted more and more with quantified data: polls, budget representations, and so forth.

The same skill concepts can be applied to quantified form as to written statements and to observed phenomena.

SYNTHESIS AND PROLOGUE

Facts don't always speak for themselves. They must be worked over and, in a sense, created into meaning. Skills are seen as tools which assist one to do the working over and the creating. No matter what form an experience takes, the one interacting with the experience brings a generalized pattern of functioning which allows some transaction to take place. The more one becomes aware of how he functions, what he does, and what he may do, the more likely he is to be able to be effective and efficient in the processing experience.

The forms in which experiences are encountered or presented may vary. This does not imply that there are distinct and separate skills to be used with each form. There is no neat progression or step-by-step model which will necessarily teach a youngster how to function with his experience. Instead of teaching youngsters how to think or how to function, teaching (and learning) may do well to focus on monitoring functioning—something which youngsters do even before entering the school.

A teacher encounters a number of myths when approaching skill development with students and within the school situation. The myths are powerful and sometimes appear as part of the conventional "wisdom"; for example, that a student must be a good reader to do well in social studies, or that values and valuing are distinct from skill development.

Students can be taught to self-monitor their own functioning with experience and can become aware that concepts and skills relate functionally. It is suggested that the teacher confront students with the issues involved in skill development.

"Skill" is an elusive term. It stands for a number of interrelated activities which include values, symbols, reasoning, questioning, and a number of affective variables.

If one is to teach concepts, then a strategy for sharpening the tools used to create, to test, to shape, and to modify experience must be a permeating aspect of the planning.

Where to? If one recognizes various kinds of concepts, is aware of a broadened view of skill development, and has wrestled with the *ends* to which he wishes to apply content, then the sign points to the need to determine the *means* or vehicles which will allow one to work with concept and skill development. We encounter the term "content," but as a means rather than an end—something to be used rather than a product to be consumed just because it is there.

REFERENCES

1. Dewey, John: *How We Think*. Boston, D. C. Heath Co., 1933.
2. Smith, B. Othanel: Logic, thinking, and teaching. Educational Theory, October, 1957.
3. Carpenter, Helen McCracken (ed.): Skill Development in Social Studies. 33rd Yearbook, NCSS, 1963.
4. Parsons, Theodore W., and Schaftel, Fannie R.: Thinking and inquiry: Some critical issues. *In* Fair, Jean, and Shaftel, Fannie R. (eds.): Effective Thinking in the Social Studies. 37th Yearbook, NCSS, 1967.
5. Crutchfield, Richard S.: Nurturing the cognitive skills of productive thinking. *In* Rubin, Louis J. (ed.): Life Skills in School and Society. ASCD Yearbook, 1969.
6. Jarolimek, John: The psychology of skill development. *In* Carpenter, Helen McCracken (ed.): Development in Social Studies. 33rd Yearbook, NCSS, 1963.
7. Fay, Leo C.: The relationship between specific reading skills and selected areas of sixth grade achievement. Journal of Educational Research, March, 1950.
8. Getting Ready to Read Workbook. Pittsburgh, Stanwix House, Inc., 1962.
9. Ross, Ralph, and Van Den Haag, Ernest: The Fabric of Society. New York, Harcourt, Brace and World, 1957.
10. Merton, Robert K.: Behavior patterns of scientists. American Scholar, Spring, 1969.
11. Kennedy, Robert: Thirteen Days: A Memoir of the Cuban Missile Crisis. New York. W. W. Norton Company, 1969.
12. Gordon, Edward J.: Conflicting values in the secondary school. Yale Alumni Magazine, January, 1963.
13. Schrag, Peter: The end of the great tradition. Saturday Review, February 15, 1969.
14. The role of the schools in developing social responsibility in a free society. NEA Journal, November, 1963.
15. Town, Salem, and Holbrook, Nelson M.: The Progressive Fifth or Elocutionary Reader. Boston, Sanborn, Carter, Bazin Co., 1856.
16. Sherwood, John C.: Discourse of Reason: A Brief Handbook of Semantics and Logic. New York, Harper and Row, 1960.
17. Ennis, Robert H.: A concept of critical thinking. Harvard Educational Review: Breakthrough to Better Teaching, 1967.
18. Chase, Stuart: The Proper Study of Mankind. New York, Harper Colophon Books, Harper and Row, 1963.
19. Stevenson, Adlai E.: The hard kind of patriotism. Harper's, July, 1963.
20. Thouless, Robert: How to Think Straight. New York, Simon and Schuster, 1950.
21. Keyes, Kenneth S., Jr.: How to Develop Your Thinking Ability. New York, McGraw-Hill Book Co., 1963.
22. Bruner, Jerome S.: On Knowing, Essays for the Left Hand. Cambridge, Harvard University Press, 1962.
23. Murphy, Lois Barclay: Self-management capacities in children. *In* Frazier, Alexander (ed.): New Insights and the Curriculum. ASCD Yearbook, 1963.

24. Adell, Marian Young: The art of questioning. NERA Newsletter, Spring, 1964. (New England Reading Association, Oreno, Maine.)
25. Chase, Stuart: How language shapes our thoughts. Harper's, April, 1954.
26. As quoted in Rudolph Flesch, *The Art of Clear Thinking*, Harper & Bros., New York, 1951, p. 49.
27. We have found two excellent resources that can be used with students: Hy Ruchlis's *Clear Thinking* (Harper & Row, New York, 1962,) and Kenneth S. Keye, Jr.'s, How. To Develop Your Thinking Ability, do a sophisticated job in an unsophisticated way. Highly readable, interesting, and practical. Student response is good. Both help in providing a cognitive base from which to work (7th through 12th grades).

"It's a blend of ground meats and tasty gravies appetizingly poured over a shingle."

(By George Booth. Reproduced by special permission of PLAYBOY magazine. Copyright © 1971 by PLAYBOY.)

7

VEHICLE SELECTION

"... Use a little wine."

... Upon this gifted age, in its dark hour
Raining from the sky of a meteoric shower
of facts ... they lie unquestioned, uncombined.
Wisdom enough to each of us our ill
Is daily spun, but there exists no loom
To weave it into fabric."

EDNA S. VINCENT MILLAY

WHAT WE TEACH *IS* IMPORTANT!

There are teachers who are "crammers" and teachers who are "lovers" and the battle between the two goes on in practically every school in the country.

The crammer is the teacher who is the fact worshipper. His daily pilgrimage is to the well of data. His converts, like squirrels in the fall, gather their sustenance for later use. The crammer may recognize the need for the loom on which the fabric of knowledge is woven and the importance of both to the lives of his students, but he is not a constructionist nor is he a weaver. In a sense, he is a sower of seed. He broadcasts his seeds and walks away from the garden. It is out of his hands. His task is done.

The lover, on the other hand, does his missionary work by preaching kindness, decency, and goodness. He *is* the loom. He works at producing a synthetic fabric but cares little for facts or for raw materials other than sheer emotion. A reductionist by commitment, his followers are emotionally blackmailed into a simplistic social study of the golden rule. He offers a faithful model of the world in the form of a bowl of cherries—pitless. His loom is a set of blinders.

Administrators are quite pragmatic in their tolerance of both advocates and mediate the contest by saying that "we need both." In a way, we do.

Both satisfy some segment of the public. One can parade as

the academician; the other as a nice guy who cares about students. And the administrator can use them as examples of a "well balanced" staff. The remainder of the teachers usually fall someplace on a continuum between the two extremes.

It should be noted that both the crammer and the lover are in basic agreement on one fundamental issue: It doesn't make much difference *what* one teaches. Both are indiscriminate in what they select to be used by students, implying that a teacher just "puts something in" and somehow it will all work out—into something.

Unfortunately, the "put something in" kind of thinking has been reinforced. It has been intimated that the teaching processes are the thing! Emphasis has been placed on the How, and Why; What has been assumed. What, Why, and How are necessarily related.

At a State Social Studies Conference, a program participant came prepared. He brought a can of French cut green beans which he placed on the podium for all to observe. He accepted the group's apparent premise that if a teacher taught "conceptually" and gave an emphasis to skills development, it didn't make much difference what the subject matter was. You could pick "any old thing" out of the broad area of social studies and do the job. "As a matter of fact," he said, "I would go one step further. I would argue (in a philosophic sense) that a single *object*—such as this can of beans—could serve effectively for establishing the subject matter for teaching social studies for a K through 12 program."

VEHICLES

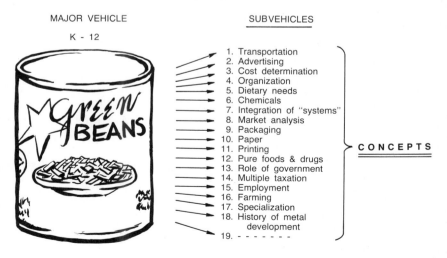

MAJOR VEHICLE

K - 12

SUBVEHICLES

1. Transportation
2. Advertising
3. Cost determination
4. Organization
5. Dietary needs
6. Chemicals
7. Integration of "systems"
8. Market analysis
9. Packaging
10. Paper
11. Printing
12. Pure foods & drugs
13. Role of government
14. Multiple taxation
15. Employment
16. Farming
17. Specialization
18. History of metal
    development
19. - - - - - -

CONCEPTS

He asked the conferees to determine what kinds of "things" they could teach about the can of beans. With the use of a little imagination, the group came up with a number of *related* "topics."

After some time was spent listing the possibilities, one of the "no-matter-what" advocates stated from the floor that the whole presentation was a "big put-on." "Sure, you *could* use a can of beans, but aren't there more important things we could use, even knowing that the concepts are the same?" he questioned.

The point was made. The term "more important" suggested that choices should be made and that some things are more valuable to use with students than others. Although not necessarily ends in themselves, the fact of inclusion implies a great deal.

Yes, one *could* use a can of beans. Whether a can of beans *should* be used is a different issue. The "subject" one selects "to teach" implies to the student what the school and the teacher believe to be important; it implies values. A choice in this area is a choice at the implementation level and lays bare an implied value system. It is no longer possible to "hide" in the gentle verbal oasis of abstract plans.

CONTENT AS A VEHICLE

At this point we get into one of the biggest hang-ups in teaching. In our metaphorical excursions and in our dispositions to use analogies and similes, we cause ourselves much sorrow. The term "content" is one such sorrow. The term implies something that is contained within a specified set of limits. The term implies being "inside" and, as such, implies a container. For example, social studies may be a container; American history may be content. But American history is a container within a container and the date 1776 may be content, and so on. The key point, however, is that of implied closure to the whole effort. The emphasis is upon an entity, a thing, and leaves little room for processes and openness.

In Chapter 5 we noted that there are different kinds of concepts serving different functions. Some are more instrumental than others; that is, some have a greater probability of being used as analytical frameworks in subsequent activities. In Chapter 6 we used an approach to skills which allows the identification of specific factors involved in retrieving and in manipulating data into conceptual "organizations." It was stressed that any concept is *both* a tool and a hypothesis constantly subject to being modified; if you will, constantly open to being changed. A content approach which courts closure seems diametrically opposed to conceptual teaching.

When we talk about *selecting* content, we are talking about selecting data or clusters of data that allow both the teacher and the students to do two things:

1. To help in the movement toward constructing and testing of concepts.
2. To help in the movement toward the use of skills in the development and testing of concepts.

We find, then, an initial base for selecting data or content anchored in its *potential* as a *carrier* or *vehicle*. It is NOT something that exists for itself; it is a means rather than an end. For example, one does not purchase a new car in order to park it once and for all in a garage. True, it may still serve a number of functions, but the initial criteria is that of its function as a means of transportation.

A teacher may insist upon having students memorize the names of the presidents in chronological order. The teacher will usually admit that this content is strictly a *means,* a way of getting to something else, such as having the students become better citizens, or being necessary to get into college, or necessary just to be "educated" in the social studies. Regardless of whether her purposes are logically valid or subject to empirical testing, the point still stands. The content is used as a carrier or vehicle to move the student to something other than itself.

This suggests that knowing what one is trying to accomplish and why one is making the attempt becomes crucial in vehicle selection. The work done in Chapter 3 on developing a rationale becomes an imperative if one recognizes the need to select in this area. If we do not know what we are trying to accomplish, we can become smothered with the poet's "shower of facts"—what the social scientist calls a proliferation of information—and end up aimlessly latching onto this or that.

The key criterion for vehicle selection is its instrumentality, its usefulness in carrying one to concept and skill development. The vehicle itself must be rather *explicit* about what it has to offer so that the relationship between it and the desired ends of the teacher can be determined. For example, in Chapter 2 the stone ax vehicle had a number of social science concepts implicit in the study, but also in Chapter 2 we noted how the bridge cheating vehicle was more functional in skill development and the teacher had to work at relating the data to desired concepts. A table of quantified data has to include data that lend themselves to skill development and/or some specific concept the teacher wishes to develop with the class.

In selecting a vehicle, the nature of the vehicle plays an important part. It may appear as an object, a study, a tape, a film, an article from a newspaper, an experience, a table of data in quantitative form, and so forth, but *its specific ingredients must relate to the ends the teacher has in view.* Obviously some vehicles are more functional than others.

For centuries teachers have placed reliance upon the textbook as a vehicle. It hasn't been stated this way but, in fact, there has been an assumption that the text will somehow provide a basic means of getting teachers to their perceived ends. The teacher's own background and experience were also considered to be prime vehicles, and when the textbook and the teacher combined efforts, it was assumed that the ends were being met. But when the ends of neither the teacher nor the textbook have been specifically identified, these traditional vehicles do not prove functional.

Most teachers are also amply provided with curriculum guides. These guides often list topics which are not functional as vehicles. The guides, too often merely an abridged textbook, simply list areas of human activity and, at the intermediate and secondary levels, put the areas of activity into some chronological time dimension. For example, an 8th grade social studies guide is likely to list such things as "The Colonial Period" and "The Age of Jackson," and so on. By some odd coincidence you will find, probably, the same sequence of listing in high school and college texts.

"The Colonial Period" and "The Age of Jackson" are more descriptive than instrumental in terms of the functions a vehicle should serve. The elementary teacher faces the identical problem. Elementary guides list such topics as "The Family" and "Indians" and, in most cases, these appear as some nebulous end in and of themselves. (Refer to Chapter 3 and the elementary curriculum analysis.)

Some of the newer guides deal with broad focus areas or themes which focus upon an aspect of human activity. For example, an 11th grade guide (significantly NOT called a course of study) lists four main focus areas for a year's work: *Man in his Social Environment; Man in his Physical Environment, Man in his Conceptual Environment; Man and Self.* Each focus area has a list of topics. Under *Man in his Social Environment* we find such things as "Conflict," "Nation," "Population," "Communication," and so on. The focus areas and possible topics *ARE NOT VEHI-CLES AND ARE NOT DESIGNED TO ACT AS VEHICLES.* They serve one *primary* organizational function — that of suggesting areas in which related vehicles can be selected.

Topics and focus areas *are not vehicles.* To delude oneself in attempting to use them as such is a confused and confusing past-time. A prime example of this confused and confusing activity was encountered a few years back in a Peace Corps training project. An extremely competent professor of American history was asked to conduct one training session and to prepare a lesson addressing some basic concept or concepts which he felt would be helpful to the trainees once they were located in rural villages in India.

He selected the Progressive Period as a focus area. Several "reference facts" were listed on the board and he lectured upon the intricacies of this particular period in the American experience.

At the conclusion of the session he informed a colleague that he had wanted to *use* his data to build the concept that "the contemporary world makes it impossible to enter any situation with a prescribed plan for step-by-step solutions."

That evening a trainee dropped into the office. She wasn't known as an intellectual giant but was a good barometer for assessing how things were going. She referred to the afternoon's session with the professor. "I enjoyed the class and he was interesting, but I don't know what all that stuff on the Progressive era has to do with what we'll be doing in India."

A staff member responded. "Look," he said, "I give you detailed instructions on how to get from here to 'X.' I point out each turn, each intersection, each distinguishable factor and then tell you that when you get to highway "y" you must stay right on the highway and must head due east. OK. You follow the directions and get on the highway. Two miles down the road there's a big detour sign telling you to go south. If you just follow my directions, you will plow right through the detour sign."

The trainee smiled: "You mean that all he was trying to get across to us was that a person has to be flexible and adjust to changing situations?"

Let's see what happened. The professor had decided upon a *focus area* but had not selected any vehicles which *specifically* allowed him to move toward developing the concept. He still clung to the view that the countless bits of data he presented would somehow do the trick. In a sense, he assumed that *he* was a vehicle and that this was enough. It appeared that *his* prime goal was *not* the development of the concept but rather the data itself. The concept was a secondary consideration. The focus area concentrated on an activity during a period of time. The professor was familiar with it, but it was too broad and nebulous to be instrumental. The desired concept was, in reality, an incidental by-product. On the other hand, the staff member knew the concept and simply selected a story as a vehicle to achieve the desired end. For the specific purpose in the specific situation, which vehicle was more effective?

It is not a question of whether the professor was wrong or that data is unimportant. We *are* suggesting that when one selects different objectives, he must seek different vehicles. This calls for something we term "teaching honesty." This is something that incorporates intellectual honesty but goes beyond and into activities that directly influence the behavior of other human beings.

An important variable in selecting an appropriate vehicle in a teaching situation deals with the often misused term "meaningful." When something is meaningful or when something is satisfactorily explained it implies that the new (be it a concept, book, piece of data) makes sense — it fits in or connects with the old. The new and the old *interact*, each modifying the other, and this leads to the formation of a conceptual scheme which did not exist before. If a vehicle is functional in terms of concept and skill development *and* if it assists in building the bridge between the old and the new, some of the basic ingredients of relevancy are operational for the teacher *and* the students.

WHAT DO VEHICLES DO?

Using the term "vehicle" to replace content, as a label, may help us to keep in mind the functions served. What do vehicles *do*? In what ways do they help in effective teaching?

Vehicles assist the teacher in managing the overwhelming amount of data encountered. In actuality, a teacher who is competent recognizes the need to establish some boundaries — even flexible ones. These boundaries help in decisions related to instructional management.

Vehicles assist the teacher in providing opportunities for students to use specific data in the development of skills.

Vehicles help the teacher to keep in mind that the selection and use of data imply explicit relationships between concept and skill objectives.

Vehicles provide variation as a base of classroom activities.

Vehicles provide ways of satisfying needs of students to have immediate "targets" that serve a definite purpose and that can be started and finished in the sense of providing psychological accomplishment. This is functional for the teacher as well.

Vehicles can be modified; that is, they can be used *in toto* or in part, depending upon the ends the teacher has in mind. This also encourages the students to *transfer* their experiences to classroom concerns.

Vehicles assist the teacher in working with materials and students in creating relevancy. Relevancy is not "found" or "given" but is created as the student becomes aware that what he has learned is transferable and of use outside the classroom.

TESTING WHAT VEHICLES DO

Most of us still quest after certainty. Intellectually we may know better, but we still look for utopian answers as to *what* vehicles should be used. This quest dismisses the criteria established for vehicle selection. It brings us back to the question of "teaching honesty." Utopias have at least two things in common; they are free from change and they assume a universal acceptance of a common value system. We simply do not live in a world amenable to utopian answers. In most cases the real world is rampaging with change and buffeted with a host of often conflicting value systems. A class is no different. We deal with probabilities and there is no guarantee that a specific vehicle will work.

The quest after certainty brings teachers face to face with the "enemy." Pogo reminds us that "we are it." Sitting in on professional gripe sessions seem to confirm Pogo's observation. Teachers, especially student teachers, are prone to lament the obstacles. The outdated and often not very exciting textbook appears to be the main target. Students and teachers are apparently demanding that the textbook function as a vehicle while being naive about recognizing its built-in limitations.

After listening to this type of complaint over and over again, a curriculum coordinator met with social studies teachers and presented his plan for saving the schools. Given the existing view of the function of textbooks and curriculum guides, educators in the social studies area could save the taxpayers millions by doing two relatively simple things: (1) Provide an almanac to all first grade youngsters and then have them memorize it for the next eleven years. This would cost about $2.00 per child. (2) Use the local telephone directory as supplemental material. This would be of no cost, or at least relatively inexpensive.

He explained that most of the data found in textbooks can be found in an almanac. The almanac had maps and charts and historical surveys. Famous people were mentioned. "As long as we don't have any framework for intelligently using such data," he argued, "the almanac is admirably suited to most existing social studies programs."

Leaving the almanac salvation approach, he focused in on the telephone directory as being a major vehicle. He wanted the teachers to become cognizant that something as innocuous appearing as a telephone directory might serve as an instrument to get to a number of concepts and skills.

He passed out the following article, asked the teachers to read it, and suggested that they think about what they would do if they found themselves in this particular situation.

The Year the Schools Began Teaching the Telephone Directory*

No one quite knew what had been the motivating factor. It seemed unlikely that the Council for Basic Education was behind it. Sputnik itself seemed a long way off. Some harsh critics, seeking a scapegoat, suspected the Telephone Company, but upon closer examination it was clear that they might have had as much to lose as they would to gain.

No, it was the superintendent's decision, and no apparent pressure group seemed to have motivated it. The memorandum went out on March 18th. It was simple and to the point.

> Beginning with the Fall term, all 7th grade classes will be held responsible for learning the contents of our local telephone directory. Each teacher, working in cooperation with his or her immediate supervisor, will evolve methods and procedures necessary to effect an efficient and appropriate achievement of the above-stated goal.

---

*Adapted from Harmin, Merrill, and Simon, Sidney: The year the schools began teaching the telephone directory. *Harvard Educational Review*, 35:3, Summer, 1965. Copyright 1965 by President and Fellows of Harvard College. The parts deleted deal with approaches to methods and are well worth reading.

You can imagine the buzzing which went on in the men's faculty room. Some said that the memo was a first step toward a merit pay plan. Others were convinced that it had something to do with Admiral Rickover. An intellectual blamed it on that "Bruner guy." In the women teacher's room there was a more sedate but nonetheless bitter inquiry. "Just what is the old boy up to now?" "Do you think there will be a system-wide test?" "I wonder if the company has brought out review books yet?" Many questions were raised in the school and in the community about this new 7th grade curriculum. It wasn't long, however, before a united front of teachers, principals, and the superintendent, worked out, in more or less trial-and-error fashion, a set of answers that became quite standard. Soon no one bothered to ask the questions any longer, for the answers had become predictable. For the historically minded, here is a sample of the more pesky questions.

Q. Why learn the telephone book?
A. It develops good study habits, which will be necessary in college, and it trains the student to concentrate and apply himself, qualities which are useful in adult life. Among other things, disciplined adults are what we want.

Q. Won't they just forget the information after the tests?
A. The less bright student will most likely forget a lot. However, we intend to have regular reviews in later grades and consequently the retention curve will hold fairly satisfactorily.

Q. Why work so hard learning the telephone book when the directories are so handy when you actually need one?
A. After all, this could be said about any subject we teach. If we want our people to look up information when they need it, why teach anything? Furthermore, life is hard, and the sooner our students learn this the better off they will be.

(The teachers received a memo in their mailboxes just prior to the ending of the school year.)

The success of the telephone directory project initiated by this office has earned the well-deserved respect and admiration of the entire community. The rigorous efforts you and your students have made have not gone un-noticed. . . .

Consequently, we are assigning to the 5th grade the community's telephone directory. . . . We are assigning 7th grade teachers the exciting task of teaching the telephone directory of our State Capitol. The 6th grades, to make the study complete, will combine their study of French with at least one unit on various sections of the Paris, France, telephone directory. This is dependent upon whether or not we can obtain government or foundation assistance to purchase the suitable directories, however.

The teachers' discussion following the reading considered such things as how curriculum decisions are made at the "top" and handed down, how the same questions always seem to be asked about curriculum, how we ask too much of kids by moving upper grade content to the lower grades, and how dependent everyone is on outside funding. The discussion was a rather superficial and unsophisticated approach to problems faced by educators. However, the curriculum coordinator was pleased to see an immediate transfer to the real situation. When he brought the group back to the question he had posed prior to their reading the article, the response indicated that the satire had been recognized. In some ways it was humorous. But the group came up with limited suggestions as to what it might be able to do if given a telephone directory and told to teach it.

The same vehicle was given to a group of parents. The same charge was made. Parents also saw the humor, but when asked to suggest what uses they saw for the directory, they approached it more seriously.

One intent parent believed that "it wasn't too far-fetched" ... that "teachers face this problem every day and I wonder what they *can* do?" Out of a brainstorming session, the following ideas emerged:

1. The maps in the front of the directory could be used to show how telephones link different parts of the country.

2. The whole concept of communication systems and their influence on personal and economic functioning.

3. The idea of the historical development and implications of the phone. (One parent recalled a telephone survey taken in 1936 to forecast the presidential vote and that the pollsters failed to realize that the poor didn't have phones so the sample was inaccurate.)

4. How about a case study of the telephone company as a business organization? a public utility?

5. Just looking at the names in the directory seems to show a "melting pot" and something could be done with this.

6. Hitch-hiking on the previous comment, a parent suggested that there might be clues to help to determine geographical ethnic

patterns in the city. Do telephone exchange numbers indicate clusters of Germans, Irish, Italians, and so on?

7. Don't overlook the yellow pages. How about advertising, business, etc. And how did the telephone company come up with the categories for listing businesses—by titles, by services, by products?

8. A comparative study of all the things listed in a telephone directory of 10 years ago, 20 years ago. Discussion of recognizing change.

9. What about direct dialing? Has the computerized age changed personal practices?

10. The different shapes and sizes of telephones (and different colors) and the numbers per household suggest some status symbols.

The brainstorming started to become exciting. There were a lot of things a person could do. He didn't have to feel trapped. You are probably aware that the parents were talking more about things a teacher *might* do rather than selecting specific vehicles. *These were lay people and perhaps this points up a major difference between a professional and a lay citizen.* Theoretically a professional knows his ends in terms of concepts and skills and is thus in a position to select appropriate vehicles. The lay person, on the other hand, sees possibilities even though finding it difficult to articulate them in terms of actual teaching procedures.

In this particular situation the parents were able to see more creative possibilities for the use of the telephone directory than were the teachers in the group being worked with. This is not to say that most teachers would have had the same difficulty. It does demonstrate the types of approaches one can see as possibilities if one is able and willing to think divergently. Teaching does something to teachers. In its day-to-day framework, teaching can become a boomerang. This may, in part, explain why a number of teachers appear to have more difficulty in seeing the learning possibilities dormant in a telephone directory, or a textbook for that matter.

Traditional "boxes" may demonstrate degrees of usefulness. But they may also dull the ability to free the thoughts. The Galloping Gourmet in *The Graham Kerr Cookbook* seems to share this concern when he writes: "Traditions are useful as armor against professional attack—they are also a form of self-induced contentment created by stamping up and down on one spot—getting nowhere, risking little, and achieving an immortal zero."

It is helpful to remember that whatever divergent thinking is and whatever is meant by creativity, such things are not necessarily gifts of birth but, in varying degrees, are *learned* activities and often are functions of situations that encourage this kind of learning to take place. We talk about such things *for* students. A more fundamental question may be directed at ourselves. What do we really have to lose by risking a bit?

Taking a Ride in Classroom Vehicles

Let's take a look at some selected vehicles that have been used by classroom social studies teachers. The examples will indicate the use of different *kinds* of vehicles. Note whether they have the potential for concept and/or skill development. Note also whether they are completely divorced from a large focus area or even from a specific topic.

VEHICLE ONE

1. The vehicle is to be used with an *11th grade* social studies class.

2. *Focus Area:* The Search for the Good Society: The American Experience.

3. *Topic:* The curriculum guide lists "The Founding of the Nation."

The school system, for whatever reason, had determined that The Search for the Good Society was to be studied in 11th grade social studies. This is what we call a focus area. The Founding of the Nation is a topic and implies a time dimension. Neither are vehicles because there are no explicit concepts or skills implied in the given statements.

The teacher determines what her ends are in terms of concepts and/or skills. Then she selects an appropriate vehicle which will allow the ends to be achieved.

4. *Concepts.* The teacher desired to provide the opportunity for the students to construct and test the following concepts:

a. Each person carries a picture of the "good" society in his head. This picture is "made," is learned.

b. Different people accept different types of evidence in order to say "I know."

c. When one talks about the "best" society or the "good" society, one must say "best or good, compared to what?" What is the goal (end) and how is the goal to be attained (means)?

d. Each society has a "view" about *how* people should live together.

The teacher wanted the students to develop the above concepts. She anticipated using the Declaration of Independence and the Constitution as subsequent vehicles. While going through a college textbook on government, she came across a dialogue which she rewrote for her students.

5. Vehicle

Aristo and Demo*

Once upon a time two men sat before a fireplace. The two men, Demo and Aristo had very little in common. They didn't "see" things the same way; they didn't carry the same pictures of the world around in their head. Sometimes communication breaks down when people have such different pictures. But Demo and Aristo at least talked to one another.

Aristo: I observe people all the time. I am interested in what they read. Do you know what I see? I see that for every person reading a good newspaper or book, there are countless others who read comics and love stories and all sorts of junk.

Demo: So? What are you trying to prove?

Aristo: It proves a great deal. It shows that you and your followers are much too optimistic about human nature. You think that humans really want to know the facts and that, once they know the facts, they will be willing to use them. And you think that they are interested in making decisions for themselves. Ha! Back in the 18th century you argued that all people could have a good life if they could elect their representatives. You talked of a society in which individuals would study all sides of a problem and then vote for that which seemed to help the general good. It amuses me that you still think this way. Haven't studies shown that your

---

°Burns, James MacGregor, and Peltason, Jack W.: GOVERNMENT BY THE PEOPLE: The Dynamics of American National Government. Copyright 1952. Adapted by permission of Prentice-Hall, Inc., Englewood Cliffs, New Jersey.

fine "intelligent" citizen simply votes the way he does because his father voted that way? And you go on believing that the individual citizen is something more than human! Ha!

Demo: I admit that I was overly optimistic. But I think you are too harsh in your criticism. Tell me, because men don't *always* act in a reasonable way does it mean that they *never* act in a reasonable way? I realize that people often act out of self-interest, but do they always so act? Aristo, you seem to oversimplify things. After all, human life is complex. Our knowledge coming from the social sciences helps us to get a better understanding of human behavior and we can learn to accept man as he really is. Knowing this we can build a better society.

Aristo: You're still in the ivory tower. You talk about dreams and theories. Come down into the streets and just use your common sense. Men are not even able to take care of themselves, so how can you set up a government asking them to take care of themselves and others?

Demo: Look, we cannot get away from having a government by men. Using your own logic, Aristo, if people are so bad wouldn't it be unwise to put all one's faith in one man or in a small group of men. This seems a good reason for making all government accountable to the people. Thomas Jefferson wrestled with this issue. If you recall, he said:

> "Sometimes it is said that man cannot be trusted with the government of himself. Can he, then, be trusted with the government of others? Or, have we found angels in the form of kings or dictators to govern him? Let history answer this question."

A recent thinker by the name of Niebuhr seemed to say the same thing: "Man's capacity for justice makes democracy possible, but man's inclination to injustice makes democracy necessary." Think about such things, Aristo!

Aristo: No...no...no! You don't understand. I am only talking about your "average" man in the street. To put faith in him is to put faith in a government of incompetents. Sure, this average man could take a stab at running a simple government like a small rural community. But things are complex today—large cities, specialization. The average man would blow the whole thing.

Demo: It is you who miss the point. This average man of yours is not expected to supply answers or to give judgment on all governmental decisions. What he does may be limited. But his is not to say that it isn't important. He helps to determine which leaders shall lead and for what purpose. Democracy recognizes the need for leadership and the need for the "expert."

Aristo: Come now, it is only common sense that a government should be run by the best.

Demo: Fine. How do you measure the best? And won't we find the best of the best and come back to one man rule? Who are the best? Of course, I assume you put yourself into that category! The best? whites? males? poets? businessmen? laborers? school teachers? athletes? Sure, a person may be the best in a particular thing, but is this to say he is best in everything? No, Aristo, if a government is *for* the people, it has to be *by* the people. I think we both want the best, but I think we have to decide upon a *means* of deciding the best and you haven't given this much thought.

Aristo: Your faith in the people dumfounds me. You mean to say that people can choose between rival leaders? Ah, this calls for knowledge and judgment — two things most people lack.

Demo: We are not communicating. If my shoe pinches, the only one who can tell is me. I don't know anything about making shoes — about different kinds of leather, style, and so forth. And I don't know everything that goes into the making of a law. But I *do* know if a shoe doesn't fit. And I *do* know whether or not a law works. To quote another friend:

> "Experts do not like being told that the shoes they so beautifully make do not fit. They are apt to blame it on the distorted and misshapen toes of the people who have to wear the shoes."

Aristo: Never mind your quotes! I live in a world in which we have to make fast decisions.

Demo: There is need for better decisions, perhaps. But don't delude yourself. Your system is not so efficient as it seems. You just have better ways of covering up your mistakes.

Aristo: You haven't convinced me. Democracy is not something that most people want or deserve or else they would be more concerned about it. They really don't give a darn. Now, *you think that* over!

Both men sit looking into the fire. The embers still glow.

6. *Activities:* Questions for class discussion

   a. If you add the suffix "cracy" to Demo and Aristo, does it help in understanding the dialogue?

   b. The phrase "pictures of the world" in one's head might refer to what? pictures of what? Why is it difficult to communicate with people holding opposite or different pictures?

   c. If one is "optimistic" about human nature, what might he believe?

   d. When Aristo refers back to the 18th century, to what

specific period in American history was he making reference. Does the Declaration of Independence *infer* what Aristo claims?

e. What factors are involved in a person's voting patterns? How *do* people reach decisions?

f. What questions of *logic* appear in the dialogue?

g. What is meant by social science and how might new findings or recent knowledge about human behavior possibly help in determining how a "good" society might function?

h. Aristo asks Demo to come down out of his ivory tower — to leave his theories and to come into the streets, to use "common sense." What is the difference (if any) between the two types of knowledge? Which — theory or practicality — (or what combination of both) might be reliable in regard to human behavior?

i. Aristo claims that the country has changed. Do changes in ways of living place different demands upon the average citizen? (Who is the average citizen? If there are new or different demands, what are they?)

j. What is the citizen's role in *making* and in *evaluating* governmental policy?

k. What problems does one encounter when he uses the phrase "the best"?

l. If one analyzed the dialogue by listing the types of evidence both Demo and Aristo accepted, would it be possible for the same evidence to be interpreted in different ways?

m. "The embers still glow" might suggest what to students of government today?

The teacher did not identify specific behavioral objectives, and this would be necessary in developing her methods. But she *did* take into account the focus area, the topic, concepts and skills, and she selected her vehicle accordingly. How else might the vehicle have been used? Could it have been reworked for an 8th grade class? 5th grade?

The dialogue vehicle may have been too long. It may have

been too sophisticated for some students. For the sake of argument let's grant both counts. Are there vehicles within the vehicle? How about a single quote from either Jefferson or Niebuhr? What might one be able to do with the shoe analogy? Could the dialogue vehicle, or parts of it, be related to the Declaration of Independence as a *vehicle*? The Constitution as a *vehicle*?

Many vehicles help to generate new vehicles!

VEHICLE TWO

The following is a lesson plan used in a suburban elementary school. It was used at both the 3rd and 4th grade levels. See if you can determine what *vehicles* were used. Parenthetically, most teachers are told that elementary youngsters have a "short attention span." We have found that if one uses a *number* of *short* vehicles which keep the pace changing but which are related to the desired objectives, there is little problem with interest and/or attention spans. We are tempted to comment that a limited "attention span" may refer to the younger students not having learned as yet to cover up their boredom.

Focus Area: Culture   Lesson Plan
Topic: The male and female behavior   Social Studies

I. *Objectives*
   Major concept: Man's differences are learned because he has had different lessons.
   Supporting concept: The world into which one is born gives us different roles to play.
   Supporting concept: The roles each of us play help us to think that *all* other people behave the same way.
   Supporting concept: The roles we play are learned. Unless all other people learn the same way from the same lesson, the role will be different.
   Skill to be introduced: The making of a theory and the testing of a theory.

II. *Approaches*
   1. Make believe the students are trying out for parts in a play. They are trying to get one of the *roles*. The author writes the play and what must the actor do?

The particular play has six characters: a father, a mother, a son, a daughter, a grandmother and a grandfather. Discuss briefly how the author has a general idea of roles to be played but the actor helps to complete the roles.

Question to the class: How would one *expect* each of the above characters to behave? For example:
Father: works, punishes, makes decisions, etc.
Daughter: plays with dolls, is shy, cries, etc.

2. List on the board the following characteristics and activities and ask the students to indicate with an M or an F whether they would most likely apply to a male or a female:

a. Raising children f. Cooking and keeping house
b. Working to get food g. Soldiering
c. Gentle   h. Liking athletics
d. Fishing   i. Making major decisions
e. Crying   j. Driving a car

After determining whether the students understand the terms, ask them to "make some conclusions" about the ways males and females behave. Have them complete the following:

Most males. . . .
Most females. . . .

3. *Making a Theory:* Explore with the class how one goes about making a "guess" and bring up the idea that some guesses may be better than others.

 a. "Accidentally" stumble over the wastepaper basket. Ask the class "to make a theory" about *why* you stumbled. The theory can be "tested" by getting more information. Students can ask the teacher only questions that can be answered "yes" or "no" to see if their theory holds up. (Anticipated theory: "You didn't see it.")

 b. *Transfer* the discussion back to male and female roles. Did the class make a theory about the ways males and females behave? How might we test this theory?

4. *Data:* Take descriptions from anthropology of the Arapesh, Mundugumor, and the Tchambuli tribes. Each group lived in New Guinea. (Locate on the map for the sake of placement.) Give the students the data:

Arapesh ("A")	*Mundugumor* ("B")	*Tchambuli* ("C")
Both male and female are gentle, "motherly"	Both male and female are harsh and violent	Men stay at home while the women work
Both raise the children	Both slap and abuse the children	Men wear adornments; women do not
	Females work in the fields and support the family	Women support the community
	Females and males fight each other	Males dance and entertain

Refer back to the characteristics and activities of males and females listed on the board. If the students lived with "A" or "B" or "C," would they categorize the characteristics in a different way?

5. *Review*

a. Review what the class said about the author who creates the role and what the actor does with the role.

b. Review what the class has said about "theory making" and discuss the theory they had already made about how males and females behave.

BUT, now we find peoples behaving in a way that doesn't fit into our first theory; the theory doesn't hold up.

WHAT NEW THEORY MIGHT WE MAKE ABOUT THE WAYS MALES AND FEMALES BEHAVE?

You have noted the lesson plan and realize that the teacher, in making the plan, had to predict a general degree of reaction from the students. If the predictions were out of line, then the teacher would have to modify — to make decisions — on the spot. Knowing her purposes and having thought through the vehicles, the teacher would at least have some base for making these decisions. Were you able to identify a number of different vehicles? What vehicles were created by the teacher? Was the teacher a vehicle in some cases? Were the students' own backgrounds a vehicle? The teacher took the New Guinea information from Margaret Mead's *Growing Up in New Guinea*, but was her purpose to have the students study place location or learn the names of tribes? How did the vehicles serve to help in "changing the pace"? Are there any implied suggestions about the type, number and form of vehicles an elementary teacher might select as opposed to the type, number and form one might expect a secondary teacher to select?

We are not debating whether this was a good lesson. You might want to ask yourself what vehicles you would have needed to help to carry you to the concepts and skills.

VEHICLE THREE

The following vehicle indicates how a teacher used part of a textbook as a vehicle. He took all the facts that were in a chapter and made one page a "fact sheet" vehicle. The sheets were distributed to the class.

Fact Sheet   Country "X"

I. *The Land*
"X" is a country of *many* islands.
Four of the islands are *quite large*.
All the islands *equal* an area the size of California.
"X" is located off the east coast of a continent.
To the west of "X" is a sea.
To the east of "X" is an ocean.
No part of "X" is more than two hundred miles from the sea.
The islands of "X" are the upper parts of mountains.
Swift streams form fertile plains.
Most people live on these plains.
Mountains cover nearly seven eighths of the land.

II. *A Trip Through "X"*
Island number 1.
Island number 1 is in the southwestern part of "X."
Most of the land on Island 1 is a plateau.
Part of Island 1 is forested mountains.

Island number 2.
Island number 2 is east of Island number 1.

Island number 2 has a rocky coast.
Island number 2 has *many* rugged mountains and rice fields.

The Inland Sea.
The Inland Sea is north of Island number 2.
The Inland Sea is bordered by three of "X's" largest islands.
The Inland Sea is dotted by *a lot of small* islands with villages.

Island number 3.
Island number 3 is "X's" largest island.
Island number 3 has "X's" largest lake.
Island number 3 has "X's" largest mountain.
Farmers work in the fields on Island number 3.

Island number 4.
Island number 4 is north of island number 3.
Island number 4 is "X's" second largest island.

III. "X's" Climate Has Four Seasons.

The teacher's initial assignment to the class: Using just the information on the fact sheet, draw a map of country "X." Twenty-eight students drew 28 different maps from using the *same* informational base. One map appeared as in the illustration on page 239.

Given the fact sheet, the teacher's initial assignment, and *one* result of the assignment, can you infer the possible concepts and skills the teacher wanted the vehicle to assist in helping to develop? If a number of people try to infer the concepts and skills, you will discover that the *same* vehicle can serve a number of diverse functions. This suggests that the teacher's role in planning activities, in conjunction with the vehicle, becomes a crucial factor in the lesson(s).

Taking the concepts and skills you inferred and taking the fact sheet vehicle plus the student maps (now vehicles themselves), what activities can you plan with your focus on Japan?

VEHICLE FOUR

A senior high school "problems" class was involved in approaching the "divisions" in present-day society and the forces bringing

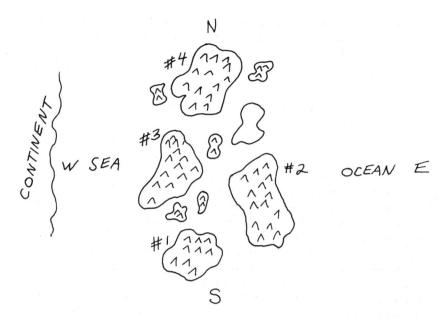

about polarization in social, political, economic, and international affairs. The teacher used Jefferson's First Inaugural Address *not* as an aspect of chronological development but as an instrument to bring focus on basic issues. If you review the First Inaugural Address you will find:

1. During the election campaign, there were some heated debates and discussions which "might impose on strangers unused to thinking freely and to speaking and writing what they think."

2. There is a principle that, although the will of the majority prevails, the minority possess equal rights by law. To violate these rights "would be oppression."

3. There is a call to unite in heart and mind, to "restore social intercourse."

4. A country which does not tolerate religious intolerance has gained nothing if there exists a political intolerance "as despotic, as wicked, and capable of as bitter and bloody persecution."

5. "Every difference of opinion is not a difference of principle."

6. If there are any people who wish to dissolve this Union or to change its Republican form, they should be allowed to be undisturbed as "monuments of the safety with which error of opinion may be tolerated where reason is left free to combat it."

7. People are to be honored not because of birth but because of what they do.

8. Some people make the error of condemning another because they do not see the whole picture.

The teacher explained the use of the vehicle. "If history is to be used," he said, "then we had better start using it! Too often I have been guilty of using Jefferson primarily for a time link—to link together chronological packages. Using the First Inaugural Address of Jefferson points to a lot of basic things: man has struggled with these issues facing man in his attempt to be social; the social and governmental structures were created by men, not gods—people who felt the vicious whips of their fellow beings and somehow managed to function. Jefferson went through a living hell and yet so often we make everything seem so clean and neat and nice, . . . almost a preordained fact that certain people have been chosen to rise above the conflict with the 'right' neatly folded in the pocket." He explained how inaugural addresses proved to be substantial vehicles and relevant to the concepts and skills he wanted to teach *and* relevant to contemporary issues as well. He pointed out how the use of such vehicles motivates students. "I have more students really digging into history now than ever before. They are learning more 'facts' than before because they see how the facts are related and are functional!" he claimed. He added that teaching this way is also more fun for the teacher!

It is interesting to view Jefferson's Second Inaugural Address. He talks about local passions, the rights of the "aboriginal inhabitants," the difficulty in changing people, and the responsibility of the press.

Such vehicles do not have to be searched out. They exist and are readily available for the teacher. It depends upon whether the teacher knows what to do with them. Always we come back to the teacher!

You have probably realized by now that the "crammer" and the "lover" would be threatened by this approach to vehicle selection and use. It's a paradox. The crammer, if he *really* wanted students to retain facts, would be wise to pay heed. We are not talking about using less data; we are suggesting ways of putting *more* data to work! And the lover might find his avowed "ends" more possible if an honest respect for human efforts formed his "loom." The vehicles provide manageable raw materials. The use of the vehicles depends upon the loom created by the teacher. The designs in the fabric woven could show relevant relationships *if* we would try!

The Bible tells us that if we use a little wine, it will be good for our stomachs. This applies equally to our students' well being. A little "wine" — heady, perhaps, and a little warmer, but a possible way of being more alive to the tasks of making sense out of a complex world.

AFFECTIVE/COGNITIVE VEHICLES

The aforementioned vehicles share one common characteristic with the textbook as a source of data. Essentially they are cognitive in orientation; they appeal primarily to the thinking processes. Although this is necessary and good, there are times when this is insufficient to implement the teacher's attempt to make the lesson relevant. Something has relevancy when we are capable of understanding it in terms of our own experiences. A major criterion for selecting vehicles, then, is whether students will find them relevant. This requires an understanding of the affective (feelings and emotions) component of the students' behavior. This component is often neglected by teachers because feelings and emotions are thought of as being "private." We are not suggesting that teachers invade the privacy of their students' lives, but rather we are suggesting that emotions and feelings are not divorced from the cognitive or "thinking" domain and that the "relevancy" and "meaning" students so often tell us is lacking, especially in social studies, is directly linked with the omission of the affective component. A piece by Barry Rowe, which appeared in the April, 1969, issue of *Media and Methods*, exemplifies irrelevant choices made by teachers and the affective as well as the cognitive awareness of students (page 242). Or consider the top of page 244, also taken from the same issue of *Media and Methods*. Renée Gabriel and Barry Rowe are not unique in their views. Involvement in learning is desired by all students. Yet participation and involvement in classrooms have been lacking because too many teachers have been crammers. Emotional involvement

Inside and Outside

ENGLISH 1st HOUR

shakespeare was born in april 1564
in stratford-on-the-avon, then
("The Graduate," winner of
seven Academy awards, breaks
all records.)
a small country town of less than
2,000 inhabitants, in the county
(This highly acclaimed film is
considered the social comment
of...)
warwickshire. his father, john
shakespeare, was a glover who
was for
(Brilliant . . . Sardonic, ludi-
crously Funny—"The New
York Times")
a time one of the leading citizens of
stratford. in 1586 john shake-
("Hair," which started as an
off-broadway production, rivals
the)
speare was chosen high baliff
(mayor), but later he withdrew
from
(genius of Rodgers and Hammerstein. Called the tribal
love-)
civic life. records of the dramatist's
early life are scarce. at the
(rock, the record-breaker is a
pioneer in new stage effects.)
age of eighteen he married anne
hathaway, who was eight years
older
(8:00 p.m., channel 6—"The
People Next Door"—modern
drama about)
than himself. a daughter was born
in may 1583, and twins in 1585.
(a teen drug addict and how it
affects his family and neighbors.)
for the next eight years nothing certain is known of shakespeare's
(Rerun by popular demand.
Color)
life. there is a well-known legend
(which can neither be proved nor
("playboy." 16:1, January, 1969.

"Incident in the streets of the)
refuted) that he fell foul of sir
thomas lucy, the local magnate,
and
(city." "Help me, I'm hurt,"
said Paul, but his silent scream)
was forced to leave stratford. by
1592, when he was twenty-eight.
(went unheard by the insensate,
bedlam crowd. Fiction by R.
Coover)
shakespeare was becoming known
in london as an actor and a writer
of successful plays. thereafter the
records accumulate. class dismissed.

PHYSICAL EDUCATION
2nd HOUR

all right you guys first of all we're
gonna start off with jumpin'
(Caution: Cigarette smoking
may be hazardous to your
health)
pretty good now pushups ready exercise one two one two
(Jogging is good for the heart
and lungs—the organs which
may...)
okay toe touch—kneebend—toe
touch to the left first exercise . . .
("Sex Education: Blunt an-
swers to tough questions" by
J. Collier)
ready burpees one two three four
one two three four one . . .
("aerobics"—The most effective physical fitness plan ever!)
twenty-five sit-ups one one two
one three . . .
("The facts that all should know
about drugs, their effects,
and...")
now then the fundamentals of basketball this is a basketball . . .
("isometrics"—The amazing
ten-second system of no-motion
exercise...)
good enough take three laps around
the gym an' shower up.

Inside and Outside

SCIENCE   3rd HOUR

a common clay brick contains a certain amount of matter. we expect
(**Apollo 8 on Christmas voyage**)
two similar bricks together to contain twice as much matter as either
(**Has been hoped that interferons would treat many virus diseases...**)
one alone. However, no two bricks are exactly alike; they are crudely
(**The nuclear non-proliferation treaty would ban the construction...**)
constructed. let us think of new silver dimes, all closely identical
(**Cybernation is the complete adaptation of computer-like machines...**)
shiny pieces of the same stuff. it seems reasonable to suppose that
(**Cryonic resurrection is planned some years hence for the late...**)
the simple count of the number of dimes defines the total quantity
(**Voiceprint identification can identify the same way as a fingerprint.**)
of matter in the dimes. of course, we could cut some of the dimes in
(**Commercial cloud seeding has been proved effective by tests.**)
half and get a different count of the number of pieces, without changing
(**Lasers have a definite foothold in industry, especially in those...**)
the amount of matter present. that's all for today, class. see you tomorrow.

SOCIAL STUDIES   5th HOUR

the president may refuse to receive an ambassador from another state
(**Bobby Kennedy assassinated**)
if he is for any reason objectionable to the united states. in such
(**Russia invades Czechoslovakia**)
circumstances, the person is considered "persona non grata." in order to
(**Johnson out of race**)
avoid having this happen to our own appointees, the state department
(**It's down Jones. Up lending rate**)
inquires beforehand about the acceptability of the person we propose
(**Nixon wins!**)
to send. any country may demand the recall of any diplomatic official
(**Riots shake DeGaulle regime**)
it finds undesirable. under international law ambassadors and ministers
(**Martin Luther King is slain**)
and their staffs enjoy the special privileges of diplomatic immunity.
(**Pope bans birth control**)
they cannot be taxed, nor can they be arrested. when a war breaks out
(**Apollo 8 on Christmas voyage**)
between two countries, they are given safe passage home. **you are excused.**

— Barry Rowe
[*Clinton High School*
Clinton, Iowa]

(From Media and Methods, April 1969. Used by permission.)

in the classroom is a critical consideration. How one feels is often an important consideration to be confronted by individuals as they engage in thinking about specific problems. The feeling of anger, for example, may get in the way of clear thinking. On the other hand, people often will not think about a problem until they are

As I look back on my education, the basic conclusion that I reach is that

participation and involvement

are the two key words. If junior and senior high school teaching methods were modeled after those of the primary grades, especially kindergarten, student interest and enthusiasm would begin to overcome the

apathy

that seems to prevail in America's schools. In kindergarten, participation is encouraged as a means of becoming involved. Why, then, is this very basic but extremely significant teaching method discarded in favor of the archaic lecture–discussion method when a student reaches the secondary level?

Why not return to involvement and abandon the unnecessary assembling of minute details which are of no practical use?

—*Renee Gabriel*
(Clinton H.S., Clinton, Iowa)

(From Media and Methods, April, 1969. Used by permission.)

angry. Humor can also be used as an effective means of stimulating thought. Thus, many comedians can stimulate us to think about important problems by humorously employing social criticism. The following poem illustrates how at least one student felt about school:

"He always wanted to explain things.
But no one cared.
So he drew.
Sometimes he would draw and it wasn't anything.
He wanted to carve it in stone or write it in the sky.
He would lie out on the grass and look up at the sky. And it would be only the sky and him and the things inside him that needed saying.

And it was after that he drew the picture.
It was a beautiful picture.
He kept it under his pillow and would let no one see it. And he would look at it every night and think about it.
And when it was dark, and his eyes were closed, he could still see it.
It was all of him.
And he loved it.
When he started school he

brought it with him. Not to show anyone, but just to have it with him like a friend.

It was funny about school. He sat in a square, brown desk.

Like all the other square, brown desks.

And he thought it should be red.

And his room was a square, brown room.

Like all the other rooms.

He hated to hold the pencil and chalk,

With his arm stiff and his feet flat on the floor.

Stiff,

With the teacher watching and watching.

The teacher came and spoke to him.

She told him to wear a tie like all the other boys.

He said he didn't like them.

And she said it didn't matter!

After that they drew.

And he drew all yellow and it was the way he felt about morning.

And it was beautiful.

The teacher came and smiled at him.

'What's this?' she said. 'Why don't you draw something like Ken's drawing?

'Isn't that beautiful?'

After that his mother bought him a tie.

And he always drew airplanes and rocket ships like everyone else.

And he threw the old picture away.

And when he lay out alone looking at the sky,

It was big and blue and all of everything.

But he wasn't anymore.

He was square inside

And brown

And his hands were stiff

And he was like everyone else.

And the things inside him that needed saying didn't need it anymore,

It had stopped pushing.

It was crushed.

Stiff.

Like everything else."

The teacher couldn't help but be surprised. Such creativity. Such flair. Could this 12th grade boy really have composed such a poem?

It is not known today whether he actually wrote the poem himself, all alone, or not.

It is known, however, that he committed suicide shortly afterward.

Nothing needed saying anymore.

*Taken from Phyllis Battelle, *Toledo Times*, Feb. 18, 1970.

If you *feel* something after reading a poem or seeing a picture, you have operationally defined the concept of "affective." Overemphasis on the affective component, of course, can lead one to the position of lover. As we pointed out earlier, this too is harmful. What we are suggesting is that the teacher recognize the need to synthesize these two positions. The degree to which a vehicle should be affective and/or cognitive is a question we cannot answer. Teaching is a choice-making profession, and this is one of the choices to be made each day. We are suggesting that films, records, slides and simulations provide the teacher with an additional source for choosing relevant vehicles. Vehicles, remember, are SOURCES OF DATA, and data can be supplied in various forms, depending on the objectives.

Films are a major source of vehicles. Unfortunately many teachers see films (or any other vehicle) as an activity—an end in itself. After all, one can use a film, or record, or tape recording and take up a full class period. Many teachers have the mere filling up of time as their objective, although it is never explicitly stated. There are some teachers who will show almost any film available, without previewing (how can one decide whether to use a film or any vehicle without first becoming acquainted with it?) and simply because it is available and they have nothing better to do. Many future teachers, having undergone that experience as students, see little value in using films in their own teaching. This is unfortunate. There are hundreds of excellent and inexpensive films available today. Many city libraries have films for loan. How might you utilize the following examples?

"Neighbors" is a film produced by the Canadian Film Board. Utilizing real actors and animation the producers have shown two "neighbors" dissolve their friendship and begin to quarrel over a flower growing on the line dividing their property. In their quest to possess the flower the two neighbors build fences and escalate their means of offense until each is killed. The beauty of this film is that it can be used with so many levels of students. There is no dialogue and the student simply has visual data to collect. It may be discussed at several levels of sophistication from the theme of neighbors to that of international conflict and war. One teacher we know used this in conjunction with the poem "Mending Wall," by Robert Frost.

"An Occurrence at Owl Creek Bridge," distributed by Mc-Graw-Hill Films, recreates the Civil War atmosphere in an unusual way. Rather than a documentary narrative one is immediately drawn into feeling the horror of having to face death as one views a condemned soldier about to be hung by the enemy. Does he escape at the last breathless second or is one catapulted into his mind as he awaits death? This is a spellbinder and truly recreates the reality of an event as distant as the Civil War. This was a Grand Prize winner at the Cannes Festival. We have seen junior high school students spend a week discussing its implications and become motivated to seek and use data.

The Encyclopaedia Britannica Educational Corporation has many fine films. Among their best are those which have recreated events as they have actually have been described in major Supreme Court cases. In one such film, *The Gideon Case*, the issue of right to counsel is dramatically illustrated as many of the original participants re-enact their own historic roles. The conflicting evidence is presented, and the original scene of the crime is revisited. Students must confront the dilemma of making judicial decisions based on conflicting data.

Julian Bryan has produced some enchanting films for the International Film Foundation. In doing so he operated under the following belief: "I believe that we film-makers have too long preached at children, often with dull narration. We have given all the answers and left nothing for pupils to discover. How exciting now to make new short films which raise questions instead of answering them and which involve children."* Each film depicts the beauty and simplicity of other people's lives. One such film is entitled "African Village Life: Building a House." This is a study of the Bozo people building a house. There is no narration, only natural surrounding sounds. Methods of making ropes, construction of the frame, and the thatching of a roof of reeds provide data to the student about another culture's survival techniques.

Records and tape recordings are another source of vehicles. Most students are very aware of popular music and records have the advantage of being continually updated and easy to incorporate within a lesson. One teacher we know was experiencing trouble getting her students involved with anything. The students, considered "slow" or "dumb" by others, had reading difficulties. The teacher assigned them the task of putting forth their view of the world in some nonwritten form. One group of students put together a tape recording of four selections, including Flip Wilson's "Cowboys and Colored People," "Harper Valley P.T.A.," "God on My Side" by Bob Dylan, and "Silent Night/7 O'clock news" by Simon and Garfunkel. The ensuing discussion focused upon the hypocrisy of war, religion and politics and lasted two days as the group had to defend their selections.

Combining recordings and slides is also an effective way for the teacher and/or students to provide data. A recording of the Declaration of Independence, when synchronized with slides showing oppression, revolution, freedom, and so forth enhances student reaction. Pictures in magazines can be made into slides with an Instamatic camera and then particular slides are synchronized with specific words on the record. An elementary teacher used this technique when she took her students on a walking tour of their school neighborhood while they were learning map skills. The children took pictures and slides with Brownie and Instamatic cameras, had them developed and put these together with a tape recorded narration of their tour. Each of the

---

*Quoted from International Film Foundation advertising sheet.

children was given an opportunity to record his impressions on tape and to choose which pictures he wished to have shown as he spoke. The finished product was then played, and the children located what they saw in the pictures on a map of the neighborhood.

A high school teacher, after producing a slide tape concerned with the American revolution, was asked by several of his students if they could produce such a vehicle instead of doing the assigned term paper. The teacher agreed and the three boys turned out a production which was later utilized in a school assembly program. They took John F. Kennedy's inaugural address from a record and recorded "Age of Aquarius/Let the Sun Shine In" as background music. They synchronized this with slides concerning America as *they* viewed it, with what President Kennedy was asking for in his address.

A student teacher used Simon and Garfunkel's recording of, "I am a Rock." The student was teaching a sociology class and wanted the class to inquire into the nature of the relationships between individuals and society. As a result, his class raised questions concerning the nature of mass society alienation, suicide, primary and secondary social groups, competition, and communism. This one lesson created a launching pad for class sessions for the rest of the semester.

Simulation is another fine vehicle for involving students in the learning of concepts and skills of inquiry. Simulation is a means for allowing the student to live vicariously. Working within a *model* of social reality students manipulate variables, discover relationships among given data, make decisions and discover consequences implied in their decisions, all within the safety of the classroom. The research seems to indicate that the biggest advantage of simulation is its ability to promote a high degree of interest because the student becomes involved with making decisions and taking calculated risks. Facts are required to be applied in the process of making decisions rather than simply memorized.*

Inter-nation simulation, for example, simulates a "world" composed of "nations." International and domestic pressures are modeled after conflict in reality, and the students as decision-makers must work with the data supplied concerning their country's natural resources, defenses, foreign policy, and so forth, to resolve conflict. The problems of diplomacy, secret treaties, trade agreements, peace negotiations and compromise define the

---

*Cherryholmes, Cleo H.: Some current research on effectiveness of educational simulation: Implications for alternative strategies. *American Behavioral Scientist* 10: 5, October, 1966.

complexity the students must attempt to understand in order to maximize benefits for their country.

"Sunshine" is a simulation concerning race relations. Students are "born" by pulling race identity tags out of a hat at the beginning of the simulation. They are born with identities (white, black, tan, brown, level of education, income, and street address) and maintain these identities throughout the game. Sunshine is a mythical city with six neighborhoods with varying degrees of segregation and integration in housing and schooling. Pressure cards force students to confront specific issues affecting race relations. Pre- and postattitude tests on racial toleration are supplied. This can be used with both elementary and high school students.*

SYNTHESIS AND PROLOGUE

What we teach *is* important! It has a definite relationship with *how* and *why* we teach. The concept of VEHICLE frees us from the narrow view of content. It does not discard content but rather gives a greater emphasis because it is necessary to carry one to the development of concepts and skills. We have seen that one can establish a scheme for selecting appropriate vehicles and that it need not be a random activity. The teacher must know exactly why a vehicle is instrumental in her plans. And a vehicle must have some *specific* properties within itself in order to be instrumental.

We have seen what vehicles can *do* for planning. But hopefully we are wise enough not to expect a vehicle to do the impossible. It is only a *part* of the total teaching act.

You have seen different kinds of vehicles put to work in actual classroom situations: the dialogue with secondary students; Margaret Mead's studies with elementary level students; a "fact sheet" from a textbook used with a junior high school geography lesson; inaugural addresses; and even a combination of *created* and actual vehicles. It is a lot different from just passing out textbooks and reading assignments. It is perhaps the difference between a professional and a lay person.

Chapter 7 brings us to different kinds of materials available and *the processes a teacher goes through* in effecting a translation into practical vehicles for classroom use. As we will see, a teacher never releases the student role. He may refine it and share it. This is the activity called teaching.

---

*DeKock, Paul: Simulations and changes in racial attitudes. *Social Education* 33: 181–183, February, 1969. This particular journal has a description of several other simulations for various grade levels on pp. 195–199.

*"Never mind about that yet . . . first you've
got to learn to wake people up!"*

8

DEVELOPING STRATEGIES

We shall not all sleep, but shall all be changed

A child is able to go beyond the information he has been given to generate additional ideas that either can be checked immediately from experience or can, at least, be used as a basis for formulating reasonable hypotheses.

JEROME S. BRUNER

STRATEGY

This chapter deals with teaching strategies. Unfortunately the term "strategy" is derived from a military context in which a general takes the variables of a given situation into account and *plans* a system which allows the use of specific tactics in defeating the determined enemy. Occasionally this use of the term seems appropriate and is quite descriptive of the armed camps existing in many classrooms. A "win-lose" climate dictates strategies that are devastating to both teacher and students.

However, strategy has now evolved to refer to specific plans that allow the implementation of activity designed to achieve predetermined ends.

The key to an effective strategy is *organization*. Organization refers to a process rather than an entity: a reasonable, rational, and self-correcting plan for implementing student and teacher functioning. It need not be rigid, closed, and restricting. One can plan a *structure* for teaching which is flexible, open, and non-restricting and which, at the same time, does not court chaos or "Four H" random activity.

A teaching strategy takes into account the variables at work influencing one another in the specific situation. Some of the variables are external to the classroom: the nature of the community — its composition, socioeconomic levels, history, and tensions; the experimental background of the students — their attitudes, expectations, self-concepts; the total school system and its relationship with the community; personality factors involved in functioning of professionals in positions suggesting prestige and status; peer pressure among colleagues; oneself and levels of competency; and so forth. These external factors *do* influence the determination of strategy and are an integral part of the teaching situation. There are also internal teaching/learning variables which also relate one with another *and* interrelate with the external situation.

This book has concerned itself primarily with the internal considerations: rationale, syllabus, content sources, concepts, skills, vehicles, and teacher survival.

Hopefully it is obvious that we have *not* limited the concept of strategy to only one component, to whether one uses inductive or deductive reasoning with students and to what techniques are effective in approaching such reasoning. Such a narrow concept of strategy is misleading.

The *approach* in the book implies a strategy. For better or worse we have attempted our own strategy—one directed at providing you with some assistance in determining *your own* strategy. This stems from our belief that a teacher's strategy is aimed specifically at trying to assist students in developing *their own* strategy and style for meeting life situations.

Analyze what we have tried to do. We tried *not* to imply that teaching and learning are mechanical, simplistic, step-by-step activities. Instead we have deliberately tried to suggest that teaching and learning are systems of human functioning with a host of mutually influencing parts. There are no neat recipes. If teaching and learning are *creative* efforts designed to understand, organize, and use human experience, scientific materials must be handled with nonscientific approaches.

We have tried to explore with you interrelationships and possibilities. The importance of the teacher as a thinking/feeling person intervening in the lives of others—on purpose—suggests a pragmatic *and* ethical need to evolve a rationale: an honest excursion into the reason for the reasons. We have used a number of vehicles, many actually used in classroom situations with students, and we have used the vehicles in order to motivate, describe, raise issues, test, suggest; the vehicles are not models in the sense of being right and pure examples of good teaching. (There are a number of variables we would have to know in order to make such assessments.) The selected vehicles were woven in and out of descriptive material; we tried to *use* them in specific situations. We have explored content and the issues involved: history, social sciences, use. Again we tried to move in and out of vehicles; some of the vehicles directly involved *content* and the use of skills in dealing with data. Concepts and skills were woven into each focus or chapter and were purposely *not* approached in isolation. We have tried to involve you in *doing* some of the activities. We have tried to mesh questions with a concept of questioning, to use *both* inductive and deductive reasoning. There were attempts at synthesis. And we have tried to work, the best we could, with the affective areas — anger, humor, some sarcasm. We tried to share our excitement and our despair. There is also periodic data input: quotes, facts, and sources. In no place have we tried to work strictly with discovery or strictly with testing. Rather we have entered the teaching and learning system at different points of focus *but constantly in search of relationships.* The abstract and the practical were intended to feed each other. We have shared ideas with you — some that are *not* in vogue but with which we are struggling. We have tried to put our approach within the context of the total social studies domain: values, attitudes, expectations, change, pressures.

Monitor us. Use the Strategy Sheet to note how and when we moved with and used skills. Check on how many G–R concepts were used. Review the vehicles used and try to determine focus functions of each as well as other functions implied. Check whether and to what extent we have tried to make terms functional through contextual use rather than just definition. In your monitoring, identify the vehicles and materials that you could use in teaching youngsters and whether the vehicles are transferable, with modification, for use at various grade levels. List the concerns you have that we have failed to discuss.

Obviously we did not intend a methods "cook book." Those expecting a step 1–2–3–4 bake approach will be disappointed. Others may be partially satisfied, knowing that it is only a beginning.

The liability in our attempted strategy is that there is no mechanism for feedback, for self-correcting evaluation; no chance to modify, expand, delete, react to on-the-spot questions. Books suffer from this lack. Books are not always the best vehicle, but rather are only one among many and are far outdistanced by the most effective vehicle: a good teacher. Once a book goes to print, it acquires a rigidity. Fortunately, a classroom, unlike a book, does not lend itself to "binding."

STRATEGY WITH STYLE

Strategy always comes home to the teacher. Concepts, skills, vehicles, words, and raw data don't teach. They have to be worked, and it is their working that becomes the essence of an effective strategy. It is selective work, purposeful work, and related work. Too often we either neglect or play down teacher *style* when we discuss strategy. We talk about individualizing instruction and usually have the students in mind. If we are consistent, we would be wise to include teachers and to recognize that there *are* different teaching styles. There are many ways of doing the same functions, and a teacher's personality and self-functioning play a vital role. Each teacher has his own life style and this relates to his teaching style, to how well his strategy works. There's no *one* magic style that assures a connection with students. Most styles that are *authentic* are honored. Authentic *people*, not those play acting with position and role, seem to be a basic ingredient regardless of the style. We've seen kind, sweet, demure, soft-spoken, articulate styles that come through to students as little more than velvet-gloved dictation and cover-ups for teacher boredom. On the other hand, we've seen gruff and rough styles that on the surface appeared hard, closed, and uncaring come through to pupils in such a way that classrooms were open, flexible, and purposeful. Respect is earned. The Great Pretender in the classroom will make a sound theoretical strategy extremely difficult to implement. Students know if a teacher really cares about their learning, know if the teacher really cares about the subject, know if lessons are to fill time, space, and heads or are *really* lessons. Young people respond to authentic styles. Part of planning strategy is a teacher's recognition and use of his own style.

STYLE PLUS FUNCTIONS

Authentic style is important but it is not enough. It has to be applied to the pursuit of effective teaching activities.

The teacher as a *person* in the classroom is part of the strategy. And this person should consider himself more as a practicing student than a tethered teacher. He practices what he teaches. For example, he shares his ends and means with the students. No games. He shares the syllabus with the students and spends time going over it and spends time sharing the processes he went through to come up with it. He asks questions and expects to be asked questions; he shares with the students his own reactions to questions that make response difficult. When working with different kinds of concepts, he finds it natural to identify them as such—*to think aloud with the students.* He opens up to feedback from the student—in terms of his course, the content, the vehicles, the problems, and so forth. And he demands the right to feed back to the students his own concerns and reactions and doubts and feelings. He expects to be intellectually pushed, and demands the right to do some intellectual pushing back. He assesses with the class the direction of the study and assesses alternatives open. He accepts responsibility for keeping an eye on the target and for "running interference" for getting there.

He comes to class prepared and expects the students to come prepared. He stays on top of his content area and shares his *own* subject matter adventures with the class—a book, a journal article, a nagging question. They have a chance to see him involved and struggling and learning. In the long run one teaches by example and not percept. The effective teacher remains curious in a disciplined way and he pursues his curiosity in disciplined ways.

He demands of his students no *more* and no *less* than what he demands of and for himself.

He accepts the role of resource person. He provides data when needed. He's not afraid to solicit data when needed. He helps students to monitor their own academic strategy and acts more as a counselor than a judge.

He knows that a class discussion can be effective only if participants have some in-put to make. In automotive terms, he knows the difference between spinning wheels and burning rubber. And he knows when to ease up and when to bear down.

He is a synthesizer. He builds into his strategy the time to pull things together and to raise issues. He also builds into his strategy ways of differentiating between what has been learned and that which is still open—the unresolved issues, the questions for which he and the class members have no data with which to respond, the qualifications necessary for making any knowledge claim, the questions that should have been raised.

He is intellectually tough. He knows that this doesn't mean piling on more and more busy work but rather pursuing an issue in an intellectually honest way. He insists upon the attitudes and values implied by the strategy. Being tough doesn't preclude being sensitive to human needs and hope. It does mean having a thought-out criterion for human functioning and being strong enough to value it publicly and to live by it as a teacher and as a person.

He does all this in his own way and with his own style. He expects students to respond to all this in their own styles.

If the teacher is sophisticated, he realizes that he does not have control over everything that happens. The outside world is brought daily to the classroom. He and the students live in many demanding worlds and the school is just one such world. He recognizes a responsibility for those things he can most influence: his own behavior, teaching strategy, classroom atmosphere, data, concepts, skills, transfer, plans for specific implementation.

If things don't work in the classroom, he reassesses the things he *can* control and change. He is willing to modify and to adjust if deemed necessary and prudent. But, for many reasons, it is naive to believe that a teacher will "connect" with *every* student *all* the time—just as every youngster doesn't "connect" with him all the time.

RELATING TACTICS WITH STRATEGY

We have said that the key to strategy is *organization*. If there is no neat recipe, are we left with chaos? No. We *are* left with an organized framework for systematically relating a number of fluid activities.

A *tactic* refers to the moves made (or desired to be made) in a *specific* situation. The only requirements are that the tactic support the general strategy and that the tactic be functional (work) in the situation.

Let's assume that our strategy indicates that we are concerned with teaching G–R concepts that are *transferable* beyond any one specific situation. We assume that a G–R concept is comprised of a number of U–N concepts that are worked into a pattern of relationships we label G–R. We assume, in the strategy, that NO G–R concept is absolute: each concept is open to qualification and change as new data suggest. We assume that a G–R concept moves *beyond* empirical data and that there are ways of checking whether the move is valid.

Given the above, our specific planned tactic must consider all (or selected parts) of the following: generalized, repetitive, and transferable concepts; open to modification; and checked for validity.

The old term *inquiry* has been used to refer to a method or tactic used to derive an intended concept. It *denies* the efficacy of telling students the concept. In this sense, *inquiry* has been applied to tactics that move away from sheer lecturing (perceived as telling) and that move away from *deductive* reasoning.

The term "inquiry" has, in some quarters, been synonymous with the "discovery" approach. Initially, discovery referred to a student's being able to discern *relationships*. Somewhere along the line this concept was lost and in its place appeared a concept of "discovery" that meant the student was to *discover a concept*. To discover a specific concept was interpreted to mean that a student used primarily *inductive* reasoning in his discovery process. In a naive way this relatively pure inductive tactic was felt to parallel "the" scientific method. See diagram of the interpreted procedure below.

It becomes rather obvious that the student *may* be more prone to manipulative techniques under this tactic than even when he existed under the regimen of deductive reasoning. For example, the student may be asked to discover an already existing verbal

INQUIRY: An Interpretation

"DISCOVERY" TACTIC: A GAME OF HIDE AND SEEK

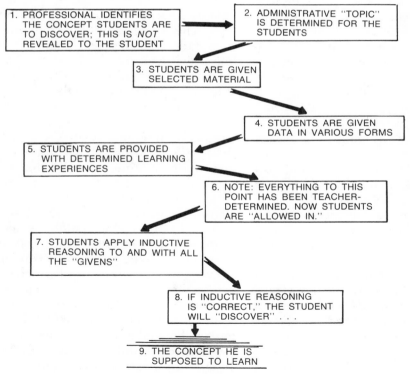

1. PROFESSIONAL IDENTIFIES THE CONCEPT STUDENTS ARE TO DISCOVER; THIS IS *NOT* REVEALED TO THE STUDENT

2. ADMINISTRATIVE "TOPIC" IS DETERMINED FOR THE STUDENTS

3. STUDENTS ARE GIVEN SELECTED MATERIAL

4. STUDENTS ARE GIVEN DATA IN VARIOUS FORMS

5. STUDENTS ARE PROVIDED WITH DETERMINED LEARNING EXPERIENCES

6. NOTE: EVERYTHING TO THIS POINT HAS BEEN TEACHER-DETERMINED. NOW STUDENTS ARE "ALLOWED IN."

7. STUDENTS APPLY INDUCTIVE REASONING TO AND WITH ALL THE "GIVENS"

8. IF INDUCTIVE REASONING IS "CORRECT," THE STUDENT WILL "DISCOVER" . . .

9. THE CONCEPT HE IS SUPPOSED TO LEARN

Note: The teacher's method is deductive while the student's method is primarily inductive.

tag for a specific concept. The data, materials, and general strategy may have already been determined for him. Implied in the tactic is that if the student uses the selected data correctly, he will derive (discover) the concept the teacher has in mind. There is more than a fair amount of control. For example, the concept, data, strategy, and evaluation are monitored by the teacher.

We are not convinced that this is what the discovery tactic or method was originally intended to do. The intent, as we understand it, was to get away from "show and tell" at all levels of study. However, in practice, we have seen discovery tactics used as a subtle form of manipulation and indoctrination. Furthermore, those who support this as being "the" scientific method have an untenable base from which to work. For those desirous of method recipes, however, it lends itself to neat stages, steps, and "right" and "wrong" use of data.

Hilda Taba states that "learning by a discovery involves inductive sequence. This sequence starts not with the exposition of the general principle, but with exposing the learner to some concrete instances of the principle that he can analyze, manipulate, and experiment with. . . ."[1] There appears to be an implicit assumption that one must *start* with the concrete, the facts, *as a necessary condition* preceding a discovery of relationships. This widely accepted assumption that reflective thinking cannot take place until there is an available body of facts leads to the stressing of factual coverage, memory burdens, and a host of discrete and unrelated information.[2] If reflective thinking and/or discovery is assumed to be *inductive* in nature, then it is relatively easy to keep the old wine in newly labeled bottles. All we have is a different reason and justification for continuing the collection and counting of facts.

We have discussed the view that science is NOT a strictly inductive process. In operation, the processes often do NOT start with facts but rather with conceptualizations which guide the need and method of turning to empirical data to reconstruct, test, or verify the *initiating* concept. Is this to deny that science is partly an inductive activity? No. The processes used are deductive — inductive working *together* in reciprocal support. Karl Popper, in his *The Logic of Scientific Discovery*, raises a question which is of substantial significance in determining tactics which effectively relate to the overall strategy. Popper argues that it is difficult to teach students the acts involved in scientific discovery BUT it *is* possible to work with students in *"testing" discoveries*.[3] As was pointed out in the chapter on skills, one can be taught to use logical reasoning by checking logical reasoning, can check and monitor what meanings are in fact related into a concept or concepts, and can check and determine if the conceptual meanings refer to the world of experience. It is possible to approach discovery and inquiry by establishing testing strategies that use inquiry methodologies.

Instead of facts being a necessary condition to thinking, we find conceptual thinking a necessary condition to effective use of facts! Generically, human thinking may have evolved in and through random factual experiencing which, in turn, fed into the conceptualizing of experiences into abstractions, into transferable and usable ideas. But we cannot make the logical leap that *all* subsequent thinking on the part of man remains unchanged in experience-processing procedures. Concepts *modify* the procedures. One does not *start* inquiry with a blank slate. The conceptions one holds become tools for fact gathering and use.

The *entrance* point to inquiry and discovery need *not* be within the framework of *inductive* tactics. Entrance may be achieved by exposing a general principle or concept to the student—as part of the real world. Students are asked not to memorize the verbal statement but rather to test the concept and, in so doing, inductively discover relationships that support, qualify, or deny the given concept. The problem is not with a tactic being inductive *or* deductive but rather with a strategy that uses deductive-inductive processes. An effective entrance point may be a *deductive* thrust which demands *inductive* reasoning, deductive subtesting, more inductive methods—a continual process of discovering and testing of the ends *with* means subsumed under what we call inquiry.

The teacher's primary role becomes one of helping to determine with students effective strategies for testing concepts. In this strategy for strategies, we still find a concern with terminology, with inductive and deductive reasoning, and with the monitoring of functions or skills needed to retrieve and process data. There is a need for information and there is a need to use identified concepts as *tools*, a transfer of sorts, in the situations allowing the testing.

This entrance tactic is consistent with an overall strategy built to have students *transfer* the use of *concepts* and *methods*: concepts *with* methods.

This entrance tactic is more manageable on the part of the teacher and the student. It helps in meeting head-on the need to understand what acting people *mean* by their actions if there is a

INQUIRY: An Interpretation

"TESTING" TACTIC: TEACHING AS EVALUATING

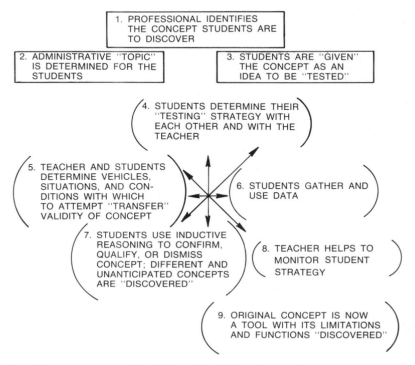

1. PROFESSIONAL IDENTIFIES THE CONCEPT STUDENTS ARE TO DISCOVER

2. ADMINISTRATIVE "TOPIC" IS DETERMINED FOR THE STUDENTS

3. STUDENTS ARE "GIVEN" THE CONCEPT AS AN IDEA TO BE "TESTED"

4. STUDENTS DETERMINE THEIR "TESTING" STRATEGY WITH EACH OTHER AND WITH THE TEACHER

5. TEACHER AND STUDENTS DETERMINE VEHICLES, SITUATIONS, AND CONDITIONS WITH WHICH TO ATTEMPT "TRANSFER" VALIDITY OF CONCEPT

6. STUDENTS GATHER AND USE DATA

7. STUDENTS USE INDUCTIVE REASONING TO CONFIRM, QUALIFY, OR DISMISS CONCEPT; DIFFERENT AND UNANTICIPATED CONCEPTS ARE "DISCOVERED"

8. TEACHER HELPS TO MONITOR STUDENT STRATEGY

9. ORIGINAL CONCEPT IS NOW A TOOL WITH ITS LIMITATIONS AND FUNCTIONS "DISCOVERED"

Note: The teacher's method is similar to that of the students.

desire to explain the actions — "to subsume them under rules which connect similar situations with similar actions."[4] Students bring their actions to a cognitive and functioning level. It also assists in selecting relevant materials, checking skills or student strategies as an ongoing process.

In a sense, this entrance tactic may be more honest and less prone to inadvertent manipulation by the teacher.

A testing strategy allows access to individualizing instruction. The *same* given concept may be tested by students differing in ability and sophistication, and the testing strategy a student uses may reflect different areas of interest. For example, a G–R concept may be tested using U–N concepts from history and may be tested through gathering data by reading. The same G–R concept may be tested "on the street" by using U–N concepts from experience and tested through gathering data from observation and listening— from "sensing." Each provides different testing grounds for the G–R concept but each requires a strategy for inquiry. And the two tests may feed or challenge one another when the results of inquiry are shared. This has implications for teaching slower students who are usually slow in terms of reading. Instead of piling on more data, a teacher can assist them in testing concepts through experience.

Both the inductive discovery tactic *and* the testing discovery tactic may be used. Neither has any exclusive "rights" within the strategy. If used well, *both* find consistency within the strategy context. The entrance point may be either *deductive* or inductive activity.

Suppose that a teacher wanted to teach the concept that rapid increase in population tends to give rise to problems not measured in numbers alone. Assuming the teacher wants students to function with concept, the teacher may:

1. Use an inductive entrance point. The teacher may present the following data as a "given":[5]

a. World population will double in the next 30 years.

b. Highways and new suburban areas consume one million acres of land a year.

c. The demand for electricity has doubled since World War II.

d. Each person accumulates, on the average, seven pounds of trash per day.

Using this data (and more) the teacher can plan activities and select materials which will assist the students in using the data (U–N concepts) to discover what the teacher has in mind. Depending upon the teacher, this can be an open or restrictive approach.

2. The teacher can present the concept to the students as a "given" and then work with the class and with individual students in determining strategies for testing the concept in order to discover qualifications of the concept, supporting data, denying data, and so forth. The entrance point is deductive.

In these examples the teacher is both a data resource and a strategy resource. In both cases the teacher monitors the functioning of the class and of individual members. Evaluation is an ongoing process involving the monitoring and is thus additional data for the student to use.

If the strategy is premised on qualitative functioning rather than upon quantitative hoarding, tactics may stress depth instead of breadth. It is sometimes assumed that breadth gives depth, but it can be argued that limited depth approaches allow for breadth in that the more one deals with ideas and data, the more expanding are the relationships discovered. This calls for selection rather than broad coverage as a focus. But the depth selection does *not* necessarily exclude covering a broad area. For example, using three amendments to the Constitution with in-depth tactics allows a broad view of pre-civil war, civil war, and reconstruction *as well as* an entrée into contemporary social problems.

STRATEGY EQUIPMENT

Remember, strategy is a plan for implementing activities designed to arrive at determined ends. Within the broad plan are subplans or tactics which guide activities in *specific* situations. A strategy is a plan, but it also includes the issues of implementation — issues that move it from the abstract to the field of action.

There are some basic "equipment" considerations to effective strategy:

1. *The broad administrative topics should be kept in mind and analyzed in terms of how they can be used.* This is a pragmatic, administrative consideration. The broad administrative topics (Spain, The Colonial Period, The Fertile Crescent, etc.) are broad boundaries to data.

2. *Identified concepts to be discussed during the study.* The concepts should be known in terms of levels of transfer (G–R and U–N concepts), and sources should be on tap. This suggests organizing a system which is readily accessible. Cards measuring 5″ x 7″ have proved effective. A G–R concept is put on each card and U–N concepts and/or sources are indicated. Cross reference can be made to administrative topics.

3. *Vehicles should be identified.* Their potential use should be recorded in terms of concepts and skills. Within a short period of time, one will have a bank of vehicles. This also calls for organization. A filing system which identifies the vehicle, its use, and type (case study, chart, map, data

sheet, article, research study, etc.) should help in making decisions about vehicle use.

4. *Motivation and/or transfer can guide one in selecting vehicles that indicate a relationship to current social concerns.* When one knows what concepts he plans to teach and the broad administrative topics, he can select a number of current vehicles: polls, quantitative charts, diagrams, letters to the editor, maps, a series of headlines, pictures, cartoons—vehicles that we call "breakers." They can be used to build relevancy, to synthesize, and to evaluate in terms of transfer.

5. *A Strategy Sheet for students will put on the line the types of functioning that the teacher hopes to monitor with students.* The Strategy Sheet is an evaluation form but NOT a basis for grading.

6. *Perhaps the most important initial piece of equipment is a brief syllabus of the course, which is given to the students and reviewed with them.* This opens up the teacher's strategy, guides planning, and helps to establish expectations for both the teacher and the students.

7. *A curriculum log is a teacher's diary.* It is the de facto curriculum recorded as it unfolds. Most people view curriculum courses of study as written guides which point out what a teacher is expected to do. A curriculum log, on the other hand, is what the teacher and the students have *actually* done. It is written after the fact. It can be fun to keep. It can also prove helpful when trying to synthesize with the students and when working on syllabus revision. A curriculum log passed on from one teacher to another as students move through the school grades would prove extremely valuable. Logically it would be a vast improvement over having a priori courses of study infer a course or a school program. Unfortunately so much of what we do is not a game of logic.

The equipment indicated in the list is not magic. It is interesting to note, however, that the first six items can be implemented, in varying degrees, *prior* to entering the fray. It *is* possible to identify the broad administrative topics from kindergarten through grade 12. In this respect, we have a national curriculum in the social studies area. With few exceptions, one can go anywhere in the country and find the same topics listed at the same grade levels. It is possible to identify content concepts as one is *taking* courses in history and the social sciences, and it is possible to initiate a classification system for the concepts. One can start building and annotating a vehicle file with vehicles from his own academic work and reading. It is possible to work out different kinds of Strategy Sheets for oneself as he takes courses—even a methods course. One can work on developing a rationale and can develop syllabi for several courses.

Granted, none of these would be rigidly fixed; but there would be an organization pattern. There would be material prior to student teaching and approaches that could be tested during student teaching. Perhaps of even greater importance would be the possibility that one's own academic work might become more meaningful if he approached his courses as resources rather than hurdles.

To paraphrase Bruner: A teacher is able to go beyond the information he has been given to generate additional ideas that either can be checked immediately from experience or can, at least, be used as a basis for formulating reasonable hypotheses.

It *is* possible.

And it *is* possible that teaching and learning can be an experience of awakening sensitivity and cognition. It *is* possible that we shall change.

SYNTHESIS AND PROLOGUE

There is no authoritative set of rules for guaranteed success in teaching the use of social studies. A plan to implement educational experiences must reflect a planned flexibility. If the horse is drowning, one has to expect to be able to change horses in midstream instead of wishfully hanging on with visions of eventual rescue and salvation. "No one knows very much how people learn or what they should learn in this broad area [social studies],"[6] and this suggests that the heart of a strategy is having a plan to at least bring to the student's awareness what, why, and how he is *doing*. This awareness includes being familiar with one's own style, with the functions of concepts, and with ways of working on experience that allow "meanings" and relevancy.

The teacher can prepare for a planned flexibility *prior* to entering the classroom by identifying concepts, vehicles, and possible components of specific tactics. College courses in education and in academic areas can be approached as teaching resources,

(Miss Peach by Mell Lazarus. Courtesy Publishers—Hall Syndicate.)

as learning that can be transfered into other learning situations. For example, an elementary teacher studying a particular ethnic group's struggle in the immigration process in an academic course and studying social studies methods in an education course should be able to consider *both* as complementary efforts. The "equipment" is forged out of such effort.

There is substantial difference between putting it all together conceptually and putting it all to work in an actual teaching situation. This raises a very practical question of teacher survival. If one knows what he is trying to do, has worked out a tentative strategy, and has the basic equipment, what obstacles might he face? How does one overcome the obstacles while retaining intellectual and professional integrity?

REFERENCES

1. Taba, Hilda: Learning by discovery: Psychological and educational rationale. Elementary School Journal, March, 1963.
2. Taba, Hilda: The teaching of thinking. Elementary English, May, 1965.
3. Popper, Karl: The Logic of Scientific Discovery. New York, Basic Books, 1959.
4. Hayek, F. A.: The Counter-Revolution in Science. New York, The Free Press, 1959.
5. Mallan, John T.: Broader perspectives. New York Times Student Weekly. February, 1971.
6. Robinson, Donald W.: Teaching by the inquiry method. NASSP Bulletin, September, 1966.

"Well, there goes the Apocalypse!"

(By Ed Fisher. Copyright 1971 Saturday Review, Inc.)

9

SURVIVAL

"Nicanor lay dead..."

We have always preferred an ignorant bad man to a talented one and hence attempts were usually made to ruin the moral character of a smart candidate; since, unhappily smartness and wickedness were supposed to be generally coupled, and incompetence and goodness.

BAYNARD R. HALL (1843)

SKUNK AT A LAWN PARTY

Teaching is initially a physical activity.

If one survives the grueling physical demands, he may find time and energy to engage in the use of intelligence. And, per chance, if one's stamina and mental mettle allow him to survive long enough in one place—long enough for board members and parents to slap "'ole John" on the back—then one might be able to engage in the intellectual.

A thinking, bright, sensitive person who commits himself to being more than a paid employee, to working with human potential within the tumult of human experience, walks into an often extremely hostile environment when he takes a job in the public schools. We don't mean the hostility of a "blackboard jungle" variety but rather the subtle and sophisticated hostility evident at so many zoos. This is not to say that the caged occupants of the zoo are "bad." It *is* to say that the situation is not good.

An exciting and intellectually alive teacher is committed to turning answers into questions and questions into activity. An exciting and intellectually alive teacher is committed as much to unlearning as he is to learning. This may not be a particularly healthy commitment in a climate that often views the ends of learning as being happiness, absence of frustration, assurance, and a billfold full of credit cards and knowledge.

Intellectually sound and effective teaching is seldom wanted. There is a big difference between teaching and looking as if one were teaching.

(Copyright 1964 Jules Feiffer. Courtesy Publishers—Hall Syndicate.)

To be good is not enough. It may in fact prove to be a liability in some school situations. Having ability is not enough. One has to be able to carve out a working environment in which ability has a chance to be put to work. Surviving in a school environment is what this chapter is all about.

THE SOCIAL STUDIES TEACHER AS A "MODEL"

Stereotypes have a way of hanging on. And they become prompters of a self-fulfilling prophecy. Researchers working on personality profiles of various occupation groups as presented through mass media found teachers to be "clean, kind, fair" but also "the slowest, dullest, weakest, and softest professionals."[1] When stereotypes are at work, one has to come close to "fitting the mold" or he's out of the game before he starts. So a teacher must be clean, kind, and fair—or he doesn't get to bat. And if he is not "slow" or "dull" or "weak" or "soft," he is likely to be "suspect." His intent is likely to be questioned—even by the "good" folk.

If one plans to survive two cold facts emerge:

1. To be good is not enough.
2. To be good may, in fact, be suspect.

These two cold facts stand out loud and clear in a profession that offers little reward for being good. The criterion for meritorious service is: how long you have been anchored and how many courses you have had. Only on rare occasions have teachers been rewarded for good *teaching*, for *doing* a job, regardless of length of service or the Saturdays or evenings spent accumulating hours. Personal satisfaction is said to replace artificial extrinsic rewards, and we would do well to recall this as we sit down to the chore of grading students.

In 1936 Howard K. Beale issued a report of the Commission on the Social Studies (AHA) titled *Are American Teachers Free?*[2] His conclusion that teachers are not free, don't know they are not free and, if they did know, wouldn't care is interesting. But of more interest might be some of the problems he faced when conducting his study. Teachers apparently didn't identify the problem of freedom as having much to do with personal conduct, controversial issues, methods, or texts. "Thousands of teachers are utterly uninformed and unaware of anything outside of their textbooks and minutiae." "The average teacher is so conventional-minded that he, like the community, honestly feels that the unconventionalities of the teacher whose freedom is denied should really not be tolerated."

Beale was not able to identify any school where teachers had been subjected to pressure because they believed in or advocated military preparedness, large armies, or the indoctrination of children with militaristic attitudes.

But this was in 1936. At least three wars later, things must have changed!

In the midwest, one school, under the gun of a war "moratorium" day, declared it was not the role of the school to be partisan. A short while later, elementary students in the system were encouraged to parade down the main street in a display of "loyalty" and support of the nation's involvement.

Cold fact number three: If one turns answers into questions and certitude into doubt, he is dangerous. It is a good bet that he will stand alone. There are varying priorities within the social studies cadre. Few teachers appreciate martyrdom on the part of a colleague. (Who will be next?) Fewer yet willfully seek out martyrdom for themselves. Hobert W. Burns once told an eager graduate class in Educational Foundations: "I have seen a number of good people stand up to be counted. And they were. Midst the cheers of the on-lookers they were counted... *out.*" This is not to be unexpected. In a profession whose court of appeal in professional activities is an elected lay board of education, the standards applied to job keeping have little to do with professional competency. Standards have a lot to do with local norms.

When it is said that teaching is initially a physical activity, we are not referring just to the "pecking" preference given the experienced teachers already in the system. The new teacher is likely to inherit what is not wanted by the others: the nonstatus courses and the "trouble" courses. If there is a shortage of classrooms, invariably the new teacher gets the traveling visa and has to move from classroom to classroom. Onerous administrative assignments often fall upon the new teacher, and these range from hall monitoring to who gets the large study hall just before lunch. Even the number of teaching preparations is a consideration.

But these are all surmountable. They, too, shall pass. It's a hazing period. It is done with sugar and sweetness and understanding. If one takes all this in the spirit of hazing, he can survive.

The physical drain, however, is more pronounced during the nonschool hours.

The organization and content of teaching are almost totally different from what had been expected. Student teaching provides some experience with the problems, but when one encounters sole responsibility for teaching world geography, or world history from minus zero through 1971, or American history starting with the explorers, it becomes evident that one isn't really prepared to cover all areas, is really not wise enough in terms of content to teach well in all areas assigned. So there is much homework to do just to keep one step ahead in content areas. One may have majored in contemporary European history or Asian studies. He may have walked away with academic honors. But he will be fortunate if his own academic background preparation is applied directly in 10 per cent of a year's work. In some topic areas he is perhaps no more prepared to teach the content than is a person coming in off the street. This can be a constant source of aggravation and guilt feelings. The conscientious teacher will find himself trying to catch up in content the first year. Concern with teaching methods, motivation, and so forth, will *not* be a primary concern unless such things are used to cover up inability to catch up.

This compelling need to learn forces a number of first year teachers to be self-learners of subject matter. Thus one's methods pivot on being kind and fair, with the hope that such behavior will keep the students from pressing too hard in areas of content. This may account for teachers' being considered dull and soft by the lay public. What the teacher learns himself the first year usually becomes his basic stock in trade. He builds on this in subsequent years.

In doing this, he is conforming to system expectations. He inherits his part in a social studies program, and his own courses usually have course-of-study guides which often are little more than an elaboration upon the table of contents of a textbook. He inherits the textbook to be used. Implicitly he receives his "marching orders" and seldom has any say in program, course, or materials. His *expertise* comes in when he is *individually* able to relate his own competencies within the prescribed framework. It is a bootleg operation.

So—the first year. He can't let on that he may be good. His success or failure depends upon local norms, on his adaptability rather than his professional competence. There are also sub-

MISS PEACH   By Mell Lazarus

YOU HAVE A "PHILOSOPHY OF LIFE," IRA?

YES, MISS PEACH..

IT MAKES ME THINK ABOUT ALL THE PROBLEMS FACING HUMANITY, AND HOW TROUBLED THE WORLD IS

THEN IT MUST BE A DUMB PHILOSOPHY OF LIFE...

MY PHILOSOPHY OF LIFE IS "DON'T THINK."

(Miss Peach by Mell Lazarus. Courtesy Publishers—Hall Syndicate.)

stantial energy demands placed upon him as he tries to adapt to the system and to the content coverage expectations.

Can a bright, sensitive, thinking teacher survive? Some do. Often there is considerable compromise. Sometimes there is abdication or a cynical resignation to "what is."

What considerations might assist in survival?

SURVIVAL

If one enters social studies teaching in order to take his own ego trip, he and his teaching efforts are dysfunctional.

If the teacher's *own* ego salvation is the primary end of his teaching and if he views himself as the real "lesson" for all others — his righteous fighting for a cause, his adamant refusal to compromise, his use of the school as *his* forum, his martyrdom as he gets outflanked and chipped, his public announcements of his shocked social sensibilities, his little sling-shot poised against the big toe of the giant, his abhorence of the stupidity of human functioning, his soul torn to shreds by the "conspiracy" — then he had best forget teaching. In the "here I am, the great human hope" stance, the lesson *is* taught, and taught well. It doesn't work.

If, however, one is committed to helping students to come to terms with themselves and their worlds, and to providing tools for shaping both, then the ego is put into the background. To teach effectively is a relative term, but the attitude basic to such teaching must embrace a statesman's sensitivity combined with a politician's hard-nosed opportunism.

If one really believes in what he is doing, it calls for maturity: reasoned and reasonable expectations, political sophistication, strategy, and preparation. It calls for putting intelligence to work (oddly enough, the same type of activity we trust our students will follow).

To survive? Basic to the issue of survival is the eternal question: *survival for what?* (This is where an honest rationale helps to keep the perspective!)

Hofstadter[3] puts the survival issue into focus. The professional man lives *off* ideas and not *for* them. "His professional role, his professional skills, do not make him an intellectual. He is a mental worker, a technician.... As a professional, he has acquired a stock of mental skills that are for sale.... At his job he is a hired mental technician who uses his mind for the pursuit of externally determined ends." Few of his goals are self-determined.

This may be significant for the teaching profession.

If one wants to survive, he does NOT use the rhetoric of change. He does not play with the sacred wordings of goals. He accepts the words and does not deliberately choose a semantic battleground to prove himself. Is the goal to produce democratic citizens? You bet it is! This may and does mean different things to different people. But the *sounds are sacred:* psychological, not logical. The selection and planning of objectives and experiences to reach such goals is the anvil, bellows, metal, and hammer that do the work of shaping the product. It is *here* that one works; it is at this point that one can be effective; it is here that the sounds are shaped into meanings. (Why become vulnerable and spend energy fighting words?)

Closely related to this are the organizational vehicles. They imply sacred structure—time-tested, valid, authentic. If American history is to be taught in 5th, 8th, and 11th grades, *fine.* Keep the trappings that appear in organizational terms. American history is a broad framework of particular groups of people experiencing what it is to be human in a particular geographic area and in a particular time situation. Arguing to change the name of the vehicle is ludicrous if the name is important to administrators, parents, and peers. Again, *it is what one is able to do within the sound* that allows meaning to be created. (Why become vulnerable and spend energy fighting words?)

Administrators will be the first to admit that it isn't an operating program change that gets them and a school system into trouble with the public. Not at all. It is the tinkering with the highly visible labels and sounds, and the modification of organizational terms and structure that throw everyone into panic. *Look* conventional. *Talk* conventional.

A politically astute teacher knows when, where, why, and how to effect change. This is a sophisticated activity. It can be effectively accomplished *if the social studies teacher goes to school using the concepts from his own supportive disciplines.* Why not use what we think we know about human behavior in trying to teach about human behavior? If our teachings are functional, can't we make use of them? And if not the teacher of the use of social studies, then who?

Survival depends upon being a good administrator *first* and a good teacher *second.* If a new teacher is organized, that is, has lesson plans, takes attendance, meets all his classes, gets to school on time, doesn't cut out early, attends faculty meetings, keeps order, and *hands in all reports neatly done and on time,* mediocre teaching is likely to be overlooked. Administrators tend to evaluate on the same basis on which they are evaluated: bodies, budgets, and buildings. Neatness, promptness, and care in administrative detail are prime requisites to being considered "good."

To argue that one is a teacher and that his preparation did not include going to a secretarial school is an old refrain. In the real situation, the logic of an argument counts for nothing.

Once one has a reputation for being well organized (and for some reason social studies teachers seem to have a more difficult time with this than do teachers in some other areas), *then* he can devote his image building to teaching activities.

The first standard for such a teaching image is being *a fact collector and distributor.* You don't teach without hard data and lots of it. *And this part of the teaching act should be highly visible.* Fact sheets, data sheets, and so forth, are equated with being academically competent. There is some justification for this. A fact of life is that most students want this kind of data and they want it visible. Parents feel that this implies "good" teaching. And most administrators rejoice with things not ideas. What you *do* with the data is a different story: deriving and testing concepts, applying skill dimensions, and so forth (your methods) will not be of much concern so long as "they" know you are using data, lots of it, and are not "wasting time" on what they perceive to be abstract activities.

If one doesn't attack the system's stated goals, or the administrative vehicles of structure, and if one believes in the use of data (and functions within this framework with some visibility), he is on his way to becoming an honored member of the teaching fraternity.

Where low visibility *is* necessary is in what one plans and does *within this framework.* An astute teacher does not flaunt his strategies to his peers or to the public, and he shouldn't hide them. But he doesn't go out of his way to say, "Look what I am doing," which implies that anyone halfway bright and committed would be doing the same thing. Having thought through a rationale and having planned a syllabus helps one keep a tidy house before venturing out to clean up the neighborhood.

Survival also depends on not doing too much — especially that first year. Part of the strategy for survival within the system is to have the odds in your favor in order to be assured initial "success": success meaning *within* the verbal goals and organizational structure, and with adherence to administrative detail and use of data.

It is necessary to have students authentically involved in the subject matter and to *justify* that changes in approach have been thought through and can be assessed. *This means sound planning.* And this means *applying the sound planning to a manageable aspect of the teaching load.* It may be fair game to be quite conventional in four classes but to determine what *one* class seems ready, able, and willing to come to terms with good learning. Initial success feeds the kids, the parents, and the administration. Don't play when the odds are overwhelmingly against a fighting chance to have something work.

Survival depends a great deal on your not being a *threat* as a *person.* We have known teachers to effectively bring about changes thought impossible in a given situation when they were *liked* by their colleagues and by the administration. Oddly enough this means treating adults and students alike: as human beings. On any faculty there will be good teachers and poor teachers. Some will be bright and some quite slow. Some will be relatively innovative and others will have found the "truth." Some will talk a game; others will do. Why expect something more than human?

Being liked doesn't mean selling out. It *does* mean consideration of others, putting respect and dignity to work in actual situations, and taking stands without absolute win-lose lines being drawn, applying inquiry methods to issues, and knowing that the name of the game is not necessarily *logic.* To be reasonable, rational, and logically valid is of no avail if affective considerations deny the effort.

Look for and welcome personal support. But don't mistake personal support for political support in the larger area of conflict. Friends are usually for quiet hours.

Sometimes new teachers assume that the students want changes. Some students have verbalized the need for change and some adults have interpreted their verbalized complaints. Don't expect too much. Students have no greater access to panaceas than do the rest of us. Sometimes exuberance leads us all to simplistic action. But most of the students are willing to go along if they know one has prepared, has thought through what he is doing, and is willing to share this with them. Students want the security of disciplined discourse, data, and some structure. Students who have made it in the system as it is don't want change! In some cases these students and their public relations network can be effective blocks to change, . . . and to sincere teaching efforts.

Contrary to some popular beliefs, administrators may *not* be the curse of the teaching profession. Administrators have been found to be relatively more open to change than is commonly believed. They do shy away from teachers who are highly visible, ego-bound, and politically naive in the sense that they don't see the system as a system. An inappropriate act by one teacher can destroy months of work! Most administrators know the name of the game but they have to come to terms with a different type of clientele—to get bond issues through, to pass levies, to keep the school system "machinery" oiled. True, they may have different functional priorities, but for a teacher to automatically assume the administrator to be the enemy is to cross off possible and needed help.

Survival depends in part, on being willing to ask for help. A know-it-all teacher is devastating to a class and just as devastating to a faculty. One must be careful, however, not to ask for help if the other person is not able to respond. To ask someone to help you form a theoretical base while he is still struggling with memorizing the names of kings is to ask for trouble. The request for *mechanical help* is not likely to backfire. Once a person helps you, there is a subtle psychological commitment to what you are trying. One can always use help of some sort. Sort out the help needed and get people involved: peers, parents, students, administrators. But make sure it is *specific* help that can be initiated, given, and completed. This way you control your own main concerns.

A teacher wishing to teach well and to apply what he wants to do with teaching/learning, will face difficulties in most teaching situations. The difficulties are not insurmountable, but they demand a *political* sophistication and an *operating strategy* if survival means more than just leaving school each day in one piece.

One basic assumption underlying sophistication and strategy is that one has something to teach—something that makes the maneuvering worth the effort.

The first condition goes back to a teacher's own intellectual preparation in subject matter. Dewey wrote:[4]

> This should be abundant to the point of overflow. It must be wider than the ground laid out in textbook or in any fixed plan for teaching a lesson. . . . It must be accompanied by a genuine enthusiasm for the subject that will communicate itself contagiously to pupils.

> The central reason is possibly not recognized. The teacher must have his mind free to observe the mental responses and movements of the student. . . . Unless the teacher's mind has mastered the subject matter in advance, unless it is thoroughly at home in it, using it unconsciously without the need of express thought, he will not be free to give full time and attention to observation and interpretation of the pupil's intellectual reactions.

In other words, only when one is alive, at home, and conversant with his area of teaching can he turn his attention *to* teaching.

We are told that we don't listen to students enough. We doubt if this is the issue. We listen in a noblesse oblige manner but have little to *share with* them. Listening is a one-way street. Sharing opens up a main artery. To be alive in our own area and to share our readings, our own in-put, our own struggles, our own concerns and efforts in the field of study may be the key. If we don't stay alive and excited in our own field, we may, in fact, have little to say, little to share, little to teach. If this is the case, the best survival strategy in the world is a hollow effort.

POLICY AND PRACTICE

The following is a case study. Try "going to school"!

Trouble was brewing. One could feel it seeping throughout the school — a sort of bubbling excitement and tenseness that almost seemed a welcomed respite from the usual humdrum activities. From catching knowing glances or from catching bits of conversation from huddles of students, it seemed obvious that even the kids were aware of some impending crisis, and semi-aware of the people and issues involved.

There was no question but that Miss DePaso was involved. She didn't court the notoriety. The whole thing was disturbing. Dr. Bigelow, the Superintendent, had contacted her earlier in the day. Apparently her name had been brought up before the board of education meeting the previous night at a closed session. Two or three members had indicated some discontent with her teaching. Bigelow hadn't enlarged upon the situation. He just requested that she drop into his office after school. And he thought it "prudent" that she not mention this to anyone. It was obvious that unnecessary complications might arise if there were numerous elaborations spread among the public.

Miss DePaso had cause to be upset. The board was not too pleased with her teaching. This didn't tell her very much — but she was sure Dr. Bigelow would straighten everything out. It bothered her that everyone seemed to know "something." She hadn't said a word. She didn't want the "complications" either, and she hoped Bigelow realized that she had kept quiet.

It was a long day. She phantasized all sorts of situations and reasons for the board's feelings. Seventh period was free and she welcomed the chance to escape to the faculty room. Hopefully she would have some time to identify the pieces of the puzzle—maybe even put some of the parts together before having her audience with the Superintendent.

When she walked into the room she was confronted with an embarrassed silence on the part of her colleagues who shared the 45 minutes. She was new to the system but not new to teaching. Two years of experience had been gained in a smaller town in the northern part of the state.

She poured some instant coffee and lighted a cigarette.

Mrs. Iva Bouche had difficulty in restraining herself.

"What do you plan to do, Miss DePaso?"

"Do? Do about what?" Mary responded. She still was irked by the use of formal names.

"You know . . . about the situation."

Mary played dumb about the "situation" but asked Mrs. Bouche how she had found out anything. It was supposed to be kept within the immediate family.

Iva admitted that most of what she had heard was of rumor vintage. But Marcia Lymph, the girls' physical education teacher, played a body-purity-flavor fixation with her smoke rings while casually interjecting a news bulletin.

"We had a meeting this morning, Mary . . . a real wingding. Obviously the good doctor was flogged by the Board for some of your indiscretions. All the department chairmen were called from classes and sat through a quiz on the use of textbooks."

"The use of textbooks?"

Marcia muscled back in. "That's it, doll. Teaching without a text is like showering without a . . . a. . . ."

"Drip," Mary supplied. "Tell me," she asked. "What was the consensus of the department chairmen?"

Louella Leach, like Mary new to the faculty, suggested that the chairmen had gone on record supporting the use of at least one single text. Mary was surprised. Her chairman, Mr. Maselow, had told her early in the year that the use or nonuse of specific texts was up to her; and, anyway, if this was a problem, why hadn't it been brought up sooner. Everyone on the staff knew how she was handling the course. Why the flak now in March?

The bell sounded and Mary headed for Dr. Bigelow's

office. She was confident that the Superintendent and her principal, Edgar Jensen, would put things into a sharper focus; hopefully, a sane and sharp one. She had important things to do—two youngsters were coming in for help, there were two tough preparations facing her for tomorrow and this would take time at home and at the library. Maybe after supper she would be able to make a dent in the backlog of papers that needed correction. She hoped that the meeting wouldn't take too long.

Both Bigelow and Jensen were in the office waiting for her. The Superintendent was just finishing a phone call which obviously was concerned with some snafu regarding bus transportation. Bigelow was earnestly informing the other party that there was a man hired to specifically handle transportation and that complaints about the transportation should first be directed to him. Jensen smiled at Mary and motioned for her to sit down.

Bigelow finished and turned to Jensen. "I'll tell you, Edgar, people don't know what a big business this education has become. Thirty-five buses out three times a day. They damn near run the school, let alone determine curriculum."

"Yup, it is a problem, Dr. Bigelow. Incidentally, Father O'Malley called earlier and asked if it would be possible to reroute the buses on route A in order to facilitate getting his kids to St. Mary's by 8:15. He asked to speak with you but you were tied up with the budget meeting so I took the message. It's a problem." With this keen observation, Jensen moved his chair back.

Bigelow hesitated a moment. He turned to Mary.

"Miss DePaso, you're new to the system and I don't feel that I know you too well. However, Mr. Jensen informs me that you are a good, dependable worker and that the youngsters seem to like you. All in all you've done quite well this year. So. So, I am sure that this little suggestion which I am going to make won't cause any uneasiness on your part...."

Bigelow went on to explain that some members of the school board had indicated that they felt every teacher should have and use one basic text. He hastened to assure her that supplementary reading was more than welcomed— "but not as a replacement for a single text. As a matter of fact," Bigelow commented, "our department chairmen seem to be in complete accord with the board's view."

Mary asked *when* the department chairmen had reached

such accord and Bigelow told her about the morning meeting—one "necessary to get policy straight in a professional manner."

Mary told Bigelow that his "small suggestion" did cause some uneasiness on her part. "I feel that there is more to this than just the use of a single text," she maintained. "It seems to me that you are questioning my way of teaching. It is as though you're saying, 'Look, you're not doing your job.'" She paused. "To be honest, I am curious. Just who were the members of the Board who indicated displeasure? Was it a majority opinion?"

Jensen shifted in his chair and Bigelow glanced not too swiftly at his watch. With mustered patience, Bigelow explained that he did not feel that his revealing specific names or numbers would alleviate the difficulty. He also added that he, personally and professionally, felt that the Board was making a sound point.

By this time Mary DePaso was more than a little upset. She addressed herself specifically to Bigelow. "Now, both Mr. Maselow and Mr. Jensen [the department chairman and the principal] knew all year what I was teaching and how I was teaching. They knew this way back in September. I have had, up to this point, no reason to believe my teaching was unsatisfactory. Both these gentlemen have observed my classes, but I don't recall any board member doing similar observations. I must wonder how they can come to such a decision when they don't even know about the extensive paperback library in my classroom, the research material we have developed, or my plans...." To Mary, it was obvious that such a library provided opportunity to allow for individual differences, different levels of student sophistication, and so forth.

She was frustrated. Her remarks concluded with a comment that her teaching was "more open-ended."

Bigelow felt obliged to make some justification. "Mr. Jensen and I talked this whole thing over this morning just prior to meeting with the department chairmen. We feel that a youngster really doesn't get a sense of security in your classes—security in terms of knowing specifically where he—or you—are going. And, furthermore," he leaned heavily on the desk, "how can you possibly evaluate knowledge when everybody is doing something different? Your tests don't have specific 'fact' questions. Well, as you say, it is open-ended."

Mary made no move to leave. In the silence she recalled what Bigelow and Jensen had said when they had interviewed her for the position. They viewed their positions as being "service positions"—designed primarily to help the teacher to teach. She had accepted this. But now? She did feel that she wanted to respond to Bigelow.

"I'm not sure," she said, "that the social studies as an area of study ever guaranteed *anyone* a security blanket in the sense that either students or a teacher ever really knows specifically where they are going."

Bigelow interrupted. He shrugged. "In other words, Miss DePaso, you are saying that you don't know what you are trying to do and that you don't know what the results of your efforts will be. And you are saying, if I read you right, that in your courses accurate evaluation is impossible!"

What do you do? Mary knew that in one way she *was* saying this, and then a thought came to mind.

"But, how do you know what my tests are like?" she asked. "To the best of my knowledge neither you nor the school board has seen them."

The Superintendent explained that the best public relations a school has is manifested through what the students say. Most parents meet the teachers over dinner each day through their children. Things get out. He gave, for an example, T. Edgar Spoctor's daughter Diane. Spoctor was not on the Board but he was a leading executive in a local foundry. His daughter had been a traditional "A" student before coming to Mary's class. A drop to a "C" was disturbing. And Bigelow assured Mary that Spoctor wasn't the only one. "This type of pressure can build in a community and destroy the school's credibility."

Mary countered with: "Yes, Diane can memorize exceptionally well, but she doesn't use her information. She doesn't relate it. She doesn't. . . ."

Bigelow, glancing at his wrist watch and then at the wall clock, reminded Mary that she had said her evaluation might not be accurate.

Mary thought: Suppose his wrist watch had not jibed with the wall clock, how would he determine which one was off?

"Actually, we don't have enough time to really argue this one out, do we?" Bigelow looked for Jensen to come back into the conversation. "But," turning to Mary, "what the board feels it must know is that you are covering the material that is basic in your course. You don't use a single basic text and you can't make relative evaluations from a single text—one given to everyone—so how does the board know that all of your students are getting the essential knowledge? We have to demonstrate achievement. After all, the public is part of public education, you know." Jensen nodded his complete approval.

The long pause seemed to indicate that someone should summarize or offer an agreeable compromise. Mary broke the silence. She offered to go before the board and explain her position. Bigelow shook his head.

"No. That's all we would need. If you said to them what you just said to me, they would cut you to ribbons, and besides. . . ." He saw little wisdom in such a move. The bond issue was coming up for a vote again. And everyone knew that it had to get through this time. This was so important that it "almost demanded a professional obligation not to indicate any manifestation of internal problems at this time."

He asked Mary to move slowly. "If your way is right," he said, "we'll eventually come to it."

Mary did not pursue taking it to the board. Later Mr. Maselow suggested that she take it to the faculty professional meeting since "all teachers have a stake in what happens."

Bigelow, Jensen, and the other administrators were paying members of the professional group. They attended the meeting.

Mary DePaso presented her situation. After she completed, Bigelow asked for the floor to address the group as "a faculty member and not as an administrator," and he then reminded the teachers of the pending bond issue and of professional obligations to the "larger, overall purposes of education." He suggested that small articles of the family linen, especially the unmentionables, might be more profitably washed at departmental meetings. "Naturally, man wants to avoid conflict, so why endanger the public school by bringing its problems—professional problems—before the public?" He recalled for the group the political savy in "kissing the babies and keeping it clean."

He went on to talk about the much deserved Easter vacation which was just around the corner, commented on how well some students did on the state merit examinations, asked support for the PTA Follies.

In the parking lot after the meeting, Mary DePaso asked Marcia why the staff hadn't rallied to her support.

"Why?" Marcia shrugged it off.
So we leave Miss DePaso standing in the parking lot.

We know that she is not an autonomous professional. She works in a complex situation and doesn't have control over many of the variables which influence what and how she teaches. Like all teachers, she is part of a system — a complex of *interacting* and mutually influencing parts. And each part is a system in itself.

From the case study (an actual situation with some slight modification to protect the guilty) two different arguments may emerge: One position may be that if the teacher is in such a maelstrom of pressures, there isn't much that the teacher can do other than give in or leave — kind of a "love it or leave it" approach. Why try to modify the system when the odds are preponderously stacked against the effort? The second position may be that, given the realistic facts of life, the teacher, once aware of these facts, cannot absolve himself from *some* areas of responsibility just because he doesn't like the whole situation. Once aware of the variables at work (himself included), the teacher is responsible for that part over which he has a relatively strong amount of control — the educational program in his or her immediate classroom. And if not this, at least a responsibility for his *own* professional efforts.

Let's *use* the case study as it stands. If we were to use it with our own students, we would hopefully do more than just read it, emote, and share the lament. Hopefully, we would try to *analyze* it. For example:

1. *Identify the factors that appear to be at work in the situation.* Within the "whole," what things appear to be going on — things that can be checked with specific data? Possibly:
   a. Control and use of rumor.
   b. Loose use of terminology: the tags — "teaching," "knowledge," "public," etc.
   c. Conflict situations bring focus to *specific* activities.
   d. Formal policy emerges *after* a problematic situation.
   e. A stand on a particular infers larger policy positions.
   f. ......

2. *Identify the facts.* What information lends itself to verification?
   a. No established formal policy regarding use of texts.
   b. Board passed a policy requiring the use of a single text.

    c. Issue of the teacher's methods brought up at the board meeting.

    d. No complaints had been received although the methods had been used since September.

    e. The Superintendent states that he agrees with the board.

    f. ......

3. *Identify specific and general issues.*
    a. Specific:
      (1) Teaching methods
      (2) Teaching materials
      (3) Student and teacher evaluation
      (4) Professional responsibility of individual teacher
      (5) Processes available to individual teacher to present case
      (6) ......
    b. General:
      (1) Responsibility of the board of education
      (2) Responsibility of the individual teacher
      (3) Responsibility of the professional group
      (4) Determination of the ends and means of education
      (5) Determination of priorities: bond issue, classroom situation, etc.
      (6) ......

4. *Identify relevant facts.* Classify under the following categories:

Fact	Time Factors	Specific Issue	General Issue	Interpretation
Department chairmen in accord with board	Position determined *after* board meeting	Professional responsibility of individual teacher, and others	Professional role in making policy	Democratic involvement of professionals; rubber stamp forfeit of professional role

5. *Identify additional data needed.* The data identified should be accessible.
    a. Historical perspective of board functioning in relation to areas of policy making
    b. Formal and informal community education pressure groups
    c. Past experience with bond issues in the community

    d. Methods used to determine selection of department chairmen

    e. Superintendent's relationship with the board

    f. ......

6. *Identify questions to which empirical data can be applied.*

    a. What, specifically, are other teachers in the department doing?

    b. Can Miss DePaso's students be "compared" in any way with students taking the same course from other teachers?

    c. Has the board made any overt effort to be specific about the goals and objectives of the school system?

    d. Has the faculty professional group negotiated any areas dealing with professional rights and responsibilities?

    e. What processes are *operationally* used in the selection of textbooks?

    f. ......

7. *Personal factors which may or may not be logical.*

    a. Perception of roles: DePaso, Bigelow, Jensen, Maselow, board members?

    b. Assumptions basic to positions taken?

        Example: DePaso: Position – Use of multiple materials; no guarantee of specific direction or outcomes

                       Assumptions identified in regard to:
Teaching
Learning
Evaluation

              Bigelow: Position – Students need the security of knowing where they are going and they need to get essential knowledge

                       Assumptions identified in regard to:
Teaching
Learning
Evaluation

8. *Identify questions for which empirical data are not available.*

    a. Will the bond issue fail if the conflict is made public?

    b. If the conflict is made public, could Miss DePaso be a positive public relations figure in the situation?

    c. *Should* the faculty professional group have taken a stand?

d. *Should* the school system make a single text mandatory?
e. *Should* the bond issue be given precedence over Miss DePaso's situation?

If we were to use a case study with public school students, we might come up with a "model" which allows some base for analysis. In the "model" given there is at least some teaching leverage in trying to identify the factors, facts, specific and general issues, and in trying to sort out relevant data, additional data needed, nonrational elements, and "value" questions. Such a model might prove helpful in determining the number and kinds of influencing variables at work in areas of social conflict. *But* theoretically one wrestles with such things in order to achieve a guide to action. Did our exercise provide any insights into DePaso or Bigelow? So one has some analyzed information — what does he do with it?

There is no argument when one faces the fact that nonrational forces such as personal needs, anxiety, and fear often prove crucial in the outcome of any level of struggle. (For example, what commitments did Bigelow make to the board? Why? Could he "save face" if he wanted to? What about Miss DePaso?) Granted the emotional plays and ploys, do we automatically dismiss attempts to try to relate thinking *with* feeling or feeling *with* thought?

In reviewing the case study, you can determine what factors Miss DePaso has relatively little control over. For example, she is not going to change the fact that pressure will be brought on the schools or the fact that there is an informal communication system. True, her awareness of these things may modify her strategy, but it is questionable whether she should let such things dominate her behavior.

Over what factors and issues does she have relatively more control? When she is asked what she is teaching, why this and not this, how she is teaching, and how she evaluates, has she developed her *own* articulated frame of reference? Was her comment about being "open-ended" any more satisfactory than comments made by the Superintendent or board? Was she asking to be allowed to do things just because *she* somehow felt they were right?

If you were a parent, whom would you most likely support? If you had not thought out your own position and had not wrestled with the implications of what you were doing, whom would *you* side with?

Suppose Miss DePaso had a *rationale* which she could articulate. Would it have made any difference in the situation? Perhaps and perhaps not. But her strategy might have been different and her professional stance might have allowed her to *transfer* (with no guarantee) the kinds of experiences she wanted for her students to a larger arena—her colleagues, the administration, the board members, and possibly the community.

Granted, most school systems have not articulated a basic rationale. Most talk about wanting "the best education possible for each boy and girl." This doesn't tell a teacher, or a parent, or a student very much—if anything. We are told that bureaucratic institutions (including school systems) find their day-to-day operations geared primarily to assure the perpetuation of the institution. The functions of the institution do NOT take top priority, are often ignored, or at best used as a verbal "front" for the real operations. A school serves a number of political, social, and economic functions besides educating boys and girls. A sophisticated administrator realizes this. And so does a sophisticated teacher. In this area, a social studies teacher should "know" what he has been taught to "know about" in the various social science disciplines.

If Miss DePaso had articulated a rationale, she could have dispassionately raised the issues basic to selecting content, materials, and methodology. She could have pressured others to respond to basic issues, to assess ends and means, and to recognize the de facto reasons for whatever decisions were made.

She could have worked with others in trying to analyze the situation much as was attempted in the analysis model presented. Educational decisions could have been differentiated from pragmatic ones. Perhaps alternatives could have been opened. It would have made the situation less amenable to hidden agendas, submerged power plays, and possibly apathy on the part of others.

It may not have worked in the sense of being totally resolved in favor of positions condoned by Miss DePaso. But if her *rationale*—used openly—established a framework for dialogue and action revealed to those interested in the variables at work, the values seeking homage, and the alternative choices available, then whether it "worked" might be put in a larger perspective.

For a teacher, the meshing of short-range and long-range goals is not a foreign experience.

AND SO...

There we are. And there you are. . . .
Where?
Have we solved all your (our) problems? If so, we would have

to change the title of the book. There *are* problems. Some problems "kill" you, and there are those that are worth engaging—those that "give life." Hopefully some of the life-givers have surfaced and are exciting because nobody has nice, neat answers. We spend most of our time "responding" to questions rather than "answering" them.

Have you considered:

Your *own* rationale?

The difference between teaching social studies and teaching the *use* of social studies?

How one can *use* history *and* the social sciences in selecting and using content?

How about concepts? How can they be used as tools? Do the different kinds (U–N and G–R) make any difference to planning?

The making of a syllabus and the sharing of your effort with your colleagues?

Identifying and organizing different kinds of vehicles?

Looking at the teaching of "skills" as a way of monitoring experience?

Using "content" courses as a *means* of helping to prepare for teaching the use of social studies?

An *inquiry* approach that "discovers" by weaving deductive/inductive/deductive . . . tactics?

Taking the vehicles used in the book and adapting them for teaching? Can they assist a student teacher to prepare?

Lining up the strategy "equipment" to be used?

Teaching attitudes and values?

Your own strategy on how to survive?

And don't "swallow" *No G.O.D.s in the Classroom.* Pick out the G–R concepts and *test* them: modify, change, qualify as you engage learning through the vehicle of teaching.

Value concept: Teaching the use of social studies *is* worth engaging.

REFERENCES

1. Wright, Charles R.: Man's Communication: A Sociological Perspective. New York, Random House, 1959.
2. Beale, Howard K.: Are American Teachers Free? New York, Charles Scribner's and Sons, 1936.
3. Hofstadter, Richard: Anti-Intellectualism in American Life. New York, Alfred A. Knopf, 1963.
4. Dewey, John: How We Think. Boston, D. C. Heath and Company, 1933.

"Stop talking down to me!"

(By Al Ross. Copyright 1971, Saturday Review, Inc.)

APPENDIX

PRE-SELF-EVALUATION

Prior to trying to work with the material in the book, try to determine your point of entry. Nobody comes to a new situation, a class, or a book with exactly the same background, experience, and knowledge. One's use of something new depends, to some extent, on what he brings to it: attitudes, frame-of-reference, preconceived ideas, information, questions, and expectations. Every student coming to your classes will also be bringing his own "baggage." In order to effectively incorporate what the students bring, some teachers give what they call an entry evaluation. Please note: The Pre-Self-Evaluation is NOT a test in the conventional sense. It does not "judge" in terms of "right" and "wrong," "good" or "bad." Rather it is an attempt to identify the variables at the starting gate — variables intricately involved in what is to be taught and what is learned.

In a classroom situation a teacher can modify ends and means to help to accommodate the students, as a class *and* as individuals. This accommodation may be done *if* the teacher isn't trapped into a preconceived curriculum developed in a priori fashion — one designed to be "set" regardless of the backgrounds, abilities, interests, and experience of the students *and* teacher. A book in many ways parallels the detriments of a closed curriculum. Authors are not in a position to get feedback from, to modify for, and to adjust to the particular reader. All one can hope to do is to encourage a reader to individualize his interaction with the written material.

The Pre-Self-Evaluation is an attempt to encourage you to take a look at yourself and at the "baggage" you bring. This awareness, hopefully, will help you in determining value and possible use.

OVERVIEW

Please circle the A if you are in general agreement with the following statements. Please circle the D if in general disagreement with the following statements. Please note: *This is for your own awareness and is not for external evaluation or ranking.*

1. Effective social studies teaching calls for organization.   A   D

2. With all the new social science data available, the teacher is faced only with the choice of adding and deleting information from the conventional program.   A   D

3. Textbooks and materials can't be the scapegoat reason for poor social studies teaching. The key to material use is the teacher's own cognitive organization and critical thinking ability.   A   D

4. The teacher is a member of his class. His intellectual and teaching behavior establish expectations for other members.   A   D

5. Scholars in various academic disciplines are uniquely qualified to determine for the social studies teacher what *should* be taught. The teacher's primary concern is with *how* instruction should take place.   A   D

6. The real issue facing the social studies teacher is NOT content *or* process but one of relating content *with* process.   A   D

7. From the teacher's point of view, all formal school lessons are *means* used to arrive at desired ends other than the material itself.   A   D

8. To observe a teacher in the act of teaching is to observe a teacher making on-the-spot decisions.   A   D

9. Prior planning helps the teacher in making on-the-spot decisions by providing a guide and criterion for such decisions.   A   D

10. The teacher functions as an administrator in a specified instructional setting.   A   D

You have five minutes to discuss your responses with other participants. Try to spend as little time as possible "scapegoating" the questions. Instead, try to determine what issues are involved. Record (after five minutes) in the space below the issues you feel are important.

ENTRY EVALUATION

What must a person know about and be able to do to effectively function in the contemporary world?

A. Please list what you believe a person must be able to *do* in order to most effectively function in the contemporary world. After listing, please place in *rank* order.

B. Please identify what you believe a person must know about in order to assist him in functioning as indicated in Column A. Please list and then place in rank order.

DO	RANK	KNOW ABOUT	RANK
1.		1.	
2.		2.	
3.		3.	
4.		4.	
5.		5.	
6.		6.	
7.		7.	
8.		8.	
9.		9.	
10.		10.	

What are the implications for teaching?

CURRICULUM TOPIC PREFERENCE

Please rank your curriculum topic preferences. Put a 1 next to the one you believe to be most important, a 2 next to the second most important, etc.

1. Police Strike in New York City

2. Physical Geography

3. World History

4. Community Helpers

5. Capitalism vs. Communism

6. American History

7. Ecology

8. Poverty

9. History of Science

10. American Values

11. Urban Problems

12. Ancient History

13. Social Psychology

14. Local and State History

15. Drugs

16. Viet Nam

17. Political Science

18. Capitalism vs. Socialism

19. Race Relations

20. Civics

Pick your top choice and list the main ideas you would teach about it:

CHOICE_____

IDEA PREFERENCE

Please circle 1 if you feel strongly that the item listed should be taught; 2 if you feel that it should be taught; and 3 if you feel it should be deleted from consideration.

1. A student should be taught to be reasonable, that is, to be open to premises and assumptions. 1 2 3

2. A student should be taught that when in situations in which he is influencing others, he should be able and willing to make public his information and his reasoning. 1 2 3

3. Students should be taught to want certain things so that they, their country, and their society can live in peace and harmony. 1 2 3

4. Students should be taught such things as the Glorious Revolution, the Colonial Period, and Ancient Rome because they are important in and of themselves. 1 2 3

5. Students should be taught that science is mechanistic and leads to a narrowing of individual freedom. 1 2 3

6. Students should be taught that the social sciences are out to determine and to control human life and thus are an invasion of individual rights and privacy. 1 2 3

7. Students should be taught the structure of government. 1 2 3

8. Students should be taught to "tell the truth and nothing but the truth" as some legal and moral systems suggest. 1 2 3

9. Students should be taught to do unto others as they would have others do unto them. 1 2 3

10. Students should be taught that the unfolding of history explains the purpose of the human effort. 1 2 3

CONCEPTS

Please circle the A if you are in general agreement with each of the statements below. Circle the D if you are in general disagreement.

1. Concepts are a form of mental organization. A D

2. The concepts one has formed influence his behavior. A D

3. Concepts are patterns of how data are related. A D

4. Verbal statements or labels for concepts are *not* the concepts. A D

5. Formal schooling appears to place more emphasis upon labels and statements than on the concepts themselves. A D

6. Once a concept is formed, it serves as a constant guide for subsequent human behavior. A D

7. Concept formation is strictly an intellectual activity. A D

8. Putting labels on concepts may assist in communicating but also may contribute to a distortion in messages given and received. A D

9. Concepts are open to constant modification as new data force changes in previous organized relationships. A D

10. Concepts help to organize one's experience. A D

11. Previously held concepts form a screen through which new data are sifted and related. A D

12. Concepts can help one to encounter and to organize new experiences and data. A D

13. If a man thinks a situation to be true, he will *act* in terms of his thoughts and *not* the objective reality of the situation. A D

14. To teach inadequate and/or incorrect (not valid) concepts is to deny one's basic tools with which to come to terms with potential life experiences. A D

15. Concepts should be viewed as hypotheses rather than as "right" or "wrong." A D

SKILLS

Circle the A if you are in general agreement with the following statements. Circle the D if you are in general disagreement.

1. What is often perceived as a single skill is usually · a complex relationship among a number of sub-skills.   A D

2. Just as the terms "power" and "conflict" are cue concepts, so such terms as "map skills" and "critical thinking" are cue skills which infer a number of subskills.   A D

3. Skills are most effectively taught when approached in isolation from other skills.   A D

4. A map, a film, a story, and a reading are similar in that they provide a data bank for the application of skills.   A D

5. The development of skill use ability requires some cognition of the function of the skill (tool) by the student.   A D

6. The primary purpose of skill development is the ability to get and to use data in the development of concepts.   A D

7. *Both* concepts *and* skills may be considered tools.   A D

8. The student's identifying the purpose of his inquiry tends to assist him in determining skill use.   A D

9. The question "Is this a good country?" provides an access to identify relevant empirical data.   A D

10. It is unlikely that skill ability will be developed when sources of data are absent.   A D

11. The ability to assess statements is a vital aspect of skills development.   A D

12. Reasoning involves an awareness of conceptual rules for how data and statements should be related.   A D

13. Allowing for various levels of student sophistication, the skills to be developed remain constant throughout a social studies program.   A D

VEHICLES

Please circle the A if you are in general agreement with the statements below. Circle the D if you are in general disagreement.

1. A topic tends to be an end in itself, whereas a vehicle is used to transport or to carry one to ends other than itself.   A   D

2. WHAT one teaches is important. It implies the values held by the school and by the teacher. It implies to the student what is really important.   A   D

3. In most school social studies programs, the topic is selected or determined *first* and thus dictates the nature of the program.   A   D

4. Just as there are cue concepts (conflict) and cue skills (critical thinking), so there are cue vehicles which suggest a number of subvehicles which are related.   A   D

5. The criteria for selecting a vehicle rests with how effective it is in allowing the student to get to the desired ends.   A   D

6. To effectively select vehicles, one must be aware of the concepts and skills to be taught. The concepts and skills become the destination for vehicle use.   A   D

7. Vehicles serve as a data banks which then act as as a general boundary for specific inquiry methods.   A   D

8. A vehicle can serve a number of functions, including motivation and synthesis.   A   D

9. Topics or focus areas are NOT vehicles. They serve administrative functions and indicate general areas in which *specific* vehicles may be selected for use.   A   D

10. A vehicle does NOT discard the conventional concept of content but rather puts greater emphasis upon data and data use — an emphasis not assured by merely having topics and focus areas.   A   D

11. Vehicles may be selected with specific reference as to how and why teachers and students can use them.   A   D

12. Vehicle selection is an integral aspect of teacher planning.   A   D

13. The relative effectiveness of two possible vehicles partially rests with their explicit potential for concept and skill development.   A   D

METHODS

Please circle the A if you are in general agreement with the statements below. Circle the D if you are in general disagreement.

1. Scientific methods always start with *inductive* activity.   A   D

2. Scientific methods move in and out of deductive *and* inductive activity and cannot be viewed as a step-by-step sequential process.   A   D

3. "To discover" implies that there is something "there" to be discovered.   A   D

4. The discovery approach is primarily rooted in inductive processes.   A   D

5. The testing approach assumes that the products of man's thinking and experiencing are part of his real world—a fact of life, but subject to change.   A   D

6. The testing approach to methods *starts* with *deduction* but encourages *inductive* divergent thinking as part of the testing strategy.   A   D

7. In the discovery approach, the teacher's primary role focuses upon materials, data, and strategy which facilitate the discovery of a predetermined subject.   A   D

8. In the testing approach, the teacher's primary role is to help students to determine a strategy for testing a concept. Concepts are always viewed as hypotheses open to modification and change.   A   D

9. The discovery method puts less emphasis upon

the development of skills than does the testing method.   A   D

10. Neither a pure form of the discovery method nor a pure form of the testing method is the "right" method in all situations.   A   D

11. *Both* methods imply the need for teacher planning as well as the need for some structure.   A   D

12. The testing method focuses upon concepts and skills more than on academic disciplines and set content. It is less vulnerable to manipulation of students toward set ends than is the discovery method.   A   D

MATERIAL SELECTION

Please circle the A if you are in general agreement with the statements below. Circle the D if you are in general disagreement.

1. Materials should be viewed as vehicles.   A   D

2. Materials should be explicit about the concepts and/or skills included.   A   D

3. Materials are data banks, but the data are related to determined concepts and skills.   A   D

4. An individual piece of material should be self-contained. It should be whole, yet implicitly relate to other individual pieces of material.   A   D

5. Effective materials assist the teacher in planning.   A   D

6. Certain materials are appropriate for certain grade levels. The appropriateness is in terms of reading levels, focus areas, and topics.   A   D

7. Some materials may give primary focus to specific aspects of skill development while other materials may give such a focus to concepts. Any one piece of material need NOT give equal emphasis to both concepts and skills.   A   D

8. Materials should be flexible enough to be used with either a discovery or testing approach to teaching methods.   A   D

9. While materials may differ considerably in terms of data and concepts, the skills components remain relatively stable throughout all the materials.   A   D

10. Effective materials should relate process *with* content.   A   D

11. Materials should serve *both* the teacher and the student simultaneously.   A   D

Assume that you are teaching social studies. And assume, as well, that the only social studies the students will formally receive (K to 12) will be in your class. Assume that circumstances allow you to teach only *one* concept, *one* skill, and *one* attitude.

Determine the one concept you would teach.

Determine the one skill you would teach.

Determine the one attitude you would teach.

Then try to analyze the *processes* you used in reaching the above three determinations. For example, what did you have to *do* in order to come up with the one concept? What do you mean by skill? attitude?

INDEX